THE
ELBOW

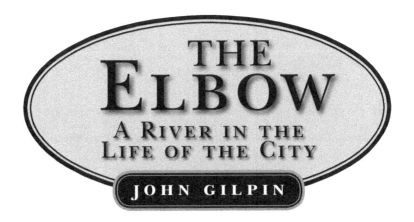

THE ELBOW
A RIVER IN THE LIFE OF THE CITY

JOHN GILPIN

SECOND EDITION

Brush Education Inc.
www.brusheducation.ca
contact@brusheducation.ca

Editorial: Nicholle Carrière, Shauna Babiuk
Cover and interior design: Carol Dragich, Dragich Design;
Cover image: Glenbow G3504 C151A3 1910a

Printed and manufactured in Canada

Library and Archives Canada Cataloguing in Publication

Gilpin, John F., 1947-, author
       The Elbow : a river in the life of the city / John Gilpin. – Second edition.

Includes bibliographical references and index.
Issued in print and electronic formats.
ISBN 978-1-55059-720-2 (softcover).–ISBN 978-1-55059-721-9 (PDF).–
ISBN 978-1-55059-722-6 (Kindle).–ISBN 978-1-55059-723-3 (EPUB)

       1. Elbow River (Alta.)–History. 2. Elbow River Valley (Alta.)–History.
I. Title.

FC3695.E42G55 2017   971.23'3   C2017-903924-5
                                                         C2017-903925-3

We acknowledge the support of the Government of Canada
Nous reconnaissons l'appui du gouvernement du Canada | Canada

To the Elbow River and its friends

CONTENTS

ACKNOWLEDGEMENTS

This book was written with the assistance of a number of people and institutions, beginning with Gerry Stotts, who first suggested that a book on the history of the Glenmore Waterworks should be written and who made a significant financial contribution toward funding the research. Significant financial contributions to this end were also made by the City of Calgary, the Alberta Historical Resources Foundation, and the Calgary Foundation. Funding from the Calgary Foundation also provided the resources to link the project to community activities in the Mission District involving the construction of the Elbow River Promenade. Community-based activities included a workshop to examine the various themes in Calgary's relationship to the Elbow River. These themes were also explored in a series of walks organized along the Elbow from the Mission District to Elbow Park. Heritage Park played a valuable role as the administrator of the funds from the City of Calgary, the Alberta Historical Resources Foundation, and the Calgary Foundation for community liaison and research purposes. The Alberta Historical Resources Foundation also provided a grant in aid of publication. The Glenbow Library and Archives, the City of Calgary Archives, the Local History Room of the Calgary Public Library, and the Provincial Archives of Alberta provided a wealth of primary sources that were the cornerstone for this study of the Elbow River. Carol Stokes at the City of Calgary Archives played a particularly valuable role by letting me know about their holdings of engineering records regarding the construction of the Glenmore Dam.

Organizing the workshop and the walks, as well as collecting historical information on the Elbow River, introduced me to a new group of people who provided information and encouragement and made the project relevant to the issue of the future of the Elbow River in Calgary. Eilish Hiebert of the Mission District Community Association, from our first meeting at the Purple Perk coffee house, contributed her organizing abilities and enthusiasm. Bill Longstaff is another active member of the Mission community interested in its heritage. Robin McLeod, as a dedicated friend of the Elbow

River, organized an expedition on the river from the Glenmore Dam to Fort Calgary. Gus Yaki led the first walk and shared his wealth of knowledge on the flora and fauna of the Elbow Valley. Tony Starlight contributed his perspectives on the Elbow as a member of the Tsuu T'ina First Nation. Bob van Wegen provided a number of community contacts and suggested sources of information. Ted Giles of Detselig Enterprises expressed confidence in the success of the book when it was only in outline form. Reg and Sylvia Harrill took time to search the archives of the Earl Grey Golf Club for source material. Dan Thorburn and his colleagues at the Calgary Foundation not only efficiently processed the grant application, but also conveyed an appreciation for the idea of writing a history of Calgary from the point of view of the Elbow River. George Campbell served as an excellent moderator for the workshop. Muriel Armstrong, Joycelin (Sara) Snaddon, and Doug Hawkes shared their memories of growing up along the river. Gerry Oetelaar of the University of Calgary Department of Anthropology and Archeology shared his insights on the human settlement of the Elbow. Paul Fesko and Jamie Dixon of the City of Calgary Water Resources Department provided valuable background on the Calgary waterworks system. Mark Bennett, executive director of the Bow River Basin Council, provided a valuable list of contacts. Sylvia Harnden of Heritage Park supplied important historical information on the park.

The first edition of this book benefited greatly from the expertise of librarians, archivists, fellow historians, and a cartographer. The second edition has benefited in equal measure from the editorial and design expertise of Lauri Seidlitz, Nicholle Carrière, and Carol Dragich. Their contributions have ensured that the original goal of producing a quality book in all respects about the Elbow River has been fully achieved.

INTRODUCTION

The genesis of this book was the suggestion from Gerry Stotts that the 75th anniversary of the construction of the Glenmore Waterworks be celebrated. Investigating the use of the Elbow River as a supply of water for the growing city of Calgary indicated that Calgary's association with the Elbow went well beyond a dam. The result was a journey both in place and time starting at the confluence of the Bow and Elbow Rivers, where Calgary was founded in 1875 with the arrival of the North-West Mounted Police, and extending upstream to that part of the Elbow that became the site for the Glenmore Dam and Reservoir after 1932.

The Elbow River was the axis along which settlement developed at Fort Calgary from 1875 to 1884. Bridging the Elbow River was the cause of conflict between the new town of Calgary built around the Canadian Pacific Railway station and the Catholic mission when it was feared that Father Albert Lacombe might be developing a rival townsite. Later, the Elbow River separated two business groups that periodically fought for control of the economic destiny of the Calgary townsite, and an economic recovery plan in the mid-1890s was based in part on using Elbow River water for irrigation. Greater Calgary, first proposed in 1906 and fully achieved after World War II, depended on the water of the Elbow.

Besides being an economic asset to the community, the river was used for recreation, its water providing Calgarians with venues for skating in winter and swimming in summer. Upon completion of the Glenmore Dam in 1932, skating disappeared. After a break of 30 years, limited use of the Glenmore

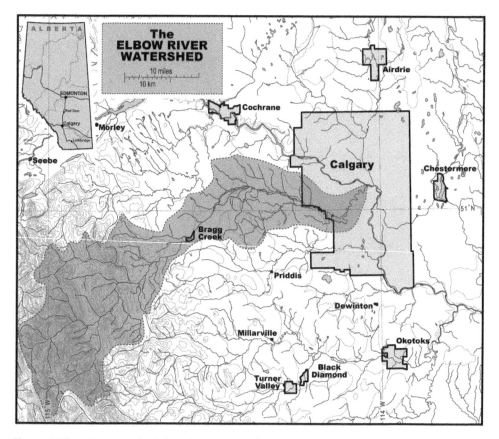

Figure A Elbow River watershed; drawn by University of Calgary cartographer Robin Poitras

Reservoir began for activities such as sailing, which minimized human contact with the water. Drifting down the Elbow River from the Glenmore Dam remains a popular summer activity.

Calgary's association with the Elbow is but an instant in this river's natural history. University of Alberta geologist Dr. John Allan concluded in 1943 that in preglacial times, 2.5 million years ago, the Bow River followed a course south of Cochrane through Glenbow Flats and along what is now the channel of the Elbow River to the present location of the Glenmore Reservoir, and then south through Haysboro to Midnapore and De Winton. The Elbow River, at this time, joined the Bow considerably west and south of its present location and north of the lands of the Tsuu T'ina First Nation.[1]

In 1961, Peter Meyboom of the Alberta Research Council incorporated Allan's conclusions regarding the preglacial location of the Bow and Elbow Rivers into a description of their postglacial development.[2] He suggested that the present Elbow Valley above the Glenmore Reservoir and the former river channel between the Glenmore Reservoir and Chinook Centre shopping mall could be considered surviving elements of the preglacial drainage system. Other features of the landscape were the result of the creation and drainage of glacial Lake Calgary in postglacial times approximately 12,000 years ago. Lake Calgary was the result of the retreat of the Balzac, Crossfield, and Morley glaciers. As the lake drained, the Bow River channel shifted northeast via a series of meltwater channels, which Allan described in some detail. These changes created the "elbow" on the Bow River at the Pearce estate and the elbow on the Elbow River where the Glenmore Reservoir is today. Allan identified four abandoned channels and suggested the sequence of their abandonment. He explained the changes in the direction of both the Elbow and Bow Rivers by "stream captures" rather than because of deflections caused by an ice barrier created by a retreating glacier.

The work of Allan, Meyboom, and others in the 1960s was brought together along with new research by Michael Wilson in his 1985 thesis entitled "Once Upon a River."[3] He disagreed with both Allan and Meyboom with respect to the preglacial location of the Bow Valley, which he suggested flowed due east from Calgary, with portions of the old valley serving as the present-day channel for the Red Deer River from Dinosaur Provincial Park to beyond the Alberta–Saskatchewan border. He retained the idea that a series of meltwater channels had developed, with the existing Elbow River between the Glenmore Dam and its confluence with the Bow River being one of those channels. The reach of the Elbow River between the Glenmore Dam and its confluence with the Bow River thus was originally created by water flowing south from Lake Calgary. The flow was later reversed when a massive influx of water from melting glaciers to the west of Calgary was carried northeast, altering the course of the Bow River to the south. The melting of the glaciers in the Calgary area thus located the Elbow Valley where it is today between Weaselhead Flats and the Elbow River's confluence with the Bow, giving it a distinctive geological history compared to the rest of the Elbow River system.

During the Holocene Epoch, which covers the last 10,000 years in geological time, Lake Calgary dried up and the flows of water from the glaciers, which had retreated to the mountains, were reduced. As a result, the Elbow Valley was occupied by a much smaller river that could not change the location of the valley but could significantly modify the valley floor. Up until the 1880s, the Elbow River meandered through the valley, creating a series of oxbow lakes that in some cases played a role in the area's human history. The newest oxbow lake is located in the Weaselhead area, while the present-day Heritage Park Marina, Stanley Park, and Roxboro Park were the locations of much older oxbow lakes that have disappeared as a result of human settlement of the Elbow Valley.

Periodic floods referred to as "freshets," from the French word *freschete* or *frais*, meaning "fresh," are also a feature of the Elbow River's natural history. At various times, these events transformed the river from a community benefactor into a raging menace. On one of these occasions, the river was described as a predator in search of people to drown and buildings to submerge. The lesser evil of the annual spring floods was reduced water quality from the end of May to early July. During those times, the large quantity of suspended solids gave the water a cloudy appearance and made it unpleasant to drink.

Early surveyors noted the great fluctuations in the flow of the Elbow River. C. M. Walker, Dominion land surveyor, in a report on township 21, range 6, noted that on May 27, 1911, "there was no flow in the main branch of the river and that three days afterward, when the snow began to melt, the horses in trying to ford the stream were swept off their feet and carried 50 yards [45 metres] downstream; also that a rise of two feet [0.6 metres] in the water in six hours is not unusual."[4]

In its various incarnations, the Elbow River has evoked fear, respect, indifference, pleasure, frustration, appreciation, and distaste while being drank, swam in, skated upon, avoided, polluted, floated upon, and crossed.

CHAPTER ONE

Calgary on the Elbow

1875–1884

The Siksika (Blackfoot), Kainai (Blood), Piikani (Peigan), Nakoda (Stoney), and Tsuu T'ina (Sarcee) frequented the confluence of the Bow and Elbow Rivers long before it became the haunt of the North-West Mounted Police in 1875. The Tsuu T'ina word for this location was *kootsisaw*, meaning "meeting of the waters."[5] First Nations peoples were attracted to the location because of its suitability as a crossing point on the Bow River rather than because of its confluence with the Elbow. It met the criteria of having a ford accessible by gentle slopes, in this case, by the Nose Creek Valley to the north and a former channel of the Bow River to the south. To the First Nations, rivers were landscape features to be crossed rather than travelled upon. The low water flows and meandering tracks made prairie rivers unsuitable for travel. Individual features of rivers were, however, important navigational landmarks for travellers. The names for rivers adopted in the settlement period were based, in many cases, on the names given to these features. The crossing at the confluence of the Bow and Elbow thus developed into a major intersection for First Nation trails radiating out in all directions.

David Thompson was the first European to come close to the confluence of the two rivers when he wintered with the Piikani on the Bow River in

1787–88. Peter Fidler reached the Bow River downstream from the Elbow on Sunday, December 9, 1792, during his trip from Buckingham House on the South Saskatchewan River. Having camped for the night a little northeast of Calgary, he travelled downstream on the Bow, stopping slightly upstream from the mouth of the Highwood River.[6] Thompson returned to the Bow on November 17, 1800, in the company of Duncan McGillivray and four other men; he reached the Bow River at a point opposite the location of Calgary.[7] From this location, he surveyed the northeast side of the Bow River below the bend, and then following a route via the Highwood River and Tongue Flag Creek, returned to the Bow a short distance above the Ghost River, thus effectively circling the Elbow River. At the end of his career, Thompson prepared a cumulative record of his travels between 1792 and 1812. It delineated the Bow River to its headwaters, so this was potentially the first map showing the Bow's conjunction with the Elbow River but not the Elbow's actual course. According to the Geographic Board of Canada, the river Thompson marked as Hokaikshi was the Elbow River.[8]

More than 50 years passed before another European came even close to the confluence of the two rivers. Members of the John Palliser expedition, which travelled in western Canada between 1857 and 1860, followed routes that entirely missed the confluence. James Hector's journal for August 15, 1858, recorded his party's arrival at Swift Creek, which they followed en route to Old Bow Fort on the Bow River, near present-day Cochrane. Such a route would have taken Hector and his group across the upper reaches of the Elbow. Swift Creek, as marked on the Palliser map, places it where Fish Creek is today.

The relative isolation of the Elbow River from events associated with the transformation the West came to an end in 1871 with the arrival of whisky trader Fred Kanouse. He had been sent north from Fort Whoop-Up by John Healy and Alfred Hamilton to establish a trading post on the Elbow River.[9] Hamilton and Healy were whisky traders based in Fort Whoop-Up who wanted to reestablish the alcohol trade in the Elbow Valley. The post was located somewhere between the present-day Mission Bridge and the Glenmore Reservoir. A second post was established in 1871 by Dick Berry, another whisky trader, but it was abandoned when Berry was killed by members of the Kainai Tribe, who also burned the post to the ground. During

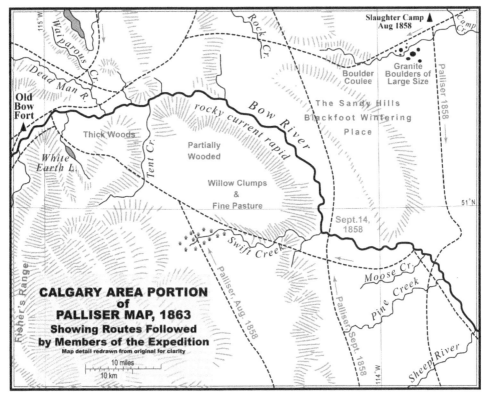

Figure 1.1 The routes followed by members of the Palliser expedition, as indicated on the map, took them around the confluence of the Elbow and Bow Rivers. As a result, the Palliser map of the area did not include the Elbow River. Members of the expedition would have been more familiar with present-day Fish Creek, which they identified as Swift Creek, having encountered it on at least two occasions.

Source: This map is a reproduction drawn by University of Calgary cartographer Robin Poitras. The original map from which the copy was made is entitled "A General Map of the routes in British North America explored by the expeditions under Captain Palliser during the years 1857, 1858, 1859, and 1860." Glenbow Library and Archives, G 3466 S12 1865 P168 1968

the trading season of 1872–73, Hamilton and Healy sent Donald W. Davis back to the Elbow River post. As soon as the winter trading season was over, the Elbow River post was abandoned—more than 2,000 buffalo robes were loaded into wagons and the remaining trade goods removed. It is unlikely the post reopened for the winter of 1873–74. Even with the post closed down, the whisky trade was still active. As Sam Livingston, a prospector and trader who settled near Fort Calgary, indicated in a letter to Alderman Archibald Francis Wright of Winnipeg in December 1874, in "these parts, there [was] plenty of it at every post. There [was] whisky concealed all over the country since last summer, and it [was] raised when required."[10]

The effect of the whisky trade on the First Nations brought the Missionary Oblates of Mary Immaculate to the Elbow Valley. In 1872, Chief Crowfoot asked Bishop Vital Grandin to help protect his people from the ravages of the poisonous brew. Bishop Grandin agreed to the request, and Our Lady of Peace Mission, the first Roman Catholic mission in southern Alberta, was established 25 miles (40 kilometres) up the Elbow River from the Bow. The task of building the mission was assumed by Alexis Cardinal, who constructed a small cabin over the winter of 1872–73. In the fall of 1873, Father Constantine Scollen and Father Vital Fourmond arrived to take charge.

Besides whisky traders, the neighbours of Our Lady of Peace Mission included Samuel Henry Harkwood Livingston, better known as Sam Livingston. Born in Avoca, Ireland, in 1831, he immigrated to the United States when he was 16. He moved west, following the gold rushes to California, Oregon, and Montana, and then to the Cariboo in central British Columbia. In about 1862, he continued his gold prospecting activities in the Great Slave Lake and Lake Athabasca areas, eventually establishing himself at the Methodist mission in Victoria, east of Edmonton, where he began to transport freight for the mission. By 1874, he had relocated his operations farther south near Our Lady of Peace Mission, placing him closer to the trade routes with the plains First Nations.[11]

The decision by the North-West Mounted Police in June 1875 to locate a police post midway between Fort Macleod and Fort Edmonton set the stage for the convergence at the confluence of the Bow and Elbow Rivers of the Oblates, the I. G. Baker Company (sometimes written as I. G. Baker & Company), F Troop of the North-West Mounted Police, and the Hudson's Bay Company.[12] The Oblates were the first to arrive in July 1875, followed by the I. G. Baker Company, which had been hired to build the police accommodation. F Troop commander Éphrem-A. Brisebois, who had a reputation for not following orders, moved the location to the confluence of the Bow and Elbow Rivers.[13] Following this decision, the Oblate mission was moved upriver in the fall of 1875.

Major-General Sir Edward Selby Smyth, in his 1875 report, praised the location of the Bow River post, which he said was situated beside Swift River. This caused some confusion over the actual designation of the river and the location of the post.

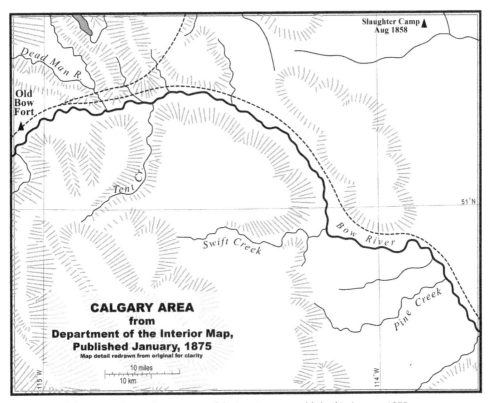

Figure 1.2 Calgary area, from a Department of the Interior map published in January 1875

This map is a portion of one published in January 1875 by the federal government on the eve of the arrival of the North-West Mounted Police. It illustrates the Department of the Interior's continued reliance on the Palliser map of 1861 for the geographical details of the Calgary area. This map may have been the source of the statement made by Major-General Sir Edward Selby Smyth in his 1875 report that the Bow River post was situated beside the Swift River.

Source: This map is a reproduction drawn by University of Calgary cartographer Robin Poitras. The original map from which the copy was made is entitled "North West Territory including the Province of Manitoba exhibiting the several tracts of country ceded by the Indian Treaties 1, 2, 4, and 5. January 20, 1875." Glenbow Library and Archives, G 3471 E1 1875 c212

The Elbow River was not indicated on any maps published by the federal government before 1875. Maps published up to that date were based on the 1861 map of the Palliser expedition and thus failed to disclose the existence of a river between Tent Creek (present-day Jumpingpound Creek) and Swift Creek (present-day Fish Creek) on the south side of the Bow River.[14] By 1877, however, the name "Elbow" was in common use on maps and in government reports.[15] Elbow was the English translation of the Blackfoot word *moki-nist-sis*. In 1883, the Department of the Interior published the first

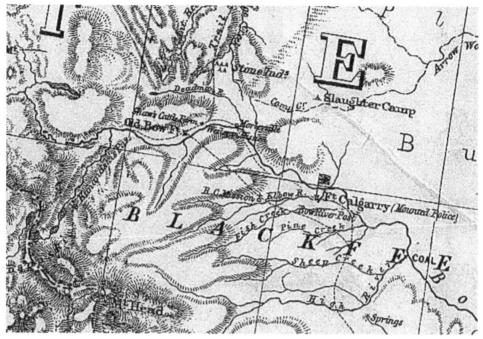

Figure 1.3 This map is a portion of one published in 1877 and is one of the first to include the Elbow River. Some confusion persists as to the spelling and location of Fort Calgary. It is located closer to the Weaselhead Flats area than the confluence of the Bow and Elbow Rivers. The map also indicates the location of the Bow River post, the original location of Fort Calgary, as being at the confluence of Swift (Fish) Creek and the Bow River.

map indicating the location of the Elbow River and accurately describing its route to the Bow River.[16] Maps of the Calgary area published after 1877 also adopted the names Fish Creek for Palliser's Swift Creek and Jumpingpound Creek for his Tent Creek.[17]

The Montana-based I. G. Baker Company was responsible for the construction of the North-West Mounted Police post.[18] It had already established itself as a contractor with the North-West Mounted Police, having built Fort Macleod and been a supplier of other goods and services. One-time whisky trader on the Elbow, Donald. W. Davis, was employed as the company's local manager. During the construction of the police post, the I. G. Baker Company also built a store on the west bank of the Elbow River south of the post. The company incorporated Fort Calgary into a transportation system using the Whoop-Up Trail, which extended north from Fort Benton, Montana. The commercial opportunities created at Fort Calgary attracted the Hudson's Bay Company, which established a post across the Elbow River from Fort Calgary. The new settlement functioned as a stop along a transportation system that developed as a result of the expanding use of steamboats and railways in the American West. Steamboats were able to navigate the Missouri River on a regular basis, with Fort Benton becoming the head of navigation by 1846. This centre of navigation for riverboats was now just over 100 miles (160 kilometres) from the Canadian border in southern Alberta. Beginning in the late 1860s, American traders entered the area and established several trading posts to obtain furs and buffalo robes from the Siksika in exchange for whisky. The route followed the traditional trails of the First Nations so did not affect the location of the trails to Calgary.[19] Even the North-West Mounted Police obtained its supplies from merchants at Fort Benton since it was closer than Fort Edmonton and the supplies were cheaper.

William Scollen, the stepbrother of Father Constantine Scollen, was one of the new additions to the community along the Elbow River, having arrived in September 1877 with the intention of becoming a farmer on the fully developed agricultural frontier.[20] Since he lacked the means to immediately accomplish this goal, he took a job as the "master" of the Our Lady of Peace Mission farm. He was provided with a residence, presumably close to the mission buildings, and was able to purchase a mare, colt, and wagon. He also learned some Cree and began to learn French, which he practised by singing hymns every night with the fathers.

Calgary in the 1870s was not, in Scollen's view, the "gold coin country" he had been led to believe it was. Its deficiencies were not the result of either its climate or the infertility of its soil, but were the consequence of the economic dominance of the I. G. Baker Company, the conduct of the North-West Mounted Police, and the First Nations. The I. G. Baker Company, which he called "Uncle Sam's business-like merchants" or simply "those Yankee traders," represented an American yoke around Calgary's neck. The company had caught the North-West Mounted Police on its arrival and had held on like leeches ever since. The company provided the force with all its supplies, shutting out local farmers and forcing local residents who worked for the company to take their wages in goods. The company also did not purchase the items it supplied to the police from local farmers. Its final sin, according to Scollen, was its receipt of virtually all the Canadian treaty money paid to the First Nations. In his view, its influence would only end when "Canadian merchants [rose] out of the trance they [were] in and [drove] the plough-share of enterprise through this Jew-liking Yankee ring that has been welded around the hard-working, industrious settlers of this country since 1874."[21]

The conduct of the police compounded the problems of the farmers since they made no effort to support the local agricultural community through the purchase of supplies and also had their own tradesmen, such as blacksmiths. Off-duty officers made matters worse by engaging in farming and ranching, and then selling their produce or cattle back to the force. To get justice for the farmers, the police had to be stopped from farming. At that time, Scollen observed "there are not less than twenty policemen ploughing up 100 acres [40 hectares] of land for government purposes."[22]

The threat of the First Nations was the third problem for settlers around Fort Calgary. The fear of an uprising was fuelled by problems in Montana and confrontations between John Glenn, a prospector and trader who settled permanently on Fish Creek in 1875, where he established a farm, and Sam Livingston with the First Nations. In one letter home, William Scollen recounted how "an Indian Chief walked up to [Glenn] bringing with him a young warrior and a squaw [woman] and told them to help themselves to old Glenn's potatoes . . . Glenn walked into his house and brought out his Winchester rifle and cartridge belt, then told the Indians to hurry outside of his fence, which they did in quick time."[23] The police, rather than protecting the settlers from the First Nations, took their side. In his view, they did so because they were afraid or "through some lustful desire to conciliate the feelings of some Indian girl."[24] Scollen's brother and his fellow settlers were the only people in the community for whom Scollen had any respect.

In March 1880, he was able to obtain his own farm, which was located along the Elbow to the west of the mission site where the Glencoe Club is today. According to Scollen, the land had been owned and cultivated as early as the fall of 1875 so had some improvements in the form of a fence enclosing a parcel of cultivated land. He did not, however, build a new house at that location and continued to live in the residence he had occupied since 1877.

Antoine Godine and his family were some of the first Métis to settle land along the Elbow River. Godine's first farm, established in 1876, was south

Figure 1.4 This view, which appeared in the June 28, 1890, issue of the *Dominion Illustrated*, was described as a view of Calgary in 1875 from a painting by an old trader. It is very similar, however, to a view of Fort Calgary painted by William Winder, the original of which is part of the Glenbow collection (NA-98–10). Winder was a member of the North-West Mounted Police from 1873 to 1881. The Elbow and Bow Rivers in this view from Scotsman's (or Fraser's) Hill appear as a single river flowing northwest. It illustrates the extent of development before the announcement that the Bow Valley would be on the route of the Canadian Pacific Railway. The North-West Mounted Police post, a significant First Nations presence, and, above the islands, a heavy log boom on the Elbow River that had been placed there in 1875 to block the timber that was floated down the river for construction purposes are important features of this image.

of the Hudson's Bay Company store, north of the escarpment, and east of the Elbow River. The farm was sold to George Emmerson in 1877, who in turn sold it to Louis Roselle and his family in 1880. Roselle worked for the Hudson's Bay Company for 26 years following his arrival from Montreal in 1842. He then spent one year as a buffalo hunter before settling into the life of a freighter in Calgary, which involved trips to both Edmonton and Fort Macleod.[25] In 1875, Baptiste Anouse Jr. established a farm close to where the MacDonald Avenue Bridge is today, an area that would eventually be surveyed as the southeast quarter of section 15. Born in Edmonton in 1857, Anouse Jr. made various improvements to his property while working as a freighter for the Hudson's Bay Company.[26] His father, Baptiste Anouse Sr., lived on land south of the Elbow in what would become the northeast quarter of section 10. Paul Faillon had established his residence in the northwest quarter of section 10 in September 1877 after having negotiated an agreement with Father Scollen that his claim would only include the land south of the Elbow River.[27] The last major land claim made before the railway announcement was that of Cecil Denney in the fall of 1879. The Denney estate was located east of the Hudson's Bay Company post and included what is now the northeast quarter of section 14 and that part of section 13 located south and west of the Bow River. Denney arrived in 1875 as the deputy commander of F Troop and succeeded Éphrem-A. Brisebois as commander of Fort Calgary in 1876.

PEOPLE'S EYES ARE NOW TURNED TO CALGARY

The decision in 1880 to change the route of the Canadian Pacific Railway (CPR) to the south via the Bow Valley transformed the fortunes of the settlement on the Elbow River. For the first time in its history, the settlement became a significant destination for settlers and investors. Increased activity by Dominion Land Survey was evidence of its new importance. In 1880, Montague Aldous surveyed the Fifth Principal Meridian, which passed less than 2 miles (3 kilometres) east of Fort Calgary. Aldous and Lachlan Kennedy carried out the outline surveys to create townships 23 and 24, range 1, west of the Fifth Meridian in 1881. The subdivision of township 24, range 1, west of the Fifth Meridian into 36 sections was delayed until the summer of 1883, leaving the community members to determine for themselves the legal description of their land in anticipation of making land claims.

Legal land descriptions were important because of the May 7, 1880, revision of the Dominion Lands Act. Prior to that date, settlers on unsurveyed land could obtain title under the terms of the homestead provisions of the Dominion Lands Act after the land had been surveyed, even if the land had been designated by the federal government for railway or other uses. The revised act removed this protection. It was designed to protect the interests of long-time settlers in a region, while at the same time preempting the activities of land speculators. The CPR was given all the odd-numbered sections north and south of the main line for a distance of 25 miles (40 kilometres) through regulations adopted in January 1882.

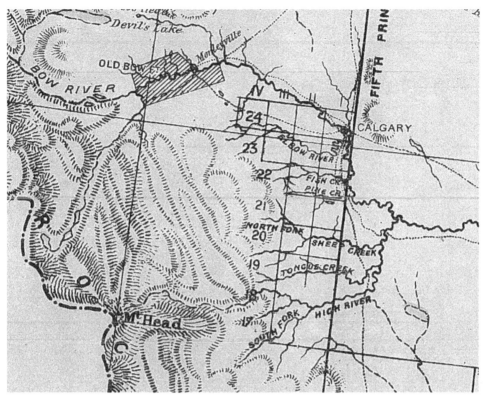

Figure 1.5 This map, published in 1881, shows the work carried out in the Calgary area in 1880 and 1881 by Dominion Land Survey, which was shifted south to accommodate the decision to relocate the route of the CPR through the Bow Valley. This survey began with the delineation of the Fifth Meridian in 1880 by Montague Aldous, which was followed by township and range surveys in 1881 by Aldous and Lachlan Kennedy.

Source: General Map of Part of the North West Territory and of Manitoba Published by authority of the Right Honourable Sir John A. Macdonald KCB Minister of the Interior, December 31, 1881. Glenbow Archives and Library, G 3470 1881 c212 copy 3

Calgary was also affected by the federal government's plan to control the development of land at critical points along CPR lines where it was anticipated that terminals would be established. This policy was applied in Regina, Swift Current, and Medicine Hat in addition to Calgary. Calgary's inclusion in the program was first suggested by Indian commissioner Edgar Dewdney, who also held the position of lieutenant-governor, in a letter to Sir John A. Macdonald, who served both as prime minister and Minister of the Interior, on March 24, 1882.[28] He recommended that provisions of the Dominion Lands Act as revised to May 7, 1880, be applied to the four townships located

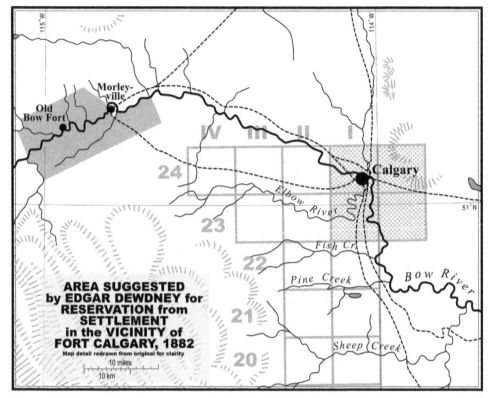

Figure 1.6 This map shows the area reserved by the federal government in 1882 at Calgary following the decision to route the CPR through the Bow Valley.

Source: This map is a reproduction drawn by University of Calgary cartographer Robin Poitras. The original map from which the copy was made is from Library and Archives Canada, RG 15 volume 1181 File 2229.

north, south, east, and west of Fort Calgary. Dewdney's letter expressed the hope that the existing claims of settlers would be respected but stated the need to take control of land development at Fort Calgary since "people's eyes are now turned to Calgary [and] attempts will be made to secure the location of what [he] thought [would] be a most important point particularly of the railway taking the southern route."[29]

Macdonald agreed with the suggestion and directed his staff to ensure that the designated area be reserved for future use or sale by the government. Residents of Calgary and vicinity, along with residents at other locations affected by this policy, were informed in the fall of 1882. The notice stated that two townships were reserved from homestead and preemption

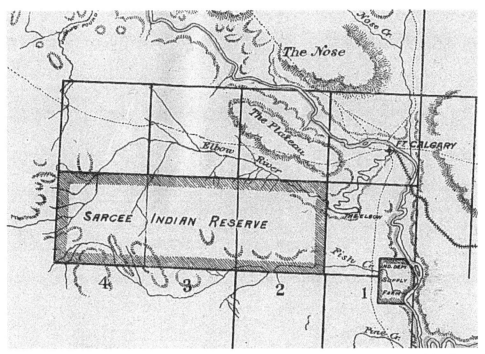

Figure 1.7 This map, published in 1883, shows the progress of the CPR to a location just west of the Elbow River. The location of the "elbow" on the Elbow River is indicated, along with the survey of the lands of the Tsuu T'ina Nation.

Source: Map of the Districts of Assiniboia and Alberta Showing Dominion Land Surveys to the 31st December 1882, Department of the Interior, Dominion Lands Office February 20, 1883. Glenbow Archives and Library, G 3470 1883 c212

entry where the CPR crossed Medicine Hat Coulee, Seven Persons River, and Swift Current Creek (the Elbow River). The federal government continued to be confused about the name of the river that would be crossed in the vicinity of Fort Calgary, where a future town was expected to be located. The townships so reserved could not be distinctly designated in advance of the survey, but squatting within 6 miles (10 kilometres) of the crossing of the Elbow, which the federal government called Swift Current Creek, was not permitted. The notice further advised that squatters already upon the CPR reserve or otherwise would in no case be protected. It was signed by North-West Mounted Police commissioner James Morrow Walsh and dated October 28, 1882.[30] In theory, the railway reserve covered an immense area east and west of the Elbow River and north and south of the Bow, but its enforcement—keeping settlers from establishing residence by setting up a tent or

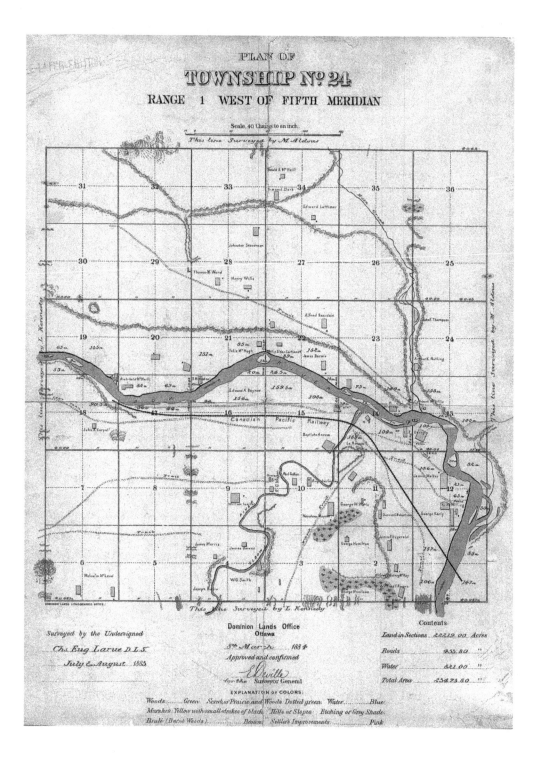

building a dwelling—was confined to that area in township 24, range 1, west of the Fifth Meridian, west and north of the Elbow River, and south of the Bow River to Shaganappi Point, which was known as Calgary Bottom. Even within this area, the federal government was primarily concerned with preventing potential land claims in sections 15 and 16.

The decision to impose the land reservation and the response of Calgary citizens were first noted by the *Fort Macleod Gazette* in its September 14, 1882, issue. The *Gazette* lamented the fact that quite a good-sized town would develop if people were allowed to continue building houses and stores. It encouraged the citizens of Calgary to send a petition to the federal government for the immediate creation of a townsite, which it was confident would be granted without delay. The response of the community to the notice as described in the October 24 issue of the *Gazette* was to organize a protest meeting and draft a petition. The main speaker at the meeting was Major Baines, who made the point that the multiple land reservations made it difficult for true settlers to make a contribution to the development of the land.

Enforcement of the CPR reserve was the responsibility of the newly reinforced Calgary detachment of the North-West Mounted Police. Fort Calgary was designated as a district post, and in August 1882, E Troop, under the command of Superintendent John Henry McIllree, arrived to increase the police presence at the confluence of the Bow and Elbow Rivers. Since the buildings at the police post were considered entirely inadequate to accommodate the division, McIllree was instructed to commence construction upon his arrival and to retain for use during the winter, any buildings that could be made habitable with little or no expense. Firms James Reilly & Co. from Sherbrooke, Quebec, and Logan & Doherty of Ottawa were contracted to build the new post.

Figure 1.8 The final step in the land survey of the Calgary area before the issuing of titles was the subdivision of township 24, range 1, west of the Fifth Meridian into 36 sections. Charles-Edward LaRue carried out the township survey between July 20 and August 6, 1883. In addition to subdividing the land, he also indicated in his official record of the survey, the nature of the landscape, the location of watercourses, and improvements that had been made by settlers. His official record of the survey was used to prepare a map of the township that was approved and confirmed as correct by the surveyor general of Canada on March 4, 1884. No titles to property in the township could be issued until LaRue's survey had been approved. *Source:* Glenbow Archives and Library, Plan of Township No. 24, Range 1, West of Fifth Meridian, Dominion Lands Office, Ottawa, 8 March 1884

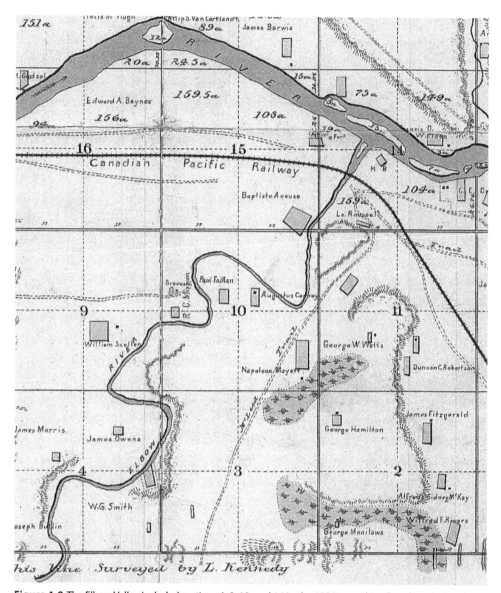

Figure 1.9 The Elbow Valley included sections 4, 9, 10, and 14 in the 1884 township plan, though the plan was not entirely accurate as to the ownership of land in all these sections. Augustus Carney was identified as having settled on a portion of the southeast quarter of section 10 located south of the Elbow River, when in actual fact, that land had been settled and improved by Baptiste Anouse Sr. Carney, who was described as a claim jumper by William Pearce, received the title to the southeast quarter of section 10, having acquired it in some manner from Napoleon Mayett.

Police efforts to keep sections 15 and 16 free of settlers included making agreements with individuals in which they agreed that their residence in the area did not give them any subsequent claims to the land.[31] Enforcing the land reserve was, however, not the primary function of the North-West Mounted Police, that was more concerned with what Commissioner Acheson Irvine called the "transformation of the West being wrought by the coming of the railway."[32] Changes included the disappearance of the buffalo and the accelerated pace of the advancement of civilization. When settlement developed gradually, the "Indians almost imperceptibly became accustomed to and acquainted with the white settlers, and on the other hand, the settlers to the Indians."[33] However, with thousands of settlers arriving via the railway, there was concern that there would be a "certain proportion of rough classes of men, requiring a strong force of police to ensure the law of the country being carried into effect."[34] As well, settlers near First Nations reserves would require protection, whereas the "Indians must also be protected from any unfair or dishonourable dealings being practised toward them by renegade white men."[35] The rapid settlement of the West would also increase the amount of public private property, which would require protection by the police.

With the announcement that the CPR would be built through the Bow Valley, the I. G. Baker Company, the Hudson's Bay Company, Louis Roselle, Baptiste Anouse Jr., and William Scollen all made attempts to delineate their land holdings and, with the exception of Scollen, made land claims. The I. G. Baker Company was the first to petition the federal government for the right to purchase its land. On March 27, 1882, the I. G. Baker Company applied for permission to obtain ownership by homesteading or by purchasing 1,300 acres (526 hectares) in the vicinity of Fort Calgary.[36] Its application noted the fact that the company had erected several substantial buildings and fenced a considerable piece of land between the Bow and Elbow Rivers for farming and grazing purposes. It considered its land holdings part of the commercial operations that the company had developed since 1875. The claim covered virtually all the land west of the Elbow, including portions of sections 14, 15, and 16. In support of its application, the I. G. Baker Company attached depositions by W. G. Conrad and Donald Davis, as well as deeds of sale between the company and Baptiste Anouse Jr. and John

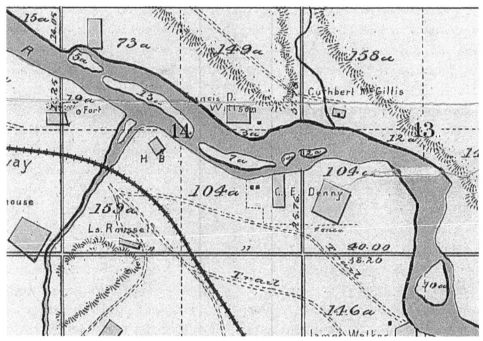

Figure 1.10 The most contested part of township 24, range 1, west of the Fifth Meridian was the land south of the Bow River in section 14. The I. G. Baker Company claimed all of section 14 west of the Elbow River and south of the Bow, along with portions of sections 15 and 16 south of the Bow. The company was eventually permitted to purchase 16.5 acres (7 hectares) south of the CPR line on the west side of the Elbow.

The Hudson's Bay Company claimed all the land in section 14 with the exception of the land occupied by the North-West Mounted Police post and the I. G. Baker Company store. This claim was not given any serious consideration, but the company was offered 14.5 acres (6 hectares) around the site of its post. Wesley Orr acquired the land when the Hudson's Bay Company refused the offer.

Louis Roselle, whose farm was located immediately north of Scotsman's (or Fraser's) Hill, claimed all the land on either side of the Elbow in the southeast quarter of section 14 except for the land surrounding the police post and the Hudson's Bay Company store. After Orr and Archibald McVittie purchased the Roselle claim in the summer of 1883, they tried to create a townsite that straddled the Elbow River. Orr eventually received title to the portion of the Roselle claim east of the Elbow River.

The Denney estate originally included the eastern half of section 14 south of the Bow River, as well as part of section 13 south and west of the Bow. The federal government rejected the Denneys' claim to section 13, and the claim was confined to the west half of section 14 south of the Bow. The Denney estate was acquired by John Stewart, who promoted it as the future location of Calgary. 1884.

Monroe. The deeds of sale were intended to extinguish the land claims of other people who had actually settled on the land. The company was advised that no action could be taken on its application pending the completion of the subdivision survey.

The Hudson's Bay Company followed suit on October 12, 1882, when land commissioner Charles Brydges claimed all of section 14 with the exception of the land occupied by the North-West Mounted Police and the I. G. Baker Company, as well as two sections of land in the same township for the Hudson's Bay Company. In support of its claim, the company enclosed a map prepared by Dominion land surveyor Montague Aldous showing the location of the Hudson's Bay Company post relative to the future subdivision of the land.[37] The company's interest in claiming land at Calgary in 1882 represented a dramatic reversal of its previous view of the land's value before the railway was rerouted through the Bow Valley. The willingness of the company to permit Louis Roselle to settle adjacent to its post was evidence of this former lack of interest. The company based its claim on the fact that it had been in continuous occupation of the site since 1874, having arrived even before the police and the I. G. Baker Company. Brydges also argued that the Hudson's Bay Company should be able to claim land at Calgary under the terms of the Deed of Surrender of 1869, by which it sold its interests in North-Western Territory to the Government of Canada. The company required the land so it could expand its operations. The Hudson's Bay Company received the same response as the I. G. Baker Company had in February 1883.

Louis Roselle began his efforts to obtain title to his land with a memorial to Sir John A. Macdonald on February 16, 1883, for the right to purchase the southwest quarter of section 14, except for the areas belonging to those parties who had constructed buildings there before the fall of 1877. He therefore recognized the claims of the North-West Mounted Police, the Hudson's Bay Company, and the I. G. Baker Company. A map prepared by Dominion land surveyor Archibald McVittie was attached to illustrate the location of his claim relative to the rest of the Elbow River settlement. Ottawa lawyer Dalton McCarthy of McCarthy, Osler, Hoskin & Creelman, whom Roselle had retained, was advised in July 1883 that until such time as the subdivision survey of township 24 was made and approved, no action could be taken on

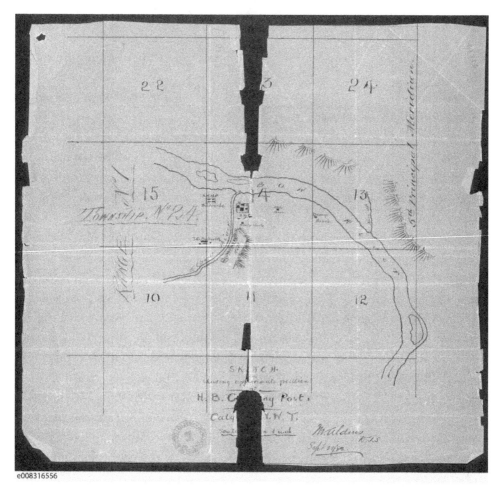

e008316556

Figure 1.11 This map was prepared in September 1882 by Montague Aldous at the request of the Hudson's Bay Company in support of its claim to section 14.

Source: Library and Archives Canada, RG 15 volume 283 File 51314

Roselle's request. Baptiste Anouse Jr. also endeavoured to obtain title to the southeast quarter of section 15 despite the fact that the I. G. Baker Company professed to have extinguished his claim.[38] He retained the same legal firm as Roselle to deal with the federal government and received the same response as Roselle.

William Scollen, as part of an effort to adjust to the arrival of the CPR in 1880, took advantage of the presence in the community of Dominion land surveyor Lachlan Kennedy and asked him to find out where the boundary

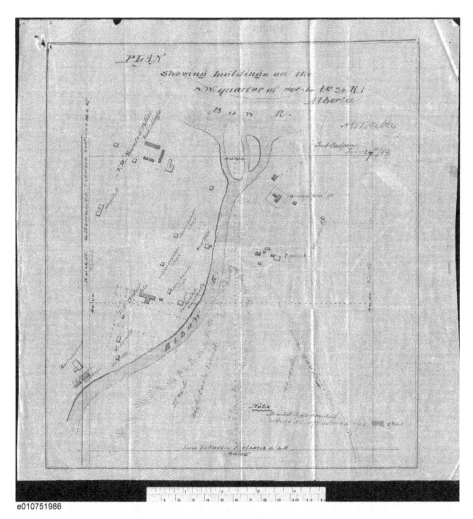

e010751986

Figure 1.12 This survey was prepared in February 1883 by Archibald McVittie at the request of Louis Roselle in support of his claim to land in the southwest quarter of section 14. The map illustrates the extent of the community that had developed along both sides of the Elbow River immediately below its confluence with the Bow.

Source: Library and Archives Canada, RG 15 volume 632 File 237386

line was between sections 9 and 10. Kennedy was not able to give Scollen a definite answer, but in 1881, a Dominion land surveyor hired by Scollen confirmed that Scollen's house was in section 10 rather than section 9. In the spring of 1882, he built a new house on the other side of the dividing line between the two sections.

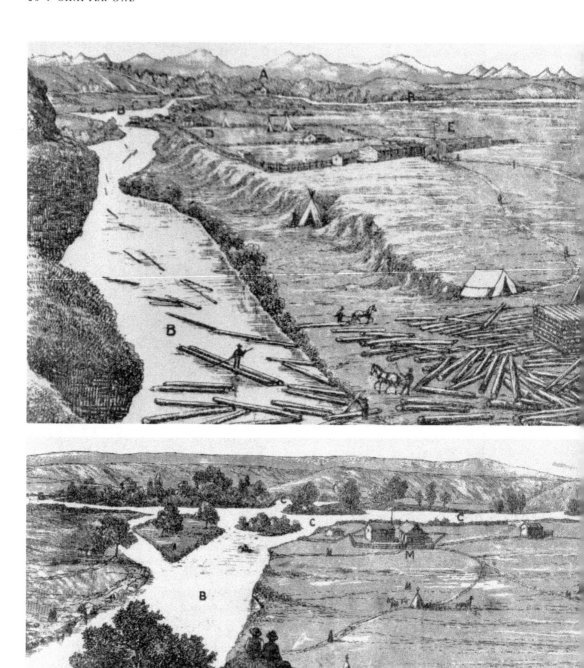

Figure 1.13 This view of the confluence of the Elbow and Bow Rivers as sketched by General Thomas Bland Strange appeared in the *Canadian Illustrated News* on December 30, 1882. It shows the quickening pace of economic activity in anticipation of the arrival of the railway. The points of interest in this scene were identified as follows:

A–Catholic mission; B–Elbow River; C–Bow River; D–restaurant; E–I. G. Baker Co. store; F–old church; G–Cochrane Ranche butcher shop; H–Cochrane Ranche steam sawmill, operated by Colonel Macleod for the Cochrane Ranche Company; I–Frogg's ferry; K–North-West Mounted Police post; L–boom bridge; M–Hudson's Bay Company store; N–Captain Denney's house.

Source: Glenbow Library and Archives, NA-83-1 and 2

Settlers in search of land after the CPR made the decision to use the Bow Valley included Napoleon Mayett and Augustus Carney. Mayett began his occupation of the southeast quarter of section 10, the present location of the Union Cemetery, in February 1881,[39] whereas Carney claimed land that he had occupied as early as July 20, 1882, in the northeast quarter of section 10 south of the Elbow River, which was also the same land claimed by Baptiste Anouse Sr. Carney was considered a claim jumper, "having been warned off by the Police who informed him that he would have no claim."[40] Carney appears to have made a deal with Mayett, since he received the title to the southeast quarter of section 10. James Morris, James Owens, James Butlin, and W. G. Smith moved up the Elbow River past the mission and the farm of William Scollen to the area of the present-day Elbow Park and Elboya neighbourhoods, which would eventually become section 4 in the township survey. Their occupation of this land took place between May 1882 and June 1883.[41] James Owens is the best known of these individuals, having come to North-West Territories as a member of the North-West Mounted Police and visiting Calgary for the first time in 1879. Following his discharge, he received the northwest quarter of section 4 as a grant of land by virtue of his status as a veteran of the North-West Mounted Police. He later established a racetrack on his land, which became an important centre of community activity before the Victoria Park Racetrack was built. Sam Livingston, who had lived at various locations in the Calgary area since the early 1870s, may also have moved on a permanent basis to the land that would eventually become the Glenmore Reservoir.

Other newcomers to Calgary before the arrival of the railway simply wanted to acquire land for a residence and/or business premises at the location of the future townsite. This group included the Cochrane Ranche Company, which established a sawmill operated by James Walker, as well as George Murdoch, a harness maker from New Brunswick, who arrived on May 13, 1883. Murdoch's journal for that date noted that he reached Calgary at 11:30 p.m. and camped opposite the fort, where he cooked scones in his wagon and maintained a fire all day on account of the rain. He noted the fact that there were "lots of dead cattle all along the bank of the River Bow, rotting and stinking."[42] On May 13, Murdoch forded the Elbow River to the fort side, rigged up his wagon box, and borrowed a tent as a temporary shelter. New settlers in similar circumstances reinforced the development of a community on both sides of the river.

THE IRON HORSE PLANTS HIS FEET IN CALGARY

Construction of the prairie section of the CPR ended with the crossing of the Elbow River on August 12, 1883, and a new construction company took over the task of completing the main line to the summit of the Canadian Rockies. The first CPR bridge across the Elbow was a wooden trestle, which was a temporary structure to permit the passage of construction trains and put the line into service. One of the excited observers to that event was Isaac Freeze, who had arrived on the east side of the Elbow River in advance of the CPR. In a letter home, he observed that on "Saturday the iron-horse will plant his first footsteps in once-distant Calgary."[43] The CPR built a rail yard, a "Y" to turn its locomotives, and a temporary station west of the Elbow River near the boundary line between sections 14 and 15. It moved its construction camp from the east to the west side of the Elbow River. No immediate decision had yet been made as to the official location of the proposed townsite.

The CPR was quickly followed across the Elbow River by many businessmen, who erected tents or frame buildings on the land south of the CPR tracks close to the I. G. Baker Company store and George Murdoch's land. Andrew Armour and Thomas Braden began the publication of the *Calgary Herald, Mining and Ranch Advocate and General Advertiser,* as the newspaper was first known, on the west side of the Elbow using a hand press, which arrived on the first train carrying freight for Calgary. From its first edition on August 31, 1883, the *Herald* chronicled the progress of the community and was on guard against any impediments to its becoming a town of note. This first issue featured an article dealing with Calgary's townsite and economic prospects, highlighting its location at the confluence of the Bow and Elbow Rivers, both of which were pure, clear, and cold and capable of supplying water power for an unlimited number of mills and factories. The river junction as a suitable location for a future western metropolis was enhanced by several beautiful islands that were well wooded and admirably suited for parks. The *Herald* maintained the opinion that the Elbow River was an important feature of the community.

Construction activities in the fall of 1883 on the west side of the Elbow included a new post office on a lot staked out in front of the I. G. Baker Company store. The first floor housed the post office, while the timber agent and Inland Revenue offices were on the second. With the post office's construction, the *Herald* hoped the authorities would forward the $500 worth of stamps boxed up in Winnipeg that awaited the building's opening. This would end the necessity for Calgarians to purchase US stamps and end the loss of revenue to the Canadian government. Businessmen McLean and Thomas constructed a two-storey building, with the lower storey used for a retail store, while the top storey was laid out for offices, nearly all of which were rented to the professional gentlemen of the city. The Methodist Church made plans to build on a lot between the I. G. Baker Company and the *Herald* offices and ordered the lumber for construction in September 1883. Construction on the east side of the Elbow included a new Presbyterian church.

Building on both sides of the Elbow continued until November 1883 when an unidentified representative of the government refused to permit the construction of any more buildings on the west side until the difficulties about the townsite regarding the CPR's land claims and the selection of a location for a station were adjusted.[44] This decision interfered with the building plans of a number of organizations and individuals, including the Methodist Church, which had to commence building its church near the tent it had formerly used on the east side of the Elbow. Permission had originally been given to allow building on the west side of the river, but it was withdrawn during the delay occasioned by the nonarrival of the lumber.

Construction activity, or the lack thereof, highlighted one of two problems identified by the *Herald* that faced the community. The first problem was the failure of the government to make a decision regarding the location of the townsite. The September 14, 1883, issue of the newspaper noted that "as yet nothing definite is known about the townsite as regards either place or times when it will be located. Vague reports have been in circulation that the difficulty between the Government and the CPR has been arranged and that the survey will be made immediately. This had the effect of reducing investment in the town."[45] The *Herald* encouraged the use of section 15 as the townsite since, in its view, that would preserve Calgary's relationship to the Bow and Elbow Rivers, which the *Herald* regarded as an essential feature of the town's location. Wesley Orr and Archibald McVittie, who showed the newspaper's proprietors a plan to subdivide the Roselle claim, brought them some relief from their anxiety over the issue. McVittie, on behalf of Orr, had made an offer to purchase Roselle's land in the southwest quarter of section 14. Roselle's land extended along both sides of the Elbow River and included land claimed by the I. G. Baker Company. In the *Herald*'s view, the land on both sides of the Elbow River and at the confluence of the Bow and Elbow Rivers would make an ideal location for a townsite. The paper predicted that if Orr and McVittie were successful in having the land placed on the market while the CPR and the government quarrelled over the proposed site, "we shall have quite a town built upon the above property."[46] Orr failed, however, to actually pay Roselle as per their agreement, with the result being that Roselle made arrangements with other individuals, including George Murdoch, while he continued to try to resolve his original land claim.

Orr and McVittie's efforts to establish the townsite were in vain because they could not obtain title to Roselle's land. McVittie, in Roselle's opinion, had also failed to live up to the terms of the purchase agreement by not making an immediate payment of $10,000. Roselle thus felt free to sell his land to other people. The *Herald*, in its September 28 edition, called once again upon the "manipulators" to make a definite determination regarding the Calgary townsite. The manipulators, in the *Herald*'s view, included W. B. Scarth, the manager of the Canada North-West Land Company, whose arrival in the community to make a decision had been rumoured for some time. But, stated the *Herald*, "Mr. Scarth doesn't come and consequently, our people are at their wits end to decide what to do. Winter is coming on and many have no adequate shelter from the cold not having any land to build on and not knowing where to build."[47] The *Herald* further suggested that there might be truth to the rumour that Scarth was an innocent victim of manipulation by the federal government, which was delaying the transfer of the land to the CPR. If the government was to blame, the *Herald* concluded, "we call on them as citizens of the Dominion and contributors to its support to remove the burdens and difficulties under which they are labouring, and if the blame is laid at Mr. Scarth's door, we warn him that those who are made to suffer now will remember it by and by."[48]

By October 5, the *Herald*'s plea for action was apparently answered as it reported that Archibald McVittie had been ordered by CPR chief engineer Mr. Hamilton to lay out a townsite at an undisclosed location. This decision indicated to the *Herald* that the government had at last "awakened to the wants of Calgary and as they have given us the daily mail, we hope they will allow nothing to interfere with the survey and that by our next issue, we may be able to announce that our town has been located and lots will soon be placed on the market."[49] The *Herald*'s jubilation, however, was premature, and on October 12, it reported that the survey had been stopped pending the visit of Richard Angus, William Cornelius Van Horne, and Mr. Egan. They arrived and left without indicating whether any decision had been made.

The parade of officials through Calgary appeared unable to resolve the issue and included CPR land commissioner John McTavish in late October. His apparent failure to make a decision was attributed to "some real or pretended claim to the section."[50] By the end of October, the *Herald* feared that the CPR would choose to locate its town on section 17, thus preventing the development of Calgary as a "compact town divided by the Elbow, but united in a common interest" and ensuring that it would be a "long, straggling place, with one part working against the other spread over too great an area to have much in common."[51]

Our Kingdom for a Bridge

The lack of an adequate vehicle and pedestrian bridge across the Elbow River was the *Herald*'s second preoccupation. The only links between the two parts of the expanding community developing on either side of the Elbow in the summer of 1883 were the CPR trestle bridge and a footbridge, which had probably been built in the fall of 1882 by James Macleod and was located south of the CPR trestle near the present location of the Mac-Donald Bridge. The community's efforts to improve the footbridge's safety were thwarted by the theft of the ropes that had been added to the bridge in lieu of a wooden railing. The *Herald* feared that people were at risk of falling into the river and appealed for the ropes' immediate return.[52] In September 1883, Mr. Grant of the North American Construction Company, which had built the CPR main line to the Elbow River, made an offer to build a substantial wagon bridge across the Elbow River for $1,000.[53] The

Herald encouraged citizens to take advantage of Grant's expertise in bridge construction and request the necessary funds from the Northwest Council, which was then in session in Regina. Colonel James Walker, who was a member of the council, followed through with the suggestion and initiated a request for $1,000 from the Department of the Interior via Edgar Dewdney, the lieutenant-governor of North-West Territories.

While waiting for a response, lamps were purchased and placed at either end of the footbridge and improvements were made to the deck, railings, and approaches. By September 21, the town, in the *Herald*'s view, had a "neat and safe" bridge for which "we have no reason to complain."[54] Not everyone in the community agreed with this assessment, though, as indicated in a letter to the editor signed "Expectancy." The author of the letter was convinced that the footbridge was becoming more dangerous and feared that a life or two would be sacrificed before the necessary improvements were made. The letter repeated the suggestion that the efforts of the local citizens be supplemented with a government grant to erect a proper bridge before the ice formed.[55]

Any complacency that the *Herald* may have felt regarding the bridge issue was shattered on October 31 when the Elbow River joined the federal government and the CPR as one of Calgary's tormentors and drove the town's level of frustration to new heights. Floating ice swept the footbridge downstream, lodging it against the railway trestle and causing an ice jam that threatened to destroy the trestle bridge. Superintendent McIllree was notified, but before the North-West Mounted Police could arrive to remove the obstruction, the construction crew that was driving piles for the new CPR iron bridge took the matter in hand, and with the aid of a piledriver and locomotive, removed enough of the ill-fated footbridge to ensure the safety of the CPR trestle.

It was a tragedy of Shakespearian proportions. In an editorial entitled "Our Kingdom for a Bridge," the *Herald* noted that the "bond of unity between Calgary East and Calgary West [had] been swept away by the Elbow's icy torrent, much to the sorrow and lamentation of Calgary Citizens."[56] This left the railway trestle bridge as the only means of "pedal transport to an afflicted public and before the [citizens crossed] the raging torrent by this means for some previous moments [they lingered] shivering on the banks and [feared] to launch away."[57] The problems of using the railway trestle were immediately solved by the establishment of a ferry service, which the *Herald* described by drawing upon Greek mythology. "No sooner," the newspaper wrote, "had some of the classic souls of Calgary yearned for Charon, the grim ferryman of the Styx and Atheron to appear on the Elbow . . . than one of our enterprising ship owners appeared on the Elbow's stormy banks with a yawl boat and an *ad valorem* tariff for the transportation of Calgary's precious freight."[58] The creation of a winter ice bridge reduced the burden imposed by the exorbitant ferry rates, at least until the spring of 1884.

The delays in selecting a permanent townsite and the destruction of the footbridge, plus a litany of other afflictions, intruded into the *Herald*'s Thanksgiving Day editorial. In its view, the "thanksgiving spirit naturally got a bit sluggish as [Calgarians] thought of the townsite still being a thing of beautiful uncertainty, of the Elbow's footbridge being washed away by the merciless torrent, of there being no representative in the Legislative Council, of the utterly supreme indifference shown to our crying wants by the Dominion Government, of the garden fields of the North West being swallowed up by ranch companies, of our being strangers to the bountiful harvest, and of a thousand other abuses of which [they] were the victims."[59] The spirit of thanksgiving, however, "went up in the tube as [Calgarians] generously thought of the bountiful harvests garnered into storehouses by his relatives in the east, of the tidal wave of immigrants that is prophesied to sweep over the North West and the golden harvests that in the future are to be garnered from our illimitable western fields, and the numerous other blessings that are to be."[60] After this dispassionate review of the situation, the *Herald* concluded that thanksgiving on the part of Calgarians was thoroughly warranted, even if the blessings justifying such a mood had been postponed.

With the destruction of the footbridge, the status of James Macleod's request for a government grant became more urgent, particularly to J. K. Oswald and Richard Hardisty. Oswald advertised himself as a justice of the peace, notary public, issuer of marriage and other licences, real estate agent, land and mining commissioning agent, and the agent for the CPR's land department, as well as the agent for three coal mining companies. Hardisty was in charge of the Hudson's Bay Company's interests in Calgary and was thus also interested in the construction of a bridge. Macleod reported to Oswald and Hardisty that there had been no progress on the grant application for $1,000 for bridge construction and advised that the community had a better chance of receiving financial assistance if it raised half the required amount and then petitioned the Department of the Interior for the rest.[61] Oswald and Hardisty followed up on the suggestion, and a petition was duly prepared and sent to the Department of the Interior on November 6, 1883. It described the circumstances in which residents of Calgary and district found themselves as a consequence of the flood. As Macleod had suggested, the petition proposed the construction of a "good and substantial passenger and traffic bridge" for $1,000 or $1,200, the cost of which would be shared between the citizens and the federal government with equal contributions of $600. The petition was received on November 19 and immediately forwarded to Lieutenant-Governor Edgar Dewdney. The letter of transmittal from John H. Hall, the secretary of the Department of the Interior, noted that the territorial government had only expended $4,000 of the total amount of $29,000 provided to it by the federal government, thus implying that it had the funds to respond to Calgary's need for a bridge. Oswald also began a subscription list to raise local contributions.[62]

The *Herald* applauded this initiative, noting that although there was a certain amount of diversion to be had by fording rivers, creeping apprehensively over an ice track, and crossing an elevated railway bridge with considerable alarm, these activities became somewhat monotonous over time, making Calgarians desirous of a foot and passenger bridge.[63] The community moved quickly to raise its share of the cost of the project.

By mid-December 1883, Oswald reported the collection of close to $700 and advised those residents interested in getting a bridge built to stop complaining at once and "show their energy in a solid, practical manner by calling by [his] shack and putting their names down for a good, round sum and then if we get [a] subsidy from the government, the work can start at once."[64] With no response from either the territorial or federal government by the end of December, Captain John Stewart, the new owner of the Denney estate on the east side of the Elbow River, offered to guarantee the balance of the funds required.

LAND CLAIMS RESOLVED

Despite the *Herald*'s view that the federal government and the CPR were not making an effort to resolve the townsite question, events were actually moving swiftly behind the scenes. Between July 23 and August 6, 1883, Charles-Edward LaRue completed a subdivision survey of township 24, range 1, west of the Fifth Meridian that placed the federal government in a legal position to issue titles to that land. LaRue's responsibility was to divide the township into 36 sections, describe the general characteristics of the land, including the quality of the soil, and indicate the location of watercourses, trails, and land that had already been broken for farming purposes. The surveyor recorded his observations in a field notebook that was used to compile the official map describing the various natural and human features of the land. LaRue's field notes indicated that the Elbow River was the feature around which the town had already started to develop, though it was "more extensive and more popular on the east side of the Elbow River on section 14."[65] Like Edgar Dewdney, he said that Calgary's location made it a community of destiny. Its geographical position, picturesque sites, proximity to the Rocky Mountains, supplies of wood and timber, and ample supply of pure water would ensure that the town of Calgary would become "one of the most important places of the North West." The preparation and publication of the township plan was completed on March 8, 1884.

The federal government also sent William Pearce to Calgary in late September 1883 to investigate the general issue of land claims. Pearce evaluated various Calgary claims with respect to the revision of the Dominion Lands Act on May 7, 1880. Pearce also made specific recommendations regarding the location of a townsite. He advised the federal government "that the west half of section 15, all of section 16, and the south half of section 17 would make a very fine townsite."[66] CPR land commissioner John McTavish began implementing Pearce's plan in mid-November 1883, when he brought Baptiste Anouse Jr. to Pearce's office in Winnipeg to cancel his claim to the southeast quarter of section 15.[67] A surrender document was drafted and signed by Anouse Jr., which in Pearce's view cleared the way for the federal government to issue a title to the CPR for section 15. Following the visit of Anouse Jr. and McTavish, Pearce advised the Minister of the Interior to move quickly to cooperate with the CPR to create a townsite by subdividing

Figure 1.14 William Pearce first arrived in Calgary in 1883 to adjudicate land claims in his capacity as a member of the Dominion Lands Board. He eventually moved to Calgary on a permanent basis in 1887, where he played a major role in various aspects of its development. He was a strong advocate of irrigation and created, or at least attempted to create, the first large-scale irrigation company using the waters of the Elbow River. As the irrigation value of the Elbow River gave way to its use as a water supply for Calgary, Pearce changed with the times and advocated the river's use for this new purpose.
Source: Glenbow Library and Archives, NA-339–1

section 16. He suggested that if the CPR were given section 15, the government could develop section 16, thus moving the townsite from section 14. The federal government followed his advice and passed an Order-in-council in January 1884.[68] The decision was conveyed to the CPR before the formal passage of the order. On December 12, 1883, the *Herald* reported the joyous news that at last, word had come to "lay out 15," or at least two blocks of it, for the townsite, and Archibald McVittie's force went to work. The federal government followed Pearce's suggestions and began laying out section 16 as a townsite, moving the community farther away from the Elbow River.

John Stewart, the new owner of the Denney estate, which originally consisted of the east half of section 14 and part of section 13 south of the Bow River, made one last attempt to keep the townsite east of the Elbow. In late December 1883, he subdivided a portion of his land and, on January 2, began advertising this location as the "people's choice" for the town's permanent location east of the Elbow. The advertisement further claimed that more than 200 lots had already been secured at prices that were within easy reach of people of all classes. His efforts to make his land more attractive also included offering lots for civic purposes such as a school. His plans included developing the islands at the confluence of the Bow and Elbow Rivers for residential purposes.

John Stewart received title to the eastern half of section 14 south of the Bow River on May 2, 1884, well after it would have been of any value to keep Calgary east of the Elbow. His claim to part of section 13 south of the Bow was acquired by the CPR and eventually purchased by William Pearce in 1886 for $10 per acre ($25 per hectare). Wesley Orr was able to complete his purchase of the Louis Roselle claim when he followed through with the original purchase agreement that had been negotiated in the spring of 1883. The Hudson's Bay Company's claim to section 14 was rejected on the grounds that the trading post had been established after 1870 and that the company could not be classified as settlers. The Hudson's Bay Company refused the offer to purchase the 14.5 acres (6 hectares) covered by its improvements, and the land was sold to Wesley Orr and Mary Schrieber. The I. G. Baker Company claim for 1,300 acres (526 hectares) was never given serious consideration, but the company was permitted to purchase 16.5 acres (7 hectares) at $50 per acre ($125 per hectare) of land in the immediate vicinity of its original store, located along the banks of the Elbow, in recognition of its usefulness to the Government of Canada and because its relations with the First Nations had "always been honourable and satisfactory."[69]

Father Albert Lacombe, who had taken charge of the Catholic mission on the Elbow in 1882, moved quickly to secure land for the mission. He and Father Leon Doucet claimed the northwest quarter of section 10 north and west of the Elbow River and all of the southwest quarter of section 10 as individual homesteads. After they received title to the land, they transferred it to the ownership of the Oblate Order.

William Scollen encountered the greatest difficulty in acquiring title to his land, and as a result, he added the CPR to his list of persecutors. He discovered upon applying for his title that, in the government's view, he had not moved onto the southeast quarter of section 9 until after May 7, 1880, which meant that his land was now railway land. He refused to accept this decision and immediately began making appeals to Sir John A. Macdonald and other federal government officials for redress based on the argument that he had made a significant effort to determine the location of his residence and on the justice of his cause as a loyal subject of the Queen.[70] He also enlisted the assistance of his brother, Father Scollen, and Father Lacombe in his effort to escape the clutches of what he called "this bloodsucking monopoly."[71] He eventually purchased 80 acres (32 hectares) from the CPR in 1890, and the rest of section 9 was retained for the future development of Mount Royal.

By the mid-1880s, Sam Livingston had settled on land farther up the Elbow River, past the homesteads of Smith, Owens, and Morris in section 4. He obtained title to his property after participating in a squatter's revolt.[72] Although it was part of Calgary, his property was also part of the rural community of Glenmore, the centre of which was Glenmore Protestant Public School District No. 114. The first meeting of the ratepayers for the school district was held at the residence of Hugh Munro within the Glenmore area on February 21, 1888, and Hugh Munro, James S. Moore, and Sam Livingston were elected as trustees. The district came into existence with the publication of a notice in the May 26, 1888, issue of the *Northwest Territories Gazette*. An important part of this rural community was the Chipman Ranch. In 1888, Richard George Robinson came from England to become its manager. Purebred horses were the mainstay of the Chipman Ranch, which was later taken over by Robinson and his sons and renamed the Elbow Park Ranch. They branched into raising cattle while continuing to breed horses.

The occupation of the Elbow Valley as far as Weaselhead Flats was completed with the creation of the Tsuu T'ina reserve. In 1877, the Tsuu T'ina were one of the signatories of Treaty 7 under their chief, Bull Head. The government decided the Tsuu T'ina reserve should be located on the south side of the Bow River, across from the Siksika reserve at Blackfoot Crossing. The Tsuu T'ina were, however, reluctant to settle at this location because their relations with the Siksika were unfriendly. Under the leadership of Chief Bull Head, they resisted the efforts of the federal government to move them and, on June 27, 1883, a new treaty was made with the Tsuu T'ina that gave them a reserve that included both the Elbow River and Fish Creek. The location was rich in game and was closer to their traditional hunting grounds around Moose Mountain. It ensured the Tsuu T'ina would be an integral part of Calgary, despite the view held by many of its citizens that this should not be the case.

INCORPORATION

The efforts of the local residents to take some control of the development of their community began on January 7, 1884, when James Reilly convened a public meeting to deal with several community issues. The arbitrary nature of the CPR's decision to locate its depot a mile from the Elbow River, and thus some distance from the existing centre of population, was his main concern. The construction of a bridge across the Elbow, a petition to the CPR to move its depot to a more central location, and the creation of a civic committee to pursue incorporation were his other suggestions for community action. The proposed civic committee was elected on January 14 with Colonel James Walker, Captain John Stewart, George C. King, and Dr. Henderson representing the east side of the river and George Murdoch, Thomas Swan, and J. D. Moulton representing the west side. Conspicuously absent was Archibald McVittie, who continued to represent Wesley Orr, whose unresolved land claim on both sides of the Elbow was the location of the settlement where several of these people lived. The civic committee established that those portions of sections 12, 13, 14, 15, and 16 located south of the Bow River and the north half of sections 10 and 11 would constitute the municipal corporation of Calgary. A census indicated a total population of about 500, but only 428 were on the list because some people were not at home when the enumerators called. Incorporation was requested by 278 people, 73 of whom resided on the west side of the Elbow River and 205 on the east side.[73] The need to adjust the boundaries, Wesley Orr's objections, and the revision of the municipal ordinance delayed incorporation until November 1884. By the time this had occurred, the loyalties of Calgary residents were to the CPR and section 15 townsite and not to the old location on section 14.

Spanning Our Noble River

The bridge problem noted by James Reilly was already being dealt with by a committee chaired by Richard Hardisty. By early January 1884, the committee's efforts had resulted in a commitment from the territorial government to contribute $300. On January 16, the committee called for sealed tenders by February 1 for a bridge across the Elbow River at a point north of the railway bridge and presumably aligned with Stephen Avenue, since the bridge was later referred to by that name. Plans and specifications were made available at Archibald McVittie's office. The civic committee made its contribution to the project by taking advantage of Lieutenant-Governor

Dewdney's presence in Calgary on January 24 to request an increase in the amount of the government grant. Dewdney advised the civic committee that the total grant for bridges throughout the territories was $7,000, most of which had already been spent, and that the money was not intended for bridges in towns but on country roads. The $300 grant for the bridge, which he increased to $500, was provided from the 50-cent per gallon tax on permit liquor collected by his government.[74]

James Christie was awarded the contract for the bridge's construction with a budget of $2,375. The *Herald* believed that "the matter [was] in good hands and [it expected] a bridge in keeping with the place spanning our noble river."[75] By early April, sufficient progress had been made to warrant Richard Hardisty forwarding progress reports from the engineers and the contractors to Hayter Reed, along with a request for payment of the $500 grant as soon as possible because "owing to the present dangerous state of the river, it is very necessary the bridge should be finished without delay."[76] Dewdney was not persuaded to send the funds immediately and advised the bridge committee that the cheque would be sent upon the receipt of certificates stating that the bridge had been completed.

On May 6, the required certificates were sent by the contractors and engineers, who declared that the bridge would be ready for use the following day. The new bridge, which had been built partially with tax revenue derived from the sale of alcohol, presumably went into service the same day the *Herald* ran an article attacking what it called the "permit farce." The prohibitory laws of North-West Territories allowed the entry of alcohol into the territories for medicinal purposes. The *Herald* observed that "Calgary must be a very unhealthy place," which stirred Dewdney's soul to "its profoundest depths" and motivated him to permit 60 cases of liquor to arrive by a Saturday night train to recover the "health of the denizens of this valley."[77] Instead of the liquor meeting the needs of this supposed medical crisis, according to the *Herald*, "it has been productive of numerous fights, black eyes, a broken nose, and many other calamities."[78] The permit system, in the *Herald*'s view, was a huge farce and a great curse, but the newspaper failed to mention that it had also provided a bridge.

Within a matter of weeks, however, the Elbow River proved even more dangerous than anticipated by the bridge committee. Its transformation into a threat to Calgary's key transportation assets began on June 21, 1884, with the onset of the annual spring rain and flood season. The rising waters of the Elbow were made more dangerous than usual in that spring by logs that had been placed on the Elbow's banks above the railway bridge. T. P. McHugh had brought them downriver just before the commencement of the rains for use as lumber and fencing material by the North-West Mounted Police. The rising water picked up the logs and carried them downstream, where they piled up against the railway bridge. By June 25, the bridge had sunk 5 feet (1.5 metres) in the centre, and the logs were battering the new Stephen Avenue Bridge, eventually piling up higher than the bridge itself. The *Herald* predicted that the train from the east would have to put its passengers and mail off on the other side of the river so they could then be brought across the Stephen Avenue Bridge, should that structure still be standing. Shortly after the *Herald* went to press on June 25, its fears came true, and the new Stephen Avenue Bridge also became a victim of the torrent, with its east end thrown completely around, coming to rest on a small island.

Initially, there was some hope that the Stephen Avenue Bridge could be repaired and offers of assistance were forthcoming from Colonel William Herchmer of the North-West Mounted Police, the firm King & Co., and the Hudson's Bay Company. Work began immediately to try to salvage this artifact of community cooperation. With the bridge out, the *Herald* returned to its familiar lament about the problems of crossing the Elbow River, noting that Calgarians would "appreciate this as the approach to the ford on both sides is very bad, rendering crossing anything but pleasant."[79] On July 23, however, the *Herald* reported that the attempt had failed and "unless our member for the Northwest Council can induce that body to give a liberal grant toward the rebuilding of this bridge, the town will be put to a great inconvenience for some time to come."[80] The *Herald* hoped that the town council, when organized, would be able to obtain a loan to carry out the work of rebuilding. It also had suggestions for how the new bridge should be built, pointing out the "desirability of putting up a Howe truss bridge of a single span with the abutments some distance further from the banks on each side than before. Such a design would leave a clean sweep for the river both when floods come and when the ice breaks in the spring."[81]

Figure 1.15 This was the scene on June 26 or 27, 1884, following the destruction of both the railway and Stephen Avenue bridges. The remnants of the recently completed Stephen Avenue Bridge are visible on the west bank of the Elbow. The *Herald*'s view that the bridge could be repaired was clearly too optimistic.

Source: Glenbow Library and Archives, NA-1315–10

Figure 1.16 The new iron railway bridge constructed in the summer of 1884 to replace a wooden trestle bridge constructed in the summer of 1883. A new vehicle/pedestrian bridge was constructed in 1887. This bridge was replaced in 1897 by one made of steel.

Source: Glenbow Library and Archives, NA-3026–15

Once the bridge repair effort had been abandoned, it was quickly replaced with a ferry built by Jarrett and Cushing. The ferry was 30 feet (9 metres) long and 12 feet (3.5 metres) wide and seemed to operate with considerably fewer problems than had been the case in the fall of 1883. Lacking the funds to make a third attempt to bridge the Elbow, the citizens of Calgary shifted their attention to the construction of a bridge across the Bow River, which they hoped would be built by the federal government. The CPR, no longer trusting the tranquil waters of the Elbow, immediately began the construction of an iron bridge. The flood of 1884 had shown that the Elbow River was as capable of disrupting the operations of the CPR as was the Bow.

CHAPTER TWO

The Elbow and the
New Town of Calgary

1885–1905

The Elbow River was both a nuisance and a benefit to the new town of Calgary. It necessitated the construction of bridges to unite its eastern and western portions and to link the west end of the town directly to the new cemetery and Macleod Trail. The Elbow River divided the real estate interests of Calgary's business community, which competed for control of the economic future of the entire townsite. Wesley Orr, John Stewart, James Walker, and William Pearce were the leading members of a group of residents who lived east of the Elbow River. Wesley Orr had taken up permanent residence in Calgary in 1885 and no longer depended on Archibald McVittie to represent his interests. He took on an active role in municipal politics, serving as a member of the town council from 1888 to 1893 and as mayor in 1894, 1895, and 1897. While involved in civic politics, he pursued an aggressive program of economic development for Calgary. William Pearce, having played a critical role in moving the new town west of the Elbow River, took up permanent residence on the eastern outskirts of Calgary in 1887 after purchasing a portion of section 13 south and west of the Bow River from the

CPR. James Walker owned the land in section 12 south of the Pearce estate, which was also outside the limits of Calgary before 1907. James Lougheed and other west-end real estate boomers had purchased land in either the CPR portion of the townsite on section 15 or the federal government portion of the townsite on section 16.

The Elbow River united the business interests of this group of individuals when an irrigation plan requiring water from the Elbow was promoted as a strategy to deal with a drought and economic depression in the mid-1890s. Lougheed and Orr cooperated to organize western Canada's first irrigation convention. The entire community initially supported an irrigation company created by William Pearce. Pearce, however, became entangled in a dispute over the federal regulation of water resources, which pitted the federal government and him against the town and farmers in the Springbank area. As the flood of 1897 illustrated, however, the perception of the Elbow as being either a benefit or a curse could change in an instant.

BEWARE OF FATHER LACOMBE

Father Albert Lacombe was the first person to take action on the need for a new bridge across the Elbow River to replace the one that had washed out in 1884. In February 1885, he proposed that one be built at the mission site.[82] This idea was supported by farmers who were interested in having a shorter route to the townsite on the west side of the Elbow via Mission Hill rather than having to take the longer route through modern-day Ramsay and Inglewood. The project was supported by James Geddes, the Calgary area member of the Territorial Council. He favoured the mission location because the residents of High River, Sheep Creek, Pine Creek, and Fish Creek would save 2 miles (3 kilometres) by using that route to travel to Calgary.[83]

On February 13, Father Lacombe wrote to Edgar Dewdney, who held office as both lieutenant-governor and Indian commissioner, to confirm an earlier commitment Dewdney had made to assist in funding the project and to remind him that he had already raised $500 from the community and anticipated further contributions. Dewdney responded on February 17, confirming his promise and stipulating that the bridge be located at a point that would ensure it would not be washed out soon after construction as had happened in 1884. On February 19, handbills were distributed in the community advertising a meeting planned for that evening to presumably organize a committee to carry the bridge project forward.

The *Herald*, while acknowledging that it was a good idea to have as many bridges as possible in a well-watered country, was resentful of the actions of Father Lacombe. In the newspaper's opinion, the residents on the east side of the Elbow River in section 14 were more deserving of a bridge than the residents of section 10 where the mission was located. The *Herald* saw the bridge at the mission as detracting from efforts to develop the Calgary townsite. The cause for concern was the fact that the mission property had been subdivided but was not included within the boundaries of the new town. Other locations for a crossing on the Elbow River and a road south to Macleod Trail, such as the farm of Augustus Carney, were suggested. The motives of Father Lacombe were also questioned by the *Herald*, which suggested that he was driven by a desire to improve the value of the mission's real estate and not that of the farmers south of Calgary.

The town meeting was duly held and a bridge committee created that endorsed the idea of building at the mission location. In view of the comments made by the *Herald*, Father Lacombe was not included as a committee member. As Father Lacombe explained in a letter to Dewdney, "people seemed suspicious [of] my intentions, thinking that I wanted to build the bridge on the property of the mission, any how and by all means."[84] He resented the efforts of the *Herald* in particular to foster an atmosphere of mistrust and suspicion. As he noted in the same letter, the plan to place a bridge at the mission "was well and fine for [a] few days, but after jealousy and suspicions were aroused, then they opposed [the plan] as you can see by the article published in the *Herald* of yesterday."[85] He declared to Dewdney that "he never thought to make the Catholic mission speculate with the bridge. When [he] was the first to speak about a bridge on the Elbow, [he] was moved only by the desire to favour everyone, the town and the farmers around . . . Calgary."[86]

With the *Herald* leading the opposition to the involvement of any Calgary resident or the municipality in the construction of a bridge at the mission site, a second community meeting was held in the schoolhouse to reverse the decision of the first bridge committee and reopen the question as to the best way to spend the $500 promised by Dewdney. The meeting was called,

Figure 2.1 This photo shows the first bridge at the mission site, the construction of which began in the summer of 1885 at the initiative of Father Albert Lacombe. The Town of Calgary objected to its construction since it felt that a bridge at the old location was a greater priority. The construction was supervised by Edward McCoskrie, who proved less than competent in carrying out the task. The bridge was replaced in 1900 by a steel through truss bridge.
Source: Glenbow Library and Archives, NA-1753–51

in effect, to take the project away from Father Lacombe. Augustus Carney wanted to know why the committee appointed to choose the bridge site considered only the mission location when there were better sites farther down the river and just as handy to town. He pointed out that one of the disadvantages of the mission site was its use of McTavish Street, which crossed the CPR tracks and thus would be frequently obstructed by trains. McVittie, as spokesman for the bridge committee, defended the choice of the mission site because it would ensure support from the Oblates, which the committee thought would not be forthcoming if the bridge was located somewhere else.

Father Lacombe immediately denied the truth of McVittie's comment and then expressed his regrets that some remarks that had appeared in a local paper seemed to misrepresent his views. He had not, he thought, "given occasion to anyone to think that he was trying to have the bridge built at the mission property. If the meeting decided to build it elsewhere, he was as ready to favour it and do what he could for it as if [it] were on the mission property."[87] Father Lacombe also read a letter from Dewdney stating that if a suitable bridge was built over the Elbow that was durable, in a good site, and able to resist ice jams, a grant of $500 would be made from public funds.

The outcome of the meeting was an endorsement for building a bridge between sections 14 and 15 and the creation of a new bridge committee that would reconsider the best location for a bridge between the mission and the Elbow's confluence with the Bow River. The new committee was made up of Calgary residents, with the exception of Carney, all of whom had already decided where the bridge should be built. Father Lacombe declined membership for a second time because of the pressure of work and to avoid being accused again of trying to influence the committee's decision.

The *Herald*'s coverage of the meeting repeated its objections to the mission's bridge plan. "Simply put," stated the *Herald*, "the residents of the town had better not subscribe to it until they have built the bridge to section 14, since if they did, they would find they would have to pay for two bridges instead of one."[88] The only case in which a site outside the town's corporate limits could be chosen by a committee "with a regard for the pockets of the citizens, is where an outsider volunteers to subscribe the whole amount necessary to construct the bridge."[89] Therefore, any money subscribed to a second bridge would be an added burden to the citizens since the town was already committed to building a bridge across the Elbow within the corporate limits. The *Herald* also pointed out to the committee that if it recommended building a bridge within the town's corporate limits, the municipality would probably get the $500 grant offered by Dewdney. If the committee chose a site outside the corporate limits, it would not only impose the cost of building two bridges onto the residents of the town, but perhaps deprive the town of the grant.

The *Herald* also made what it probably considered an effort to placate the feelings of Father Lacombe by suggesting he had served too long in the area and had won too universal a respect to have his motives or actions brought into question. It continued to misrepresent the motives of Father Lacombe by suggesting that it was a perfectly legitimate thing in its view for a man to hope that public works would benefit his property.

The effort to redirect the grant funds was complete when representatives of the bridge committee advised the town council that plans to build a bridge at the mission site had been dropped in favour of the old site. The town then assumed responsibility for negotiating with the territorial government for the funds promised to Father Lacombe by Lieutenant-Governor Dewdney. The town clerk advised Dewdney that the proposed bridge would avoid the problems of the old site since its location would be close to the railway bridge where the banks were high on both sides of the river. A bridge at this location also had more advantages for the town since it would benefit residents who owned property within the town limits. The clerk felt that it was the duty of the town council to support development within the corporate boundaries of the town and not to assist in building up an "opposition town." The mission property, he continued, was laid out in lots, and because people living there would pay no taxes to Calgary, it would be a drawback to the progress of the municipality.

Dewdney was not persuaded by the arguments of the town clerk. On March 10, 1885, the Calgary town council was informed by the clerk of the Northwest Council that since a grant for the construction of a bridge within the limits of Calgary had been provided the previous year, it was only fair that the transportation needs of the residents around Calgary be given priority. Following this decision, Father Lacombe resumed his leadership role, but as events would show, the conflict over the bridge's location was only the beginning of his problems.

An engineer from the federal Department of Public Works inspected possible sites for a bridge at the mission site. In January 1886, a meeting was held in Ottawa between Hector Langevin, the Minister of Public Works, Henry Perley, the chief engineer of the Department of Public Works, and Father Lacombe, at which time the bridge location was selected and a final cost determined. The specifications for the bridge that were prepared later that month revealed the cost would be greater than anticipated. Langevin, however, agreed to cover the extra amount by adding a further $1,000 to the federal government's share. It was also agreed that the territorial government would handle the construction of the bridge based on specifications prepared in Ottawa. Father Lacombe hoped this approach would give the people of Calgary the chance to perform the work, including carrying the stone used to fill the bridge piers.

In March 1886, the bridge specifications were sent to Edward McCoskrie, who had been hired by Dewdney to supervise its construction. McCoskrie advertised himself as a civil and mining engineer, architect, surveyor, and contractor. His clients included the Town of Calgary, for whom he had served as town engineer and architect in 1885. The federal government's specifications called for a Howe truss bridge 5 feet (1.5 metres) higher than the highest recorded flow of the river. Rather than following these plans, in an effort to save money, McCoskrie made several changes that included lowering the bridge's height, using another type of truss system, and reducing the number of vertical supports.

Henry Perley, the chief engineer of the Department of Public Works, however, refused to approve McCoskrie's changes and recommended to Langevin that the federal government's contribution be withheld pending the construction of the bridge and its inspection by federal government engineers. Dewdney was reluctant to proceed with the project given this condition. Father Lacombe, however, was not prepared to tolerate any further delays and advised Dewdney to show some leadership and not be intimidated by the Department of Public Works: "I have all confidence in your energy and capacity. If the Department of Public Works is too mean to put at your disposal the $2,000 without proviso, I wish you could go on with the bridge any how and prove once more what you can do. Yes, my dear friend, I hope we will not be deceived. You told me many times that the bridge shall be built. Now we look at your good will and perseverance."[90] Father Lacombe felt that the chief engineer of the Department of Public Works and "red tape" were responsible for the approval problems, and he had confidence in the bridge-engineering skills of McCoskrie. Dewdney followed Father Lacombe's suggestions and construction proceeded without payment in advance by the federal government of its portion of the cost.

The construction of the bridge, however, encountered several problems, which were first reported by Father Lacombe to Dewdney in August 1886, when he also indicated that nothing had been done because the contractor was "a man of no means" and had a drinking problem.[91] Father Lacombe visited the site in October and found that the difficulties with the project were even worse than he had anticipated. All work on the project had ceased, with only one-third of the project completed; construction materials were scattered about the site, some of which were in danger of being carried away by the ice jams that formed in the fall; the contractor had disappeared after having been drunk for most of the summer; and the subcontractors and labourers had not been paid. All these problems raised the question of McCoskrie's competence as a project manager. Following Father Lacombe's visit, the I. G. Baker Company was hired to complete the bridge. McCoskrie continued as resident engineer after having been informed by Father Lacombe that he was in danger of losing his job if he did not improve. The bridge was completed in June 1887 and accepted by the territorial government from the contractor in the same month. It passed an inspection by federal government engineer L. P. W. Des Brisay, and the federal government paid its $2,000 share to the territorial government in July. The final tasks required to put the bridge into operation were to give it a coat of paint and to grade the approaches. The total cost of the bridge to this point was $7,253, which was about $3,000 over budget because the first contractor had absconded with the $2,000 he had been given as an advance.

Public use of the bridge created problems after it went into service. In its June 17, 1887, issue, the *Calgary Tribune* reported that the structure was being endangered by the reckless manner in which it was used by some members of the public. "Horses and teams were racing over it in such a way as to injure any structure of the kind, and yesterday a band of wild horses was rushed pell mell across with no regard whatever to the consequences."[92] The paper noted that regulations existed prohibiting the movement of horses and teams over any public bridge at a gait faster than a walk.[93] The public, the *Tribune* pointed out, "have a common interest in the preservation of all public works of this kind, and it is to be hoped that the complaint will not require to be made again."[94] In the same issue of the *Tribune*, a local stockman pointed out that the problem was caused by people sitting on the bridge railing and spooking the animals. He advised the newspaper that "it was impossible to cross the animals if persons are allowed to post themselves up so prominently. They naturally get frightened and will turn round, and then a rush is sure to take place."[95] Francois Deschamps was appointed caretaker at the bridge and asked to report all cases in which the regulation was broken.

In July 1887, even more elaborate arrangements were made to protect the bridge from abuse by ranchers. The July 2 issue of the *Tribune* advised the public that Father Lacombe had informed them that he was compelled to place a caretaker at either end of the mission bridge to prevent parties crossing large herds of horses over it. The caretaker was instructed to close the bridge's gates whenever he saw a large herd coming and open them when the herd had been divided into smaller bands not exceeding 10 animals. This was necessary because the bridge could not accommodate more animals at one time without injury. Considerable money had been expended building the bridge, and its safety was not to be impaired. There was a penalty for anyone crossing animals on the bridge at a gait faster than a walk, though when a large number of animals was crowded together, it was next to impossible to observe that restriction. It was not considered much of a hardship to drive 10 animals at a time across the bridge. Repairs costing $500 ensured that the bridge was safe.

In February 1888, Henry Perley, the chief engineer of the Department of Public Works who had originally objected to the design changes made by McCoskrie, inspected the bridge and totally disagreed with the assessment made by federal government engineer L. P. W. Des Brisay.[96] He found that the type of truss used by McCoskrie was not adequate and that all the materials, both wood and iron, were substandard. Upon receiving Perley's report, Dewdney directed the North-West Mounted Police to place a sign on the bridge warning people that it was unsafe to use. The message on the sign was, however, ignored—people took down the sign and crossed the bridge anyway.[97] Mr. Riley of the Royal Hotel even wrote a letter to the *Tribune* stating that the bridge was perfectly safe and this was of particular concern to him since his business was in part derived from use of the bridge. The commander of the North-West Mounted Police advised that unless there was a man watching the bridge full time, people would continue to cross it. In any case, the bridge remained in use despite recommendations that it be closed until such time as the government could make the necessary repairs to bring the bridge up to standard. In June 1888, J. A. McKenzie was paid $825 to make further repairs to correct the bridge's overall construction. Ongoing repairs were required until the bridge was replaced in 1901 by a steel through truss bridge built by the Dominion Bridge Company for $2,880.

In July 1887, Father Lacombe completed his efforts to facilitate access to Calgary via the mission area.[98] He arranged to have a road graded between Macleod Trail and the southern approach to the bridge. When Father

Lacombe received information from Hector Langevin that a sum had been set aside for grading the road up Mission Hill on the other side of the bridge and that tenders should be called at once for the work, he replied that the work had already been done and sent in his bill for expenditures. Father Lacombe also wanted to create a little artificial lake at the bottom of the grade, which would greatly enhance the already beautiful scenery. A flag-pole had been placed at the top of the grade so that until the new trail was well broken in, parties coming across the prairie would know exactly where to find the roadway.

Bridge Building

Having failed to take away Father Lacombe's government grant for the bridge at the mission site, Calgarians settled for a ferry at the location of the former bridge, which had crossed the Elbow River north of the CPR line. In 1887, the east-side landowners revived interest in building a new bridge across the Elbow within the town limits. In February of that year, they petitioned the town council for the construction of a $3,000 wooden bridge with stone-filled piers and threatened to secede if the petition was not acted upon. The petition was favourably received and the required sum added to the public works budget. Early in March, the town obtained a right-of-way through the North-West Mounted Police reserve for the bridge's western approach. In the same month, the east-end landowners, in an effort to speed up construction, agreed to advance the necessary funds to erect the bridge on the understanding that they would receive $3,000 worth of town debentures in payment. Wesley Orr and John Stewart agreed to subdivide their land into town lots and register the subdivision plans within four months of the completion of the bridge. Orr registered a plan (A2) for the subdivision of his land east of the Elbow River to 11th Street SE and south from the Bow River to 17th Avenue SE in September 1887. The street names recognized the land's prior owners, including Louis Roselle. Stewart registered a plan in November 1887 for the subdivision of his land east of 11th Street to 15th Street SE and south of the Bow to 17th Avenue SE. This subdivision plan was substituted for a second plan (A3) registered in 1897. These plans established the layout for the modern-day communities of Inglewood and Ramsay and the formerly established 9th Avenue East crossing of the Elbow River.

The new bridge, described as a very solid and substantial structure, was completed in July 1887 at a total cost of $3,671. To ensure that it did not suffer the same fate as the Mission Bridge, Bylaw 64 was passed that same month. This bylaw regulated the bridge's use and appointed a caretaker to enforce the regulations. Pedestrians, people on horseback, wagons, and animals could not cross the bridge at a pace faster than a walk. Horses, cattle, or other animals could not be taken across the bridge in groups greater than 10. W. J. Compton was appointed caretaker of the bridge at a salary not to exceed $5 per month. His duties included general oversight of the bridge and ensuring that the regulations governing its use were duly enforced. Anyone who contravened these provisions was subject to summary conviction before a justice of the peace and liable to a fine not exceeding $50 or to imprisonment for a term not exceeding 21 days. Compton's efforts to enforce these regulations were hindered by members of the North-West Mounted Police, who insisted on galloping their horses across the bridge. Bylaw 279, passed in December 1895, specified that only 10 horses, 10 cattle, 50 sheep, or 50 pigs could cross any Calgary bridge at one time.

Building a bridge across the Elbow River at Victoria Park to link the railway and the government townsite with the new cemetery and Macleod Trail was, by contrast, a protracted affair. The project had been suggested as early as 1885 when construction of the bridge at the mission site was under consideration. The purchase of Augustus Carney's farm for a cemetery increased the need for such a structure. Access to the new cemetery via the 1887 bridge and through the present-day district of Ramsay via the original location of Macleod Trail was inconvenient. In recognition of this, in 1891, the Public Works Committee met with John McNamara, the owner of the land south of the Elbow River, to discuss the possibility of building a bridge on his land. The committee, however, recommended against proceeding with the project immediately because of its estimated cost of $3,500. Subsequent to this meeting, McNamara sold his land to Dr. Neville Lindsay, thus giving the doctor ownership of all the land south and east of the Elbow River in the northeast quarter of section 10 along with the land originally owned by Paul Faillon south of the Elbow in the northwest quarter of section 10.

Several citizens, however, were not willing to wait for a bridge to be built, and in August 1892, 112 citizens signed a petition requesting that the project proceed. The petitioners recognized the benefits to the town of the cemetery's new location but suggested that since it was both inconvenient and time consuming to get there, the town's task of providing a public cemetery was incomplete. Osler Street (1st Street SE) and McTavish Street (Centre Street) were suggested as the best locations for a new bridge. On this occasion, the Public Works Committee not only favoured the idea, but also suggested that the road be extended over the hill to Macleod Trail. A road along the west side of the Agricultural Society Grounds (the present-day Stampede Grounds) was considered the best route. The committee also considered Osler Street a suitable alternative. Although the Public Works Committee endorsed the project, it also advised the town council that financing the bridge's estimated cost of $5,000 would require the sale of the old west-end cemetery and a grant from the territorial government. Another precondition was that Dr. Lindsay agree to the annexation of his land so the town could benefit from its increased value. The town council was unwilling or unable to follow through with these recommendations, and the project was abandoned.

While the effort to build a bridge languished, so apparently did the development of the cemetery. A letter to the editor of the *Tribune* in July 1894 signed "Citizen" recounted the person's drive with a friend into the country that took them past the cemetery gate along what is now Spiller Road. The citizen was so ashamed of the cemetery's appearance that he drew the friend's attention away from the site to Hull's slaughterhouse located farther to the west. The cemetery's appearance was considered a disgrace to the community, with a weather-stained, unpainted house, a partially completed, tumbledown shanty stable, an open excavation intended for use as a stable, and a gateway and drives overgrown with weeds. It had the appearance of a deserted farmyard rather than a public cemetery. The writer was particularly upset at the unsatisfactory efforts of Carney to keep the property in good condition and suggested that he be replaced with "a good, industrious man who would be able to keep the few acres now used neat and trim."[99] The mayor and city council owed it to the living and the dead to take immediate action. In 1902, plot owners and other citizens organized another petition, which noted that in their opinion, a well-kept cemetery should be a matter of pride to the city and not a desolate and almost treeless place such as Calgary's cemetery had always been.[100] Suggestions for improvements included providing a water supply by digging wells, constructing a bridge at 1st Street East, and planting more trees along the roads in the cemetery.

In March 1903, the Department of Parks and Cemeteries followed through with the suggestion made in 1892 that a bridge and road to the cemetery and Macleod Trail be built as part of a cooperative program involving the owner of the land on the south side of the river. Their discussions with Dr. Lindsay led to an agreement in which he would subdivide his land to provide a road allowance to the cemetery and on to Macleod Trail. The Public Works Committee and the city engineer were directed in March 1904 to start planning its construction. At this point, the issue of the location of the bridge became a matter of dispute between Alderman Simon Clarke, who had proposed its construction, and Thomas Underwood, the chairman of the Public Works Committee. Clarke supported aligning the bridge with 2nd Street East, while Underwood favoured the use of 1st Street East because it would have less impact on Victoria Park. Alderman Clarke's view prevailed, and the Public Works Committee and the city engineer were directed to make plans to cross the Elbow River at 2nd Street East. Various delays in tendering the project, however, prevented any actual work being undertaken at the chosen site before the end of that year. The controversy continued into 1905 when Alderman Clarke, in his capacity as the new chairman of the Public Works Committee, was determined to resist any efforts to change the route. In July 1905, a petition was organized by a committee of influential businessmen to change the route to 1st Street West to save Victoria Park.[101] The *Herald* favoured the change, arguing that Clarke owned land along 2nd Street East, which explained his preference for that route. The *Herald* also objected to the way Clarke had treated members of the city council who raised objections. At the July 27 meeting, council members had been subjected to "violent and foul language." Clarke's dictatorial approach to dealing with opposition to his plan also included directing the City Engineer's Department to begin the construction of the substructure of the new bridge in the face of public opposition. The staff of the City Engineer's Department were apparently required to work on the bridge project even on August 3, which had been declared a public holiday by the city council. The *Herald* immediately charged that Clarke was exceeding his authority as chairman

Figure 2.2 The first Victoria Bridge opened to the public on December 18, 1905, after considerable controversy as to its location. Its completion solved a long-standing need to connect the western end of Calgary to the cemetery and Macleod Trail. The bridge's construction, according to the *Herald*, pitted the community against Alderman Simon Clarke, chairman of the Public Works Committee, who was accused of rude and dictatorial conduct to ensure its completion.
Source: Glenbow Library and Archives, NA-644–24

of the Public Works Committee to ensure that the entire machinery of the City Engineer's Department was being used to prevent any possible change. The issue was finally settled at the August 3 city council meeting when the council voted five to four in favour of the 2nd Street East route. One of the speakers at the meeting was Dr. Lindsay, who indicated that the agreement he had made with the city called for a bridge at the end of 2nd Street East, and he did not propose to offer any other right-of-way. If the 2nd Street East proposition was turned down, he threatened to "fence his property and sow it to fall wheat."[102] The Algoma Bridge Company, which had supplied the steel superstructure for the 1897 bridge at 9th Avenue SE, was awarded the contract to supply the steel superstructure for the new bridge. The first Victoria Bridge opened to the public on December 18, 1905.

Enemies from the East

The construction of the Calgary and Edmonton Railway was the occasion for the next round in the ongoing competition between the landowners on either side of the Elbow River. Incorporated in 1890, the railway company was authorized to construct a line from Calgary north to a point at or near Edmonton and south to a point on the international boundary. The company was also authorized to enter into an agreement with the CPR for operation of the line. In 1890, Calgary was only a station on the CPR main line and not a divisional point. That distinction belonged to Gleichen and Canmore, which received considerable economic benefits as a result. Railway terminals were the residences of the crews who operated the trains and also the location of shop facilities for servicing locomotives. In May 1890, Calgary and Edmonton Railway officials met with Wesley Orr to acquire land for a terminal since such a facility was not yet available in Calgary. Orr immediately saw this as an opportunity to reverse the decline in his economic fortunes and those of other east-end landowners that had been caused by the CPR's decision to locate its townsite and station on section 15. The future development of Calgary as a railway centre was still a matter of dispute, at least in the minds of the east-end property owners.

The Calgary and Edmonton Railway proposed to Orr that he and the other major landowners contribute land free of charge to the company for use as a terminal, half of which would be owned by the company, while ownership of the other half would be retained by the individuals who contributed the land. The argument for this was that the increased value of the land would compensate for giving the land to the railway for free. By early August, Orr was confident that not only had he obtained the Calgary and Edmonton Railway terminal, but that he had moved the future railway development of Calgary to the east side of the Elbow River. He viewed this result as the logical outcome of his three years of study and effort, along with the inherent attractiveness of his land as the natural location for a railway metropolis. In his view, he had outmanoeuvered the senators, members of Parliament, and capitalists who had paid inflated prices for land in the town's west end, confident that they could pull the strings on all railway enterprise. Orr took particular satisfaction at having dealt a deadly blow to "the town clique," a group of individuals who had never ceased to abuse and ridicule his property.[103] He accused the clique, which included Mayor James Lafferty, of using its control of the local press to write "columns of wrath" against him. Orr viewed his actions as serving not only his own interests, but also those of the entire town. Approval and applause from the town residents was the reward he expected since in his view, he had protected the town against fraud and speculation.

The town council responded swiftly to the "subtle and audacious machinations" of Orr and the other landowners east of the Elbow with disapproval and scorn. Early in September 1890, the council offered the CPR 20 acres (8 hectares) of land in the west end of Calgary in section 16 free of taxes for 20 years. The land had originally been given to the town in 1885 by the federal government for use as a park. In return, Calgary would immediately become a divisional point, with section 17 designated as the future location of the only CPR repair shops west of Winnipeg.

Both the *Herald* and the *Tribune* strongly endorsed this action. The former argued that the land would serve the immediate needs of the community better than holding it for use as a park many years hence, especially when St. George's, St. Andrew's, and St. Patrick's Islands were available for that purpose. It reversed the argument used by Orr by identifying the east-side landowners as true land speculators who did not have the interests of the community at heart. Those who supported the land transfer had no interest in speculation but simply insisted on the CPR keeping faith with the purchasers of land in the railway townsite and supporting its efforts to make Calgary a great city.

Members of the town council sought public support for their actions at a public meeting held on September 5. Those at the meeting overwhelmingly supported the council's actions as well as the argument put forward by both the *Herald* and the *Tribune* that Calgary's future was at risk because of a conspiracy launched by a small group of east-end land speculators. James Lougheed made the most direct attack on these "enemies" of the town of Calgary. This group, he argued, had conspired with the Calgary and Edmonton Railway to wreck Calgary by placing a town a few miles to the east. The east-end landowners had a moral responsibility not to cooperate with the Calgary and Edmonton Railway and thus avoid wrecking vested interests. Over the past seven years, the citizens of Calgary had made their community the most important town in western Canada, and they had the right to reap the rewards. The east-end landowners, on the contrary, had never made a contribution to the development of the town and now added insult to injury by intercepting the CPR and inducing them to place its repair shops away from the town. Because of the lack of space to build a terminal and a town on section 14, the townsite would be forced down to Colonel Walker's farm, thus making two poor towns instead of one good one. Lougheed raised the spectre of the CPR locating its shops on section 9 or even section 17, further compromising the interests of the people who had purchased land in the townsite created by the CPR in section 15. He called on Calgarians to ensure the CPR's continued support for the original townsite by voting for the motion.

The east-end conspirators vilified by Lougheed and the newspapers defended their conduct, as did Augustus Carney, who argued that they had actually made a contribution to Calgary. Wesley Orr made the same point, concluding that the newspapers were the hired minions of the west-end clique. Colonel Walker was the only speaker who rose above the level of self-interest evident on both sides by acknowledging that those who favoured locating the railway workshops in the west were real estate "boomers" and that he could be called a boomer for the east. J. R. Costigan, legal counsel for the Calgary and Edmonton Railway, and Colonel Walker attempted to arrange a compromise by suggesting that the decision regarding the location of the workshops be left to the CPR, but they were soundly defeated.

Twenty acres (8 hectares) of land in the west end of Calgary in section 16 was officially offered to the CPR immediately following the public meeting. The CPR appreciated the loyalty expressed by the offer of land. William Whyte, general superintendent of the CPR's western division, acknowledged that although there were many reasons the workshops might be more conveniently located beyond the Elbow, the CPR did not want to do anything that would seem antagonistic to the interests of the people. He had also committed the company to building repair shops between Port Arthur, Ontario, and the Pacific Coast in Calgary. William Van Horne, however, was less enthusiastic, and Calgary's official designation as a CPR terminal was not achieved until 1899. Prior to 1899, a shop was built east of the Elbow to serve the needs of the Calgary and Edmonton Railway. In 1910, a decision was finally made to build the repair shops that had been requested in 1890 in Calgary. They were located on the west side of the Elbow River and south of the CPR main line. In 1911, work began on a new yard and engine terminal south of Alyth Street in southeastern Calgary. When the new 36-stall roundhouse was completed, the older facilities at the West Calgary shop and the Calgary and Edmonton Railway shop were dismantled. The 20 acres (8 hectares) of land the city had offered to the CPR became Mewata Park in 1906. The park was subsequently reduced in size in 1915 to be used as the site of Mewata Armoury and for a highway right-of-way.

DROUGHT, DEPRESSION, AND THE ELBOW RIVER

In the early 1890s, drought and economic depression overshadowed the prospects of the entire Calgary townsite, bringing the business community together in search of a solution. Irrigation using both the Elbow and the Bow Rivers would provide the solution to Calgary's recovery and future prosperity. It was first suggested by the town council in November 1892 when the council passed a motion endorsing a system of irrigation as essential to the development of the wealth of the soil of the southern portion of the territories and the rapid settlement thereof by agriculturalists. The motion noted that irrigation in Montana, Idaho, Wyoming, and Nebraska had increased land values by $25 per acre ($62.50 per hectare). The Dominion government was urged to provide general legislation at the next session of Parliament to enable companies to construct and manage irrigation works and for granting land subsidies or other assistance to irrigation companies.

Several Calgary entrepreneurs answered the call for the creation of irrigation systems. The first company was promoted by George and Henry Alexander, who first gave notice of their plans in the December 24, 1892, issue of the *Canada Gazette*. Their intention was to apply to Parliament at its next session for an act granting the applicants the power to construct and maintain a dam or dams on the Bow and Elbow Rivers, or either of them, near Calgary and to take water from the rivers by pipes, ditches, flumes, or other means for the purposes of water supply, power creation, and irrigation. An act creating the Calgary Hydraulic Company was passed and given royal assent on April 1, 1893. The company did not, however, proceed with any developments on the Elbow River and confined its activities to the construction of a canal system that took water from the Bow, where present-day Bowness Park is located, and delivered it as far east as the Parkdale area.

The Calgary Irrigation Company was the brainchild of William Pearce. Having been discouraged from promoting irrigation while he was a government official, he took initiative as a private citizen to encourage it based on his view that it was one of the best potential investments in the West. In requesting permission from the Department of the Interior to pursue the double life of a bureaucrat and a captain of industry, he did not anticipate it would involve Dominion lands and thus interfere with the scope of his duties.[104] Since, in his view, he was not placing himself in a conflict-of-interest situation, he wanted permission to participate in the creation of the company. His formal identification as one of the promoters would confirm the community's knowledge of his role as the originator of the scheme. Fully disclosing his involvement, he argued, would be in the best interests of both the Department of the Interior and him. He anticipated that the future success of the company could create a situation in which it might have to request concessions from the government with respect to public lands. Pearce argued that even this situation would not be a conflict of interest since full public disclosure of his attempt to obtain concessions for a worthwhile undertaking would eliminate any potential concern. He believed that as long as he made his private interests known, he could be the promoter of a company that requested concessions from the government while at the same time being a government official who made decisions about the future of Dominion lands. He expected people to believe he was an honest man who could be trusted to keep the two roles separate. Thus, he saw no necessity to demonstrate his integrity to the public and resented any suggestion to the contrary. Like any good capitalist, he equated his welfare with the interests of the country.

Pearce and his fellow promoters, who included Peter Turner Bone and John Pascoe Jermy Jephson, gave notice of their intention to create an irrigation company in the November 9, 1892, issues of the *Herald* and the *Tribune*, as well as the *Canada Gazette*. The plan was that water would be diverted at some location along the Elbow east of the Tsuu T'ina reserve and at some point along a 12-mile (19-kilometre) stretch of the Bow River west of Calgary. The project, as initially conceived, was designed to provide water primarily to the town of Calgary and its immediate surroundings.

The publication of this and other notices about the creation of Calgary irrigation companies prompted a call for a public meeting, at which time promoters and their solicitors were asked to provide further information. The Calgary Irrigation Company was the main topic of conversation at the meeting. Dr. Neville Lindsay expressed the fear that the irrigation project would affect the beauty of the Bow and Elbow Rivers, which he considered the most attractive features of their townsite.[105] He also suggested that the applicants be required to give a monetary guarantee that they would carry out the work and provide an engineering report to show the scheme was feasible. Mr. Bernard suggested that any company undertaking an irrigation scheme should be subject to government control to ensure the farmers were not "mulcted [penalized] by the company by the imposition of heavy charges for irrigation."[106] John McNamara was suspicious of the motives of the applicants, whom he believed wanted to gain control of the hydroelectric potential of the Bow River, which they would then sell at exorbitant prices. He also questioned the location of the diversion on the Elbow, claiming it was necessary to go 20 to 30 miles (32 to 48 kilometres) farther west to obtain water. He also predicted that the development of irrigation would lead to all the wells in Calgary running dry.

Jephson assured those at the meeting that the company would not monopolize the water from the river, that the privileges requested were identical to other legislation already passed, and that Peter Bone, "a skilled engineer," had advised him the project was feasible. Jephson also suggested that the meeting had been called to serve the political ambitions of Dr. Lindsay, who was running for mayor in the forthcoming civic election. Pearce and Bone subsequently published a letter in the *Herald* and the *Tribune* in which they explained that they intended to irrigate approximately 7,000 acres (2,833 hectares) of land in the Calgary area, which would use only a small amount of water. The company intended to begin on a modest scale but wanted to enlarge the project to the extent that money was available, hoping that further investment would transform it into a community-based institution. Pearce and Bone illustrated the project's potential impact on Calgary

Figure 2.3 This newspaper advertisement was placed by the Calgary Irrigation Company in a special irrigation edition of the *Calgary Herald* published in 1895. The map featured in the advertisement showed the anticipated location of the canal system, which was never completed.

with a quote from the annual report of the Irrigation Branch of the United States Department of Agriculture for 1891, which noted that irrigated land was assessed at $100 per acre ($250 per hectare) and sold at $150 per acre ($375 per hectare), while nonirrigated land sold at only $5 per acre ($12.50 per hectare). A letter to the editor signed "Correspondent," but probably written by Pearce, encouraging support for the enterprise appeared in the December 14 issue of the *Herald*. It urged that corporate efforts be allowed to develop irrigation because development could then be extended to the benchlands, which were beyond the resources of individual farmers.

The legislation creating the Calgary Irrigation Company passed without debate in both the House and the Senate and received royal assent on April 1, 1893, with Pearce, Bone, and Jephson designated as the company's provisional directors. Its capital stock was authorized at $100,000 in shares of $100 each, while the amount of bonds or debenture debt was not to exceed the total amount of the subscribed capital or double the amount of the paid-up capital, whichever came first. The objectives of the company described in the Notice of Intent, including the provision to provide water to the citizens of Calgary, were authorized in the legislation. Having received the consent of the municipal council, the company was permitted to break up, dig, and trench on streets, roads, sidewalks, pavements, squares, highways, lanes, and in public places as required to deliver water to its urban customers. Public notice was required for all construction plans at least two months before the plans were submitted for approval to the Governor in Council. Construction had to begin within three years and the project completed within six years of the date of the passage of its act of incorporation.

Upon the passage of the act, Bone acquired 100 shares, Pearce 80 shares, and Jephson 20 shares. William Pearce's wife, Margaret, purchased 50 shares, and his sister-in-law, Louisa Meyer, purchased 40 shares.[107] The company thus began as a family concern and would remain so despite Pearce's efforts to the contrary. A call on the subscribed capital to the extent of 30 percent provided the company with $8,700 of working capital for the summer of 1893. The company abandoned its plan to use both rivers and concentrated its efforts on the Elbow River to irrigate land in Calgary and as far south as Fish Creek. This plan, submitted in June 1893, identified two locations for the diversion of water from the Elbow: one on the river's upper reaches north of the Tsuu T'ina reserve on the southeast quarter of section 4, township 24, range 4, west of the Fifth Meridian, and the other on the lower Elbow on the northeast quarter of section 10, township 24, range 4, west of the Fifth Meridian (which took water directly to the Pearce estate from a diversion point on the Agriculture Society Grounds [the present-day Stampede Grounds]).[108] The canal from the upper Elbow ran across the northeast corner of the Tsuu T'ina reserve, where it divided into two branches: one that ran northeast and divided again, entering Calgary at two locations, while the second branch went south to Fish Creek.

The Calgary Irrigation Company did not immediately begin construction, but continued to do further surveys during the summer of 1893 that resulted in changes to the plan that allowed for the irrigation of more land south of Calgary. The new plan moved the location of the diversion farther west on the Elbow River and extended the Fish Creek branch farther south to the Pine Creek and High River areas. This revised scheme was submitted to the Minister of the Interior on his visit to Calgary in August 1893, with the request that the company be permitted to circumvent the requirement in its charter that two months' notice be given of construction activities. Pearce justified the request on the grounds that it did not affect anyone's interests and the company wanted to commence work immediately to take advantage of the remaining months of summer. From August 1893 to the end of the construction season, $1,893 was spent to build 7 miles (11 kilometres) of main ditch plus lateral ditches and a substantial headgate to control water flow. The additional land required for the expanding system was acquired from the CPR. The irrigation company wanted to acquire all land owned by the CPR in township 24, ranges 2, 3, and 4, west of the Fifth Meridian and south of the Elbow River. Van Horne personally handled the irrigation company's purchase of the land at a cost less than that quoted by land commissioner Lauchlan Alexander Hamilton.[109]

The expanding ambitions of the company required more investors, but Pearce had much less success in this regard. Despite his conviction that he had one of the best investment opportunities in the West, his enthusiasm was not shared by any of Canada's leading capitalists. By the time Pearce completed the reorganization of his company, irrigation had taken on an even greater importance to the federal government, the town of Calgary, and many of its leading citizens. The introduction of draft irrigation legislation in the spring of 1893 was evidence of federal government interest.

Anxiety in February 1894 about the federal government's intentions regarding irrigation legislation brought about a coordinated effort on the part of the southern Alberta business community to ensure the passage of the legislation. In 1894, an initiative for joint action came from the City of Calgary and the Calgary Agricultural Society. Mayor and enthusiastic Calgary booster Wesley Orr was particularly interested in irrigation, having concluded that the city's future prosperity depended on its development. A committee was formed that received a $50 donation from the city, and a meeting was arranged with William Pearce to discuss the plan for an irrigation convention. Pearce advised the committee that a convention would serve a useful purpose since he anticipated strong opposition to the extinction of riparian rights, which allocated water to the individuals who owned the land through which the water flowed. Although Pearce agreed to procure copies of the revised legislation and to deliver a paper at the convention, he privately did not consider the event necessary to ensure passage of the legislation. In a letter to Charles B. Burgess, the Hudson's Bay commissioner of lands, he indicated the convention might be helpful in strengthening the hand of the government in its desire to extinguish riparian rights, but the views of the CPR would be the main influence in determining that decision.[110] As intended, the convention delegates endorsed the entire irrigation development program planned by the federal government, particularly extinguishing riparian rights. It was thought that the water supply was sufficient to irrigate all of the potential acreage.

The second priority of the convention was to assert local control over the management of water. This was to be achieved by the designation of the Territorial District of Alberta as a Province and the extension of its boundaries to the Fourth Meridian, considered at that time the boundary of the irrigable area. The convention also recommended retention of the clause in the draft irrigation legislation that provided for mutual associations and that the Wright Act of California be used as a guide in how those associations should be organized.

The Wright Act was a California statute passed in 1887 establishing public control over water and encouraging private investment in irrigation projects.[111] When 50 or more freeholders decided to create a district, their county board of supervisors would call a special election in which all eligible voters, not just landowners, participated. The law required a two-thirds vote to form a district, but once it was established, a simple majority could approve the issuance of bonds.

The Southwestern Irrigation League of the Northwest Territories was created to organize community support for irrigation. A central council, with headquarters in Calgary, directed the overall affairs of the league, which was to include, along with officials elected at its annual conventions, representatives of the three levels of government in Alberta and Western Assiniboia, and the presidents of all the agricultural societies and boards of trade. The convention organized a delegation to Ottawa in mid-March to emphasize western interest in the irrigation program.

As Pearce was completing the reorganization of his company and the federal government was determining its irrigation policy with the passage of the Northwest Irrigation Act, the farmers in the Springbank District, with considerable encouragement and assistance from the Calgary business community, also decided to launch an irrigation project. On July 26, 1894, a meeting was held at Springbank School to consider the best means of securing irrigation facilities for the country lying between the western boundary of Calgary, the Bow and Elbow Rivers, and Jumpingpound Creek. It was attended by a large delegation of Calgary citizens, many of whom were members of the Central Council of the Irrigation League, which had been organized at the irrigation convention held in Calgary. The leading speaker was Senator James Alexander Lougheed, who emphasized the value of irrigation, not only to every Alberta farmer, "but every resident in the towns and everyone who has a cent of money invested in the country."[112] In his view, community action was required since the federal government was not prepared to build an irrigation system in the Springbank area because "of the purely local nature of the scheme."[113] However, the federal government's emphasis on attracting private investment to fund irrigation construction in the West would not meet the community's needs. "The whole subject of irrigation," Lougheed noted, was "in its infancy in Canada, and there would be difficulty in obtaining the use of private capital to promote enterprises of this nature."[114] Lougheed discouraged any further requests to Ottawa for additional assistance since the government was unwilling to pass further legislation to promote irrigation development. The only source of assistance, in his view, was the territorial government, which had the power to legislate on the issue and possibly provide public funds to assist in construction. He suggested the community unite in a request to the Legislative Assembly to incorporate them so as to give them the power to pledge the credit of the district for the purpose of carrying out the desired irrigation works.

A committee was created to meet with the Central Council of the Irrigation League the following week. The organizers were immediately encouraged by a letter of support from Frederick Haultain, premier of the territorial government. On August 1, 1894, executive officers of the Southwestern Irrigation League of the Northwest Territories petitioned the territorial government for the passage of legislation that would permit the creation of irrigation cooperatives. It was signed by Alex Lucas, secretary of the league, Joseph McPherson and John Cowan of the Sprucevale branch of the league, and William Wallace Stewart of the Jumpingpound branch of the league. The petition noted the value of irrigation to the development of the area and that such development could not be immediately attained without legislative provisions made at once for cooperative effort in the organization and conduct of irrigation enterprises. The petition resulted in the passage of the North-West Territories Irrigation Ordinance on September 7, 1894. It outlined the procedures for the creation of a district, which began with a notice of a formal vote by area residents, followed by the drafting of a petition. In November 1894, before these procedures were completed, the Springbank organizing committee applied for permission to divert water from the Elbow River.

The haste with which the organizing committee sought to obtain water from the Elbow River was prompted by the irrigation plans of the Calgary Irrigation Company. Rather than being perceived as a benefactor to the community, Pearce was now viewed as a government official using his position to thwart the legitimate objectives of the local citizens. The community saw this as an attempt by Pearce to take away the rights of settlers, which had already been taken away by the Northwest Irrigation Act. The community saw the efforts of the federal government to implement the "first in time, first in right" principle as an extension of the conspiracy involving Pearce.

The effort to stop Pearce began at a joint meeting of the Sprucevale and Springbank branches of the Southwestern Irrigation League held in late August 1894. A petition to the Minister of the Interior was prepared, requesting him to take no action on the Calgary Irrigation Company request for more water "until the claims of the Springbank Settlers [had] been thoroughly and impartially investigated."[115] It expressed the view that the Calgary Irrigation Company was trying to monopolize all the water from the Elbow River and that William Pearce might use his political position to influence the decision on water rights. Further, it requested that a decision on the Calgary Irrigation Company application be deferred pending receipt of an application from Springbank and that an unbiased official conduct the adjudication of the applications. The Springbank settlers and their supporters either did not understand or had chosen to ignore the fact that the Northwest Irrigation Act had extinguished riparian rights.

In response to the Springbank protest, the Calgary Irrigation Company argued it had a superior claim based on the law and its greater efficiency in using the water.[116] The Springbank settlers, on the other hand, represented the minority of landowners in the area proposed for irrigation and were ignorant of irrigation engineering, economics, and law. With respect to the project's feasibility, the Calgary Irrigation Company's own review of the Springbank area showed it could not be irrigated for less than $12 per acre ($30 per hectare), which was twice the cost prescribed by the North-West Territories Irrigation Ordinance. Ignorance of irrigation law was evident in their suggestion that water could not be transferred between watersheds, so they had preference over the Calgary Irrigation Company, which proposed moving water south to Fish Creek and beyond. It was also suggested that the North-West Territories Irrigation Ordinance was beyond the authority of the territorial government and based on American legislation, which was declared to have "opened the sluice gates to all kinds of mad and fraudulent schemes, promoted by parties who were interested in other features or outcomes of the scheme, than those derived from irrigation."[117] The fact that the Springbank settlers could make better use of Jumpingpound Creek and thus had an alternative source of water, which was not the case for the Calgary Irrigation Company, was the final point in their critique. Pearce and Bone dismissed the Springbank protest overall as "mischievous" and

Figure 2.4 William Pearce made use of water from the Elbow River to create an irrigated farm at his property in east Calgary. He used his farm to promote the idea of irrigation in the West and the value of trees for the beautification of Calgary. Water was delivered to the site by a canal that took its water from the Elbow River via an intake on the Agricultural Society Grounds. The water was then carried across the grounds and across the Elbow River by a flume. A second canal carried the water along the east side of the Elbow River to 9th Avenue, and then east to the Pearce estate. The plan was registered as plan IRR D at the North Alberta Land Registration District. The irrigation system was built following Pearce's departure from the active management of the Calgary Irrigation Company.

Source: Glenbow Library and Archives, NA-2850–1

not a legitimate attempt to build an alternative system. In private correspondence, Pearce identified Senator Lougheed as the leader of the "clique" that was creating all the problems for the Calgary Irrigation Company.[118]

In the spring of 1894, Pearce decided to develop a second canal that would take water from the Elbow at the Agricultural Society Grounds and transport it via a flume across the Elbow, north via a canal along the east side of the Elbow River, and then east through Inglewood to his estate.

Responsibility for sorting out the rival claims to the water of the Elbow River was given to John Stoughton Dennis, the administrator of the Northwest Irrigation Act. His November 13, 1894, report noted that the Calgary

Irrigation Company's project was sound from an engineering point of view and been made on an accurate scientific basis. He also noted that a satisfactory start had been made on the irrigation system's construction with 6 miles (10 kilometres) of main ditch and 10 miles (16 kilometres) of laterals having been completed, as well as suitable headgates, at a total cost of $12,700. The legal position of the Calgary Irrigation Company project was equally strong with respect to its prior rights to the Elbow River and the company's right to use the water in an adjacent drainage basin. The legal issue was particularly important to Dennis, who pointed out the necessity of dealing with the first case of conflict arising from the Northwest Irrigation Act according to principles that would apply to all similar cases in the future. The final point made by Dennis was that the Springbank settlers had an alternative supply of water, namely Jumpingpound Creek. Dennis suggested a plan that combined the use of the creek with storage reservoir development on the waterway's upper portion and the use of some water from the Elbow River during its flood stage. Based on these reasons, Dennis recommended that the Calgary Irrigation Company application be given preference on the Elbow River.

Dennis's recommendations regarding the dispute over the use of the Elbow River for irrigation were incorporated into an Order-in-council approved on February 23, 1895, which also disallowed the North-West Territories Irrigation Ordinance as drafted. The order recommended the ordinance be referred back to the territorial government for revision. The Department of the Interior based its decision on the "first in time, first in right" principle as contained in the North-West Territories Irrigation Act.

The federal government's decision regarding the Springbank protest, the two applications for water licences on the Elbow River, and the status of the North-West Territories Irrigation Ordinance was made public on February 25, 1895. Protests were immediately launched by the community, which refused to accept the decision. A community meeting was organized, ending with the creation of a committee to meet with Pearce and arrange a compromise on the use of the Elbow River water. The compromise failed over confusion about its terms and objections from Bone and Dennis. The publication of the Order-in-council of February 25 in the *Canada Gazette* on May 18 removed the last obstacle to the Calgary Irrigation Company proceeding with further construction work. The federal government was prepared to ignore the community protests and support the Northwest Irrigation Act in principle, but did ask Pearce to resign from the Calgary Irrigation Company.

Despite his departure from active management of the company, Pearce could not escape being abused by the *Tribune*. The newspaper accused him of manipulating the federal government and the citizens of Calgary for personal gain and to foment revolt in Alberta as he had done in Saskatchewan in 1885. His 11 years as Inspector of Mines was given as evidence of this self-interest. Rather than promoting mineral development, he had spent his time attending to private speculations, including the acquisition of the school section adjacent to Calgary and its use as an alternative townsite. His abuse of power had continued with his promotion of the irrigation company, which had despoiled the struggling Springbank settlers of their water rights. To monopolize water rights on the Elbow, he had arranged for an amendment to the Northwest Irrigation Act that removed irrigation claims from the jurisdiction of the registrars and gave it to the land agents. He had then arranged to have himself appointed as a land agent in Calgary in 1896. The new appointment was considered a sinecure for Pearce, a way to provide for himself at a time when the government dared not allow him to continue as Inspector of Agencies but felt they couldn't dismiss him owing to his insider knowledge of the events leading up to the Northwest Rebellion. Despite this overwhelming evidence of Pearce's misuse of his office, the government would not take action despite protest from many people and groups. The question for the *Tribune* was how much influence Pearce had.

As a result of this controversy, the Calgary Irrigation Company was reorganized, with Peter Bone taking over its day-to-day management, while Peter Prince and A. E. Cross became the new directors. The Pearce family remained the major shareholder because there was no market for their stock. Pearce worked with Bone in an unofficial capacity to administer the affairs of the company. Under Bone's direction, the Calgary Irrigation Company began its ambitious construction program based on a new memorandum submitted on October 26, 1895. The company intended to use the water diverted from the Elbow to generate power as well as provide irrigation. The land included in the project, as outlined by the memorandum, included an area north of the Tsuu T'ina reserve, 12,000 acres (4,850 hectares) on the reserve itself, and additional land south of Calgary and east of the reserve, for a total of 45,000 acres (18,200 hectares). The memorandum estimated the potential number of water users at 300, who would be charged not more than $1.50 per acre ($4.50 per hectare) for water.

The first step in this construction plan was to obtain a right-of-way across the lands of the Tsuu T'ina Nation, and Pearce began the process in February 1894 by requesting a 21-year lease of the required land. The request was referred to Samuel Lucas, the agent on the reserve, who was very supportive of the project since it had many advantages for the Tsuu T'ina. However, by the summer of 1895, no formal agreement had been made. In July of that year, Bone met with Lucas and advised him that construction activities would soon commence on reserve land and that there were no legal impediments to undertaking the project since the company had the right to expropriate the land if necessary and the Minister of the Interior supported the project. Lucas advised Bone that it would be a good idea to obtain approval for the work from the Tsuu T'ina leaders on the reserve to avoid issues when construction began. Lucas agreed to take action if directed to do so by his supervisors, and Bone immediately requested that Hayter Reed, Indian commissioner of the North-West Territories, instruct Lucas accordingly. Reed was glad to cooperate since he also thought the project would be of great value, but he felt the Tsuu T'ina should receive fair return for the concession, which he thought could be in the form of free water. By September 1895, the consent of the chief and council of the Tsuu T'ina Nation was obtained and construction began. By the end of 1895, the company had completed a diversion structure on the Elbow River and 6 miles (10 kilometres) of canal.

The Department of the Interior did not pursue the issue of compensation until May 1898, when A. W. Ponton met with Bone. Ponton, a surveyor with the Department of the Interior who had not only surveyed many of the reserves, but had also laid out irrigation systems on the Kainai and Siksika reserves near Lethbridge and Gleichen. The Department of Indian Affairs countered in June 1898 with the request originally suggested by Reed that the company pay for the concession by providing free water. The Calgary Irrigation Company made no response, and no compensation was made.

Despite all its various trials and tribulations, the canal of the Calgary Irrigation Company was within one mile of Calgary by July 1896.[119] A branch had been constructed to the public cemetery on the hill immediately south of the Agricultural Society Grounds. Canals had also been dug to several farms in the Elbow Valley, including those of William Roper Hull and Dr. Lindsay. The land, according to the *Herald*, was admirably situated for irrigation. The good-quality soil and gently sloping terrain left little to be done beyond bringing on the water. A large branch from the irrigation company's main canal had also been run to A. C. Sparrow's property, where it stopped at the brow of a hill overlooking the racecourse across the Elbow River in what is now Elbow Park. An oxbow lake was located immediately below the top of the hill, in a hollow formed by high banks, which was considered suitable as a natural reservoir that could be used with very little expense. From the brow of the hill, a small ditch was dug along the hillside as far as the cemetery and William Hull's ranch and slaughterhouse. Because the ditch was so close to the city, the general opinion, according to the *Herald*, was that the city council should accept the company's proposition to bring the water to the city. The *Herald* indicated the expense would not be great and the advantages that would undoubtedly result from being able to plant trees and create gardens would more than repay the outlay. The introduction of irrigation to the city's streets and gardens, the *Herald* continued, "would entirely change the face of nature in Calgary, and the visitor from the east after crossing the dry plains of Assiniboia, would think he had struck a bit of the garden of Ontario in the wild and woolly west."[120]

The company attempted to finance the construction of the enlarged project by offering 500 additional shares in March 1896. Its prospectus noted that the richness of the soil had led to the speedy settlement of the area south of Calgary during the mid-1880s, but the extreme dryness of the following 10 years had led to crop failures. Ten years of failure because of their dependence on rain had, however, taught the settlers the value of irrigation in a land where summer drought was the prevailing climatic condition. The prospectus stressed the fact that the water provided by the canals of the Calgary Irrigation Company would be in great demand and the company's shares would thus be a good investment. However, the share offering brought in no new investors, leaving the original investors to pay for the construction costs on their own.

Lack of interest in irrigation on the part of potential investors was shared by settlers who did not buy land and water to the extent the company had anticipated and showed little interest in learning about irrigation farming. As a result, the number of water users peaked at 11 rather than 300 in 1896, and actual area irrigated was only 400 acres (162 hectares) rather than the hoped-for 45,000 acres (18,210 hectares) in the same year. This lack of interest could be attributed to the arrival of rain and the end of the drought, which had not been anticipated by the company.

With drought no longer the prevailing climatic condition of the area, Bone was forced to adopt a new survival strategy based on the company farming a portion of its own land. Joseph H. Ross, the commissioner of Public Works for the territorial government, and his deputy, J. S. Dennis, were contacted in October 1897 for assistance in implementing the plan. In the fall of 1898, the irrigation company contacted Minister of the Interior Clifford Sifton. In his October 29 letter to Sifton, Bone reviewed the history of the company, giving an optimistic view of its success by noting that an increasing number of settlers were taking up land served by the company's canals, and thus the business of the company was growing and might consequently be considered to be highly satisfactory. The low degree of utilization of the system was not attributed to the end of the drought, but to the lack of capital on the part of the area's farmers. Bone then outlined the company's plan to establish company farms that would make use of the canals, giving the farming community time to develop the means by which it could make use of the water and thus provide income for the company. The company, however, required an estimated $40,000 to develop the proposed farms. The capital could not be raised in the private sector because potential investors were of the opinion that irrigation in Canada was too much of an experiment to warrant investment in such an enterprise. To overcome this problem, Bone requested the federal government guarantee the interest on a new bond issue.

The appeal to Sifton was forwarded to Commissioner Ross, who wrote a letter in support of the project. When this failed, Bone made another proposal to Sifton in a letter dated November 29, 1898, in which he suggested the irrigation company undertake research that would assist the government in the administration of the Northwest Irrigation Act. Bone argued that since the Governor in Council had the right to define the duty of water— the total volume of irrigation water required to mature a particular type of crop—based on information derived from actual irrigation experiments, the Calgary Irrigation Company could carry out those experiments.

When the federal government rejected this proposal, Bone made a similar suggestion to the territorial government but reduced the fee he intended to charge. Unlike all previous requests for assistance, this one was successful and Bone became the director of an experimental farm. However, an increase in the amount of rain negated the need for irrigation and led to the termination of the contract.

The failure to attract new investors, low income from operations, minimal government support, and excessive amounts of rain finally forced the Calgary Irrigation Company to stop searching for ways to survive. It went into liquidation in 1905, and its water licence was cancelled in 1907.

A STARTLING VISITATION

The end of the drought was demonstrated in dramatic fashion in the spring of 1897 when the June 18 issue of the *Herald* described how Calgarians had gone to sleep that evening, not dreaming "of the sensation that was in store for the city before morning." The rising waters of the Bow River were the first to arrive and deliver what the *Herald* called a "startling visitation." The *Herald* described how the Bow, "always a powerful and turbulent stream," had been swollen by the recent heavy rains, rising that night with a sudden rapidity that alarmed residents who lived along its banks. By midnight, the Bow River had overflowed and flooded several houses on the flats south and west of the Langevin Bridge. The city's fire brigade and mounted police turned out with teams and wagons, which were kept busy nearly all night moving furniture, women, and children from the flooded districts.

The rising waters of the Elbow River followed at about four o'clock on the morning of June 19. The water's delay in arriving, observed the *Herald*, was made up for in volume when it did arrive. Ed Mellon, the proprietor of the Blue Rock Hotel located on the north side of the Elbow River at the Mission Bridge, was "probably the first to become aware of its approach, [as] it poured down to the bridge like a landslide about 4 feet [1.2 metres] high, rising about 4½ feet [1.4 metres] in half an hour."[121] Mellon, realizing the seriousness of the situation, immediately dispatched a messenger upstream to the racetrack to find out how they were doing. The messenger found that Mr. Briggs's house and stables stood in about 2 feet (0.6 metres) of water. The men at Briggs's farm, like Mellon and everyone else along the Elbow, had been sleeping soundly as the flood crest approached the city. After their rude awakening, "it was no inviting task to get to the horses and get them out, but it had to be done, and the 11 horses preparing for the Jubilee were soon safely landed in Pepper's stables."[122] The flood did not inundate Mr. Briggs's racetrack since it stood on much higher ground than his house and stables. A day's sun was expected to make conditions suitable for racing. The Elbow Valley between the Mission Bridge and the racetrack gate was a "veritable lake," but everyone was safe, including William Scollen, who was on an island. The people from the brickyard and the Kettleson family, whose very fine garden was said to have been completely ruined, temporarily abandoned their homes. The agricultural racetrack downriver from the Mission Bridge was, in the *Herald*'s words, "badly demoralized," as was William Pearce's irrigation flume. The flood also endangered the lives of two men on the Elbow who were bringing down a raft of logs for Mr. Van Wart and Mr. Thomas. They were apparently carried right through town, still clinging to the raft, and were reported by the *Herald* to be "rapidly approaching Medicine Hat."[123] The event led to an inevitable comparison to previous floods. The old-timers said Calgary's greatest flood had occurred in 1879, but the only person who could actually recall it was Sam Livingston and he was out of town when the current flood hit. The consensus among the city's oldest residents was that the flood of 1897 was a foot higher than the highest water of 1884. Much of this flood analysis probably took place at local saloons, which according to the *Herald*, were doing a thriving business because of the muddy water.

The account of the flood in the July 8, 1902, issue of the *Tribune* noted the menacing conduct of the river, which brought "a day of excitement of no little anxiety in the City of Calgary." The Bow River had become a predator that had "broken forth in its mad fury" and was "creeping up on the lands and was preying on the houses in the flooded section of the City." The Bow, according the *Tribune*, was not alone in its sinister ways. "The sober Elbow was now higher than it ever [had been] in the history of man. It, too, has flooded bridges and in a few cases is creeping into a few houses which are near its banks. It is up around the new Holy Cross Hospital."[124]

CHAPTER THREE

GREATER CALGARY
AND THE ELBOW RIVER

1906–1914

The mood of Calgary changed in 1906, along with its relationship to the Elbow River. Possibly in response to losing the battle to become the capital of Alberta to Edmonton, the city council, in cooperation with the Board of Trade, launched a plan to create Greater Calgary. The territorial ambitions of this "new" city were defined by boundary extensions in 1907 and 1910. The incorporated boundaries of Calgary went from covering three sections in 1884 to thirty-six sections in 1910. This area and beyond was occupied by many new subdivisions created to meet the demands of a land boom that coincided with the drive to create Greater Calgary. The new subdivisions along the Elbow included Parkview, Earlton, Elbow Park, Roxboro (originally called Roxborough Place), Rideau Park, Glencoe, Elbow Park, and Britannia. These all became river valley communities with the exception of Britannia. Elbow and Rideau Parks featured river lots that extended to the riverbank. F. C. Lowes was the most prominent land developer in the Elbow Valley. His promotional literature on these neighbourhoods stressed they were good investments with property values that would increase from 100 to 500 percent. The risk of flooding was not mentioned despite the fact that floods had inundated the area as recently as 1902. A total population of 50,000 was the first benchmark set by Calgary's boosters for the growth in Greater Calgary's population. This objective was promoted by a club of the same name, the Fifty Thousand Club, created in November 1906.

THE WATERWORKS QUESTION

The anticipated expansion of Calgary, both in area and population, required new utilities infrastructure to serve not only the bottomlands on the Bow and Elbow Rivers, but the upland areas such as North Hill. Initially, the disposal of sewage created by more than 50,000 citizens was considered the most important priority. Waterworks Committee chairman David Carter, however, objected based on the fact that the existing water delivery system had several problems, particularly the pumping station. The Eau Claire Lumber Company's dam did not properly supply the station with water, modifications were required to accommodate a new pump, and the well under the pumphouse from which water was being drawn had become impossible to clean and would quickly fill up with river garbage, creating a "decaying mass."[125] City engineer F. W. Thorold supported the committee's recommendation to improve the city's water delivery, citing even more problems. In his view, meeting the anticipated demands of the CPR and the proposed Alberta Portland Cement plant, plus the necessity to supply an ever-growing number of domestic users, would come close to fully using the capacity of the three pumps then in use. In addition, the full utilization of all the pumps would reduce the available water supply for fire suppression. The only way the city council could avoid increasing the capacity of the system to meet the community's future needs was for the fire department to take the pumper truck to every fire. Not only had the city's three pumps reached capacity, but at least two of them were in danger of falling into the hole that would be created if the well below the pumphouse caved in. The deteriorated condition of the wood cribbing around the well made this a distinct possibility. If that happened, warned Thorold, the water supply to the city would cease immediately, and it would take two weeks to restore service. Inaction was also not an option because the old pumphouse had become a public health hazard. People, he reported, were dumping manure and dead animals along the south bank of the Bow River, and the only way to stop the problem was to place a guard there at all times. Building a new pumphouse would allow the city to "abandon the present eye sore and put in a plant which would be a credit to the City of Calgary."[126]

The realistic options available to the city were to make major repairs to the existing facility, including relocating the intake; construct a new pumphouse at Shaganappi Point as recommended by the Waterworks Committee; build a gravity system using water from the Bow River; or make use of the Springbank Irrigation District ditch and build a reservoir on the Elbow River combined with the one in Mount Royal from which water would be piped into town. Thorold regarded any effort to rehabilitate the existing pumphouse as a waste of money. In his view, abandoning the present "eye sore" and building a pumphouse at another location that would be a credit to the city was a better alternative. The option of using water from the Bow River via a gravity system was possible but very expensive because it would require a weir to maintain the water level, an intake, a wood-stave pipeline 22 miles (35 kilometres) long and 30 inches (76 centimetres) in diameter, and at least three bridges to carry the pipeline across the Bow River. The idea of using the Springbank irrigation ditch, which had been popular in the 1890s, was rejected because of the problem of freezing in the wintertime.

Thorold also recommended the construction of a 30-foot-high (9-metre-high) dam on the Elbow River, in the vicinity of present-day Sandy Beach, using sandstone from the nearby Butlin Quarry. The 350-horsepower of electricity generated would be used to drive pumps to deliver water from an artificial lake to a reservoir in Mount Royal near the sanatorium. Gravity would then be used to distribute the water to the city from this reservoir. One of the additional advantages of this plan would be a lake created in the Elbow Valley. In his opinion, it would provide excellent boating, sailing, and bathing facilities. Streetcars could reach the lake without having to climb any hills. Pollution of the lake caused by bathing was not a consideration because it would be too large. The slow velocity of the water through the dam would make it an excellent settling basin, thus making it unnecessary to filter the water. The lack of historical flow data on the Elbow River was the only problem Thorold acknowledged with his design. His plan would work given the amount of water flowing in the river in May 1906, but it was unlikely the flow rate would always be the same. Since the federal government abandoned the systematic collection of this type of hydrographic data in the mid-1890s and would not begin again for another two years, Thorold was forced to use anecdotal evidence to make determinations about water flow in the interim. Upon the submission of his report, he resigned as city engineer, leaving the city council with the task of considering the relative merits of the Bow and Elbow Rivers as a water supply and making a final decision.

Mayor John Emerson and Alderman George Young supported Thorold's plan, arguing without any evidence that the supply of water in the Elbow River was adequate. The Fire and Water Committees were not, however, persuaded and submitted a report endorsing the building of a new pumping station about three-quarters of a mile (1.2 kilometres) west of the present site and the construction of a reservoir on the old cemetery site on Jackson's Hill. This system could be modified to provide a complete gravity system with very little waste if the future needs of the city justified the expense. The Waterworks Committee rejected the Thorold plan because of the potential impact of drought and winter temperatures on the water supply, the latter having the effect of freezing the Elbow River solid. The city did not want to deprive the irrigation-dependent farmers south of town of water during a drought nor pay the high cost of building and maintaining two reservoirs. Pollution was considered a greater problem on the Elbow than the Bow because it was small and muddied by every local storm. The height of the proposed reservoir was 30 feet (9 metres) less than the one recommended at Jackson's Hill, thus making it less useful in serving the upper elevations of the city.[127] The final decision was to expedite the appointment of a new city engineer whose first task would be to decide between the Elbow and the Bow as the source of Calgary's water supply. A second reason for the delay in making a choice between the two rivers was the need to wait for the test results of water samples taken from both rivers and a city well. The *Albertan* anticipated the results would confirm the fact that the Elbow was an inadequate source of water for Calgary. In its view, the "dull, muddy water from the Elbow could very readily be detected."[128] The city's health officer and the sanitation inspector, according to the *Albertan*, both expressed doubts about obtaining a supply of clear water from the Elbow.

While Thorold's replacement was being recruited and tests were being done on the water samples, the press and the public joined the city council in debating the relative merits of the two rivers as a water supply for the city. The *Albertan* noted there was considerable opposition to the construction of a waterworks system fed by the Elbow River based on the view that the supply was not reliable and the water was not as cool and pure as the water from the Bow River. This opinion was shared by an old-timer who told the editor of the *Albertan* that he had crossed the Elbow River in 1887, at which time there was little water and big sandbars in the middle of the watercourse. According to the *Albertan*, this view was shared by a large number of people who knew the habits of both rivers. The *Herald* joined the *Albertan* in raising questions about the quality of the water in the Elbow River. The newspaper suggested the water in the Elbow was not as clean as that in the Bow and "the experience of the oldest man in the city [had] demonstrated this beyond a doubt."[129] The consensus was the Bow River was comparatively clean and ample for all purposes.

The possibility the Bow would become increasingly polluted was raised by the *Herald* on July 7, 1906, when it discussed the construction of a sewage system in Banff. Two views were presented as to what the fate of the waste would be between Banff and Calgary. One theory was that bacteria would survive and sewage deposits upstream from the city would taint the river. A second opinion was that oxidation would take place and the water would purify itself. The *Herald* used the apparent good health of the citizens of Medicine Hat, who drank the water into which Calgary dumped its untreated sewage, as the best means of choosing between the two options. "If there were any grounds," the *Herald* concluded, "for the fear which some people express that sewage pollutes the Bow River for a considerable distance, the whole population of Medicine Hat would have died years ago."[130] Besides the mayor and Alderman Young, the only supporter for the use of the Elbow was William Pearce, who said that based on his experience, the current flow rate of the Elbow was the lowest he had ever observed.

The results of the water-quality tests resolved the debate. The water from the Bow River and the city wells was absolutely pure, reported the *Albertan*. The *Herald* was even more enthusiastic about the superiority of the water of the Bow. Bacteriologically, the quality of the Bow River water and the water from the city well were above reproach, whereas the water from the Elbow was slightly polluted. In the *Herald*'s view, it would be "unsafe to make a growing city dependent for its water supply upon an unreliable and tainted stream."[131]

R. E. Speakman had been recruited as the new city engineer by the time Calgary received the results of the water-quality tests. He immediately rejected the idea of a gravity system using a dam on the Elbow River or even an elevated reservoir near the Bow, recommending instead the construction of a pumphouse farther west and the excavation of a reservoir on the river flats for storage purposes. Alderman David Carter's sudden death on July 1 removed the one opposing voice to the plan. His replacement, John Watson, apparently raised no objection. By December 1906, Speakman was making preparations to begin construction the following year.

In January 1907, Watson became chairman of the Waterworks Committee and immediately called for the city to spend $500 to re-investigate the idea of a gravity system. He wanted surveys conducted to ascertain how far up the Bow River the intake would have to be located to obtain the necessary fall to carry water to the reservoir site at Jackson's Hill. With the approval of his suggestion, Watson retained the services of engineering consultant James Child to undertake the investigation. Child's investigation of the Bow River confirmed Thorold's conclusion that it was not suitable for a gravity system, and he requested permission from Watson to investigate the Elbow River for the same purpose. Child's reports to Watson and the city council, along with an analysis of the water from the proposed intake location, indicated the Elbow River was very satisfactory for such a system. The distance between the city and the location for an intake to provide sufficient water under sufficient pressure was half that for the Bow. Child identified a suitable location for an intake between a spring of pure water and the Elbow River channel. The water from that locale, based on its analysis by an expert, was pure and did not reveal any of the deficiencies noted in the July 1906 water analysis. No problems would be encountered in constructing a pipeline or a suitable storage reservoir in south Calgary, and he claimed that government hydrometry reports confirmed the water supply was adequate. Water was not to be taken directly from the river, but was to be carried through a series of almost-natural filter galleries before it entered the main pipeline. These galleries could be cleaned out on a regular basis and were safe from being damaged by floods. Child's report was followed by the submission of a second report by Toronto-based engineering consultant Charles H. Mitchell, who presented an equally strong endorsement for a gravity system on the Elbow River based on a cost comparison of the two proposals. The advantages of a pumping system based on the Bow River were its lower initial cost and the flexibility of extending the system if necessary. Its disadvantages were the long-term decline of water quality on the Bow because of increasing settlement and industrial development upstream from Calgary, along with higher operating costs. A gravity system on the Elbow River would not affect water quality and the water would remain absolutely pure. He claimed that government hydrological data indicated the Elbow was also capable of providing the necessary quantity of water. The gravity system was more expensive to build but had no operating costs and lower depreciation and maintenance.

Based on the reports of Child and Mitchell, Watson had Speakman's proposed system scrapped, and Speakman was dismissed. The campaign both for and against the system raged in the city council and the press, with the argument in favour of an Elbow River gravity system being advanced by Watson, Mitchell, the *Herald,* and William Pearce. The *Albertan* took a neutral position, advising citizens to read Mitchell's report since the project represented the city's biggest expenditure to date. A bylaw proposed by the city council to raise $340,000 to build a gravity system was put to a vote on June 5, 1907, and subsequently approved.

James Child was hired to supervise the construction of the new system and became Calgary's new city engineer in 1908. On August 13, 1908, an agreement was signed with John Gunn & Sons for its construction. In 1909, as the pipeline was nearing completion, Child made an operational test of the intake. The intake was opened and a quantity of water allowed into the pipeline, which subsequently froze when someone forgot to drain it. This delayed the inauguration of the system by 30 days because the frozen pipes had to be thawed, and the pumping station operated for an additional month to supply water to the city. Alderman Watson caused a further delay when he decided to make his own test of the system on April 25, opening the intake without obtaining permission to do so from the city engineer. The water again froze, leaving 2 miles (3 kilometres) of pipe to be thawed. An "expert" informed the *Herald* that Watson's actions could have potentially caused the pipeline to burst. This incident prompted Child, who was no longer willing to tolerate such interference, to submit a letter of resignation. His resignation was not accepted, and Alderman Watson was forced to write a letter of apology. His behaviour eventually led to his forced resignation in 1912.

Because the choice of the Elbow River for the city's water supply had been made in the face of evidence presented in 1906 that its water was inferior to that of the Bow, an effort was made during the construction of the gravity system to denigrate the water quality of the Bow River to enhance the public impression that the water from the Elbow was superior. This effort included an article in the July 22, 1908, issue of the *Albertan* suggesting the pride of Calgarians in the purity of their water supply "coming as it does from the clear sparkling Bow" was misplaced. According to the *Albertan*, the water "that the citizens had been drinking all summer had been passing through a pile of decomposed vegetable matter, giving off germs enough to [be] spreading typhoid over the entire city."[132] The pile of decomposing vegetable matter was hay that was placed over the intake in the fall of 1907 to protect it from freezing but was not removed in the spring of 1908. The *Herald*'s contribution to the discussion included an article entitled "Afraid of the Water," which appeared the following day. It described how the men working to remove a logjam above the intake of the pumphouse refused to drink the water from the Bow River at that location and brought a pail of water from one of the wells in the neighbourhood to drink from instead. Their statement of conditions above the intake, in the opinion of the *Herald*, was sufficient to give them the necessary excuse not to drink the water. About a week before the article appeared, the workers found a cow carcass in the logjam. The men claimed that for the two days before the carcass was freed and allowed to float away, the stench had been unbearable. The men further claimed that finding dead dogs or coyotes in the logjam was a regular occurrence. In their view, "they were not good things to be stinking around in the water."[133] The article continued with more horror stories about dead animals in the Bow River above the intake. It claimed an aged Holstein bull had been seen "committing suicide" by jumping into the river above the Louise Bridge. An attempt was made to locate the carcass, but to no avail. Dead animals were also being pulled out onto the ice during the winter and allowed to remain there until the spring breakup. No fence had been built along the banks of the Bow River near the old pumphouse to prevent the dumping of refuse, which was then washed into the river. The Eau Claire Lumber Company put up signs forbidding dumping, but no effort had been made to draw the public's attention to the fact that the city's water supply was obtained from the Bow at that location. The *Herald* article concluded with the suggestion that there were cases of typhoid in the city that had been caused by impurities in the water from the Bow River.

The pipeline portion of the water system project was completed in June 1909, by which time, according to Commissioner Graves, "gravity water" was flowing into the homes of Calgarians. A month later, Mayor Reuben Rupert Jamieson predicted that with the completion of the reservoir in south Calgary, Calgarians would not simply be using gravity water, but *aqua pura.* The reservoir, which was intended to serve as an emergency supply in the event the pipeline became inoperable and as a settling pool to improve water quality, was completed by the end of the year. On January 7, 1910, Child reported construction of the entire system came in under budget. The capacity of the reservoir was a little over 16 million gallons (72 million litres), and by choking the overflow, could be augmented to 20 million gallons (90 million litres) without danger to the system. To make the system even better, Child suggested $10,000 be spent on rip-rap for the inner faces of the reservoir dams and to create boulevards of lawn grass and evergreens along the borders. The landscaping was eventually completed and the area around the reservoir designated as Reservoir Park.

The new water delivery system was in operation for only a couple months before displeasure was expressed at its failure to completely solve the city's water supply problems. At its May 17 meeting, the city council requested the city engineer bring in a report explaining why Calgary suffered from water scarcity. Child, as the engineer in charge of building the system, was not immediately prepared to admit it was inadequate. His response noted that the problem was not the failure of the system to deliver an adequate supply of water, but rather the wasteful practices followed by the city administration and Calgary citizens in its use.[134] Examples of water waste included the use of domestic water to condense steam in the powerhouse and for street sprinkling purposes. The use of street sprinkler carts not only wasted water, but the manner in which they were filled had a detrimental effect on the entire waterworks system. The carts were simply attached to the nearest hydrant, which would draw water from a network of small-capacity mains, suddenly lowering the pressure in the entire system. This lowering of pressure made it difficult to supply water to areas such as Crescent Heights, which required water pressure of at least 50 pounds per square inch (345 kilopascals). Other cities, he pointed out, had successfully restricted the use of water. Calgary's efforts to regulate water use, which had begun in 1907 with the passage of Bylaw 1011, had failed because the bylaw was never enforced. Child implied the city council could solve the problem since it had the authority to enforce the waterworks bylaw and to change administrative practices. The city could also carry out his January 1910 suggestion to rip-rap the dams. If this was accomplished and the reservoir put into operation, it would provide an adequate balancing system to the main city supply and considerably lessen wear on the filters at the intake and the risk of water hammer—a pressure surge—throughout the system generally. His report was referred back to the city commissioners to find a remedy.

While Child emphasized the need for conservation in meeting Calgary's water needs, he also anticipated the city would need even more water from the Elbow River. He therefore suggested to the city commissioners that Calgary request all the water available from the Elbow River and that it not be "wasted" on irrigation. In May 1910, Clifford Jones, acting chairman of the Board of Commissioners, requested that Frank Oliver, the Minister of the Interior, not issue any further water licences on the Elbow River above the gravity system for irrigation purposes.[135] Oliver referred the request to Commissioner of Irrigation John Stewart, who advised the secretary of the Department of the Interior that he felt there was plenty of water in the Elbow and there was no need for concern.

Child concluded that Stewart had incorrectly calculated the capacity of the pipeline and had not addressed Calgary's concerns with respect to its future water needs. The water of the Elbow River, in Child's view, was too precious to go to waste in irrigation ditches. Child and the commissioners wanted all the water of the Elbow to be designated for the city's exclusive use. Stewart immediately rejected this view and advised Mayor Jamieson that no further action be taken. He also wanted to refer the matter to the Minister of the Interior upon his return to the city. On July 28, Jamieson wrote directly to Frank Oliver, noting the need for increased diversions from the Elbow to accommodate the city's growing population and the dryer conditions in Calgary as compared to other Canadian cities.

While the city administration awaited the opportunity to deal directly with Frank Oliver, Child made his first suggestion that the city increase Calgary's water supply by altering the existing pipeline. He suggested that water could be diverted 5 miles (8 kilometres) upstream from the existing gravity intake and conveyed in an open ditch to the Jackson Reservoir at Shaganappi Point and from there to various locations for street sprinkling purposes. Since water for this purpose was only required in the summertime, the use of the proposed irrigation ditch was practical, and it didn't matter if the water was not of the same quality as the domestic water supply.

On August 29, a meeting was held in Calgary between Minister of the Interior Oliver, E. F. Drake, Mayor Jamieson, and Child, the city engineer. At the meeting, the city officials advised Oliver of their view that Stewart was wrong about the capacity of the gravity system and its ability to supply Calgary with water. Following the meeting, Oliver requested a review of Stewart's work by Frederick Peters, the senior hydraulic engineer for the Department of the Interior, who concluded that Stewart had indeed made an error in the calculation of the capacity of the pipeline as originally suggested by Child. In late August, the federal government agreed to not grant any further water rights for any purpose that could interfere in any way with the city's water supply either at that time or in the near future. Oliver said he was prepared to consider the city's application to divert an additional quantity of water from the Elbow River up to what might reasonably be considered necessary for a city of 100,000 people but no further. Oliver, however, did not agree to turn over all the water of the Elbow for Calgary's future growth, which had been the original objective of the city administration in May 1910.

Following this decision, the city did not modify the gravity system to take additional water from the Elbow, but had to meet a new challenge to its exclusive use of Elbow River water in the form of the Western Canada Power and Development Company's plan to build a dam to generate hydroelectricity. The dam's principal promoters were James I. McLeod of Spokane, local realtor William Astley, his partner, Frank Shackle, Jerome L. Drumheller, also from Washington State, and Calgary doctor and investor George Arthur ings. The legal advisors for the company were Clifford Jones and Ernest Pescod of the firm Jones & Pescod. Jones was also a member of the Calgary city council.

On June 9, 1910, the Western Canada Power and Development Company surveyed and staked a site for a hydroelectric dam 300 yards (274 metres) below Elbow Falls, legally described as section 15, township 23, range 6. Five days later, the federal government was advised of the company's interest in purchasing the site. On July 22, the company received a report from its consulting engineer, M. S. Parker, about the potential of the site in terms of water storage, horsepower, proposed development, geological formation, and general remarks. In his covering letter, Parker noted the location was ideal for hydroelectric development because the water flowed over bedrock.

The City of Calgary responded by submitting its own memorial asking for permission to use the water of the Elbow River for power purposes by constructing a dam close to the same site. In his letter to the Minister of the Interior transmitting the memorial, Child requested information as soon as possible regarding the procedure required to obtain a licence since he wanted to start work during the summer of 1910. The efforts of the city to develop power on the Elbow River was, in Child's view, intended to notify others interested in a similar project that the city had the prior right morally, if not actually, to use the water from the Elbow. He also wanted to ensure that any project would be beneficial to the general public rather than bolster the interests of a few.[136] The application of the City of Calgary to the Department of the Interior was approved by the city council by a slim margin, with Jones abstaining because of his position as legal counsel to the Western Canada Power and Development Company. On December 1, 1910, the Department of the Interior offered the City of Calgary an agreement under the federal water and power regulations authorizing the development of water power on the Elbow River on the condition that the city spend $50,000 and $100,000 on actual power development in 1911 and 1912 respectively and have a minimum of 2,000 effective horsepower developed and ready for use by January 1, 1914. After that date, the city would be required to increase the power to a maximum capacity of 5,000 horsepower should the Minister consider it necessary or advisable in the public interest. The city immediately advised the Department of the Interior of the problems in meeting those requirements. The Department of the Interior gave the city 30 days to respond by a resolution of council of its acceptance or rejection of the agreement and to sign the agreement by March 1, 1911. A motion passed by the city council on December 19 pointed out that the city required more time to complete its study of the proposal, prepare a plan, and obtain its approval by the ratepayers. They requested the Minister of the Interior hold the waterpower site on the Elbow River for the City of Calgary until August 1, 1911, but this request was denied.[137]

The city, however, continued its efforts to obtain an extension to the agreement. The Ottawa legal firm of Lewis & Smellie was retained to present the city's case before Minister Oliver, other Department of the Interior officials, and members of Parliament. James Smellie's efforts included obtaining a letter from William Kennedy, a consulting engineer, in which he stated the absolute necessity of winter water flow data on the Elbow River for him to be able to complete his report. When the city asked for assistance from the Department of the Interior to obtain the necessary data, it was advised that the department lacked the necessary funds to carry out the work. The Department of the Interior remained adamant, and on February 3, 1911, L. Pereira, secretary of the Department of the Interior, informed Mayor John William Mitchell that because the city had not met the terms of the department's letter of December 1910, it no longer had priority on the Elbow River. This decision was not a great disappointment since the city's engineer, Child, regarded the site of little value for power, but did recommend the city secure the right to the proposed reservoir site for future waterworks extensions.[138]

Having successfully defended what Child considered an attempt by the Western Canada Power and Development Company to take Elbow River water away from Calgarians, the city returned to its prime objective of improving its water supply using the Elbow. In June 1912, Child proposed the construction of a second pipeline from the Elbow River that would have its intake about 2 miles (3 kilometres) upriver from the existing one and would be connected to a new filtration plant near the reservoir in south Calgary.[139] The new intake would be 70 feet (20 metres) higher than the old one and have a carrying capacity of 23 million gallons (87 million litres) per 24 hours. The two pipelines would deliver a total of over 30 million gallons (114 million litres) per day, which was equal to 100 gallons (380 litres) per person per day in a city with a population of 300,000. This high-pressure line would provide water for fire suppression, leaving the low-pressure line to fill the sprinkler wagons. It could also be used on a temporary basis to relieve water shortages in the newer subdivisions pending the installation of pumps at the reservoir to increase domestic pressure. The commissioners and aldermen initially supported the proposal, and a bylaw was proposed to raise $1,053,600 for construction. Child's new plan, however, was ultimately deemed too expensive, and a second plan costing $405,000 to cover the extension of the system, the installation of a filtration plant and sedimentation tanks, the enlarging and lining of the reservoir, and the extension of the existing gravity pipeline a distance of 2 miles (3 kilometres) was approved. These changes were intended to address the problems of the water's milky discolouration, apparent when the snow melted and after heavy rains. It not only made for bad-tasting water, but also affected the reputation of the city because it occurred in the summer months when there were more visitors, who would then spread the idea the city's water was of poor quality, damaging Calgary's good name. The only solution suggested was chemical treatment of the water before filtration. Child based his design on the Saskatoon filtration plant, which had been modified to increase its capacity to provide 12 million gallons (45 million litres) daily. He also recommended some minor alterations be made to reduce costs such as eliminating the hydraulically operated valves and other automatic contrivances.

Despite efforts to promote the waterworks improvements, the proposed bylaw to build a filtration plant as well as modify the intake of the gravity system on the Elbow was defeated on August 23, 1912. "It looks as though the people of Calgary did not want to drink filtered water, so I suppose we will have to drink it muddy" was the comment by Mayor Mitchell to the *Herald* following the results of the municipal vote.[140] According to Child, the defeat of the bylaw meant citizens would have to economize their use of water if the present system was to serve the CPR railcar shops as well as the new Manchester subdivision. It would be necessary to pump additional water from the Bow, thus increasing costs and reducing water quality since the water was contaminated and harder. Child resigned shortly after the vote. The level of frustration of the administration over having to deal with a problem that

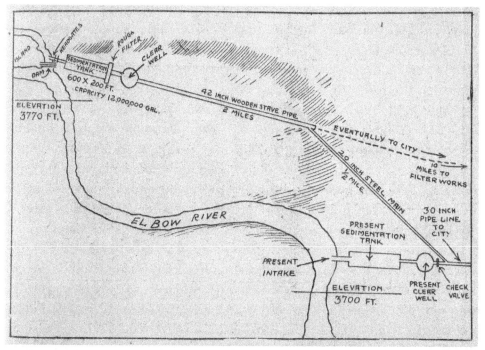

Figure 3.1 This map from the July 24, 1912, issue of the *Morning Albertan* illustrates the changes to the gravity pipeline proposed by James Child, the city engineer. A new intake located farther upriver was proposed to replace the sedimentation basin and well at the existing intake.

was a source of constant complaint was increased by the low turnout of fewer than 400 voters. The *Herald* wondered why the fact that dead fish contaminated the city's water supply during heavy rains in the early part of July had not motivated more people to vote for the bylaw. The discoloured water and the sediment it left behind had no doubt been observed, suggested the *Herald*, by people who failed to vote. Despite the results, the *Herald* suggested the city fathers press their efforts to bring filtered water to Calgary.

The implications for the city of the defeat of the bylaw were not confined to ensuring Calgary would continue to have poor-quality water and the resignation of the city's engineer, James Child. The city commissioners also pointed out that Calgary was in danger of losing its right to divert water from the Elbow since its authorization expired October 17, 1913, and "if the City lost its rights on the Elbow, it would be a serious handicap and great loss to the city."[141] Since other corporations were anxious to acquire the right to use the water, the commissioners suggested that ratepayers be asked to vote on the portion of the defeated bylaw that provided for the extension of the intake 2 miles (3 kilometres) upstream to obtain the advantage of a height of 73 feet (22 metres), which "would greatly increase the volume of water brought to the city and ensure a permanent supply for the city's requirements."[142]

With no action taken on this recommendation, the commissioners suggested a waterworks engineer be hired and the Waterworks Department be separated from the Office of the City Engineer. The new waterworks engineer would secure an additional source of water "with the least possible delay" and segment the current distribution system into separate systems so as to better deal with the requirements of each district instead of having a single feeder system for the entire city. The commissioners also suggested a bylaw to raise $1 million be submitted to the ratepayers to give the city the funds to move quickly on waterworks issues once an engineer had been hired. The city council agreed with the idea of hiring a new engineer, and Bylaw 1422 to raise the $1 million was abandoned before being referred to the citizens in a plebiscite. Arthur W. Ellson Fawkes was hired in March 1913 as the new waterworks engineer, and George Craig was hired as the new city engineer. In the same month, the commissioners submitted a new plan to deal with the waterworks question, which included the construction of a new pumphouse to take water from the Bow River and to undertake survey work on the Elbow River.[143]

The new pumphouse and filtration system could be converted into a permanent system should the city demand it. The city, however, remained committed to the Elbow River as its main source of water and "should the investigations now on hand in connection with the plentiful supply of water for the City of Calgary be in favour of the gravity system, this plant would be a safeguard in the event of an accident in connection with the gravity line."[144]

Having dealt with Calgary's immediate water needs, the city administrators turned their attention once more to designing and building a waterworks system that made exclusive use of the Elbow River as Calgary's water supply. Two options were pursued, one of which was a proposal by Fawkes to construct a concrete gravity dam near Elbow Falls at a cost of $2 million.

A second option was a joint project with the Elbow River Power and Development Company that had been created by Dr. George Ings. Neither of these options was financially feasible in 1914. Craig indicated to the mayor and the commissioners on October 26, 1914, that the existing pipeline was in satisfactory condition and only minor repairs were required to allow it to function for the foreseeable future. Four years of public debate and planning had left the gravity system much as it had been in 1910. The only addition was an elevated water tank at the reservoir in south Calgary. By the fall of 1914, the urgency for improvements to the water supply had declined with the onset of depression and war.

Very Much Refreshed

Swimming or bathing in the Bow and Elbow Rivers had a long history that can be documented back to 1883 in the correspondence of Isaac Freeze. Having arrived from New Brunswick in late July or early August 1883, Freeze camped on the east side of the Elbow River to await the completion of the CPR bridge. In a letter home, he recounted that a bath in the cool waters of the Elbow River left a person very much refreshed.[145]

Between 1902 and 1906, an indoor swimming facility was constructed by the Calgary Schools Swimming Association to keep people, particularly children, out of the rivers. In 1903, the city was asked to buy sufficient shares in the association to cover the cost of the purchase of land for the facility. The city declined, agreeing only to exempt the land from taxation and provide free water. The facility was supplemented by indoor pools built by the YMCA and YWCA.

The City of Calgary remained unconvinced of the need for swimming pools of any kind and considered the rivers suitable substitutes. J. A. McCullough and B. F. Kunz first suggested the use of the channels adjacent to St. George's Island for swimming in April 1909. In November 1909, the Parks Board directed the city engineer, James Child, to prepare a plan and cost estimates for a dam in the river's north channel at St. George's Island to provide an area for boating, as well as for deflecting dikes to protect the island. The organized use of the Bow River for bathing and boating purposes finally began with the creation of Bowness Park in 1914.

By the summer of 1914, efforts were underway by various groups to develop similar facilities in the city. In July, the Rotary Club requested that the Recreation and Playgrounds Committee clear bottles and other debris from the bottom of the Elbow River between the Elboya Bridge and the residence of C. H. Woods at 36th Avenue and 5th Street SW. They also asked that the city place ropes across the river for the safety of bathers and provide supervised dressing rooms.[146] The *Herald* lent its support to the campaign in a July 30 article that reported the lack of action by the city fathers in constructing a safe bathing place on the Elbow. According to the *Herald*, both the youth and the men of the city desired facilities for bathing and swimming. The coldness of the river water kept hundreds from venturing into its unknown depths, so arrangements that would ensure the safety of bathers of all ages were absolutely desirable. The plan envisaged the creation of freshwater pools "so arranged that the river flow could keep the water fresh but not of sufficient force to make it dangerous to the kiddies bathing."[147] Hundreds of places along the Elbow, the newspaper contended, could be converted into swimming pools at a small cost and "made safe for the hundreds of eastern folk [who] so miss the creeks and pools of other days."[148] The city responded early in the summer in the manner suggested by the Rotary Club and the *Herald*, including the provision of two dressing rooms for the convenience of bathers. A man was stationed near the swimming area and a boat kept in readiness in case of need. Parks superintendent William Reader, in his 1914 annual report, noted the public appreciation of these improvements and the fact that people continued bathing until quite late in the season. The location of the dressing rooms, the boat, and the stretch patrolled by the supervisor was probably somewhere between the Mission and Elboya Bridges.

Figure 3.2 This picnic scene illustrates the informal recreational use by Calgarians of the Elbow Valley as far as Weaselhead Flats. John J. McHugh is second from the left, and Oswald McHugh is on the extreme right. Access was provided by a streetcar line as far as Sifton Boulevard in Elbow Park.

Source: Glenbow Library and Archives, NA-2853–4

Figure 3.3 Postcards of the Calgary area produced as early as 1907 featured the scenic beauty of the Weaselhead area.

CHAPTER FOUR

WAR, RECESSION, AND THE
PROSPERITY MIRAGE

1914–1929

The commencement of World War I on August 4, 1914, inaugurated a period of retrenchment in Calgary's history that had its origins with a decline in the real estate market and the growing problems caused by the railway companies. The creation of a Greater Calgary faded as a series of economic and environmental disasters drastically reduced its imminent materialization. The environmental disasters included floods in 1915, near-flood conditions in 1916, a drought from 1918 to 1922, and a flood in 1923. By the mid-1920s, the trial by water and heat came to an end as the western Canadian economy returned to its pre-war levels at least in terms of construction activity. The idea of municipal expansion remained suppressed as the Calgary community continued to deal with the damages incurred during that period.

FLOODS, DROUGHTS, AND THE WATERWORKS QUESTION

The sequence of environmental crises began in 1915 when Calgary was threatened by its worst flood since 1902. The five o'clock "City Edition" of the June 26 *Herald* reported that in an effort to protect the new concrete Mission Bridge, the old Lowes Bridge across the Elbow River between Elboya and Elbow Parks had been blown up by the Calgary Fire Department. City crews, under the direction of the city engineer, George Craig, were taking other steps in their "desperate" efforts to save the new bridge and prevent it from blocking the Elbow River and causing flooding in the surrounding district. The space under the Mission Bridge was not sufficient to allow the passage of the large volume of water that was flowing down the river. The bridge became a dam since the water that could not flow under the bridge backed up into the adjacent subdivision. To avoid this, the falsework—the wooden frame that supported the reinforced concrete used to build the bridge until it had hardened—was cut away from the recently completed bridge, and the debris coming down the river was prevented from piling up against the structure. This was a "most difficult task," recounted the *Herald*, because the river was within a few inches of the top of the bridge arches and was apparently still rising. The city's Engineering Department was confident the bridge would hold even if the water went over the top. The possible underscoring of the foundation was the only detrimental effect the flood was expected to have on the structure. Despite the best efforts of the Engineering Department to keep the water flowing past the Mission Bridge, Elbow Park became a lake and many families were forced to evacuate. In the opinion of some Elbow Park residents, the accumulation of water was caused by the Mission Bridge acting as a dam and blocking the water.

The city's efforts to save the structure cost the life of city worker Quinton Dunn Campbell. The *Morning Albertan* described how at about 10:20 a.m., Campbell was assisting another man to chop away some driftwood on the west side of the bridge when his foot slipped and he fell into the river. His head was seen a moment later on the other side amid a lot of floating driftwood, but before help could reach him, he disappeared. His body was recovered the next day, caught against a wire at the city powerhouse in Victoria Park. It was in a swimming posture and the hip boots that he was wearing had been pulled off. The *Morning Albertan* suggested Campbell had been overcome by cramps caused by the extreme cold of the water.

By the time the water levels peaked, not only had the flood damaged Calgary's existing infrastructure, such as bridges, sewers, and water mains, to the tune of $30,000, it had also revived interest in adding a filter and sedimentary basin to the waterworks system. The water, according to the *Herald*, had been "more or less rolled and muddy since the thaw in March," and a larger sedimentary basin would provide cleaner water given the small size of the south Calgary reservoir.[149] At that time, the surging waters of the Elbow and Bow Rivers were being piped directly into the distribution system without any treatment. City chemist Fred Field, however, had reassuring news about the quality of Calgary's water despite its appearance. While admitting that the "Calgary water for the last few weeks and particularly since Saturday had been pretty nearly thick enough to cut with a knife, so far as sanitary conditions [were] concerned, it [had] been entirely healthy . . . and there was nothing to be alarmed about."[150] Although it was "disagreeable to look at and full of fine mud washed from the cut banks of the rivers," said Mr. Field, "it was all right to drink just the same."[151] He said that its appearance was deceiving because the quality of the water had gone up compared to 1914, and he found it "exceptionally free from any appreciable amounts of deleterious bacteria."[152] In fact, except for a few occasions, he had found no traces whatsoever of any bacteria that would indicate the possible presence of dangerous germs. His explanation for the improved quality of the water compared to 1914 was that there had been a greater amount of rain, which had the effect of diluting the water, and cooler weather, which prevented the growth of bacteria. Despite his efforts to make Calgarians feel better about the quality of their water, Field still endorsed the idea of the construction of a large storage reservoir.

Craig's efforts to plan and implement the necessary changes to the system had not been completed when the water crisis of 1916 occurred. In June, Department of the Interior Commissioner of Irrigation F. H. Peters, who had been driven from his home in Elbow Park in 1915, warned that conditions were ripe for a possible repeat of the 1915 flood.[153] This prediction did not come true, but the water quality in Calgary that spring, in the opinion of Mayor Michael Costello, was the worst it had been since 1883. Dr. Deane, acting superintendent of the Calgary General Hospital, found that samples of the water being consumed in various establishments in the city where foodstuffs were prepared for the public showed the water was not fit for consumption. The General Hospital solved the immediate problem of unsafe water by purchasing a Jarvis filter and making plans to install a new filter system the following year. A local bakery not only solved the problem identified by Dr. Deane by purchasing a filter system, but used it to promote the superiority of its bread because of its use of filtered water. An advertisement in the June 22 issue of the *Herald* urged people to eat Shelly's Four-ex bread since it was made from "clear as crystal" filtered water. Customers were encouraged to view the bakery's filtration plant in operation, which it claimed was the only one used by a bakery in Calgary. For the sake of their health, Calgarians were advised not to eat "bread and mud."

The flood prompted the city council to take action once again on the waterworks question, resulting in the creation of the Pure Water Supply Committee chaired by Alderman Arthur Ellson Fawkes, Calgary's former waterworks engineer. A very ambitious program was recommended and no doubt promoted by Fawkes. The plan was rejected in favour of a more modest solution that city engineer George Craig had been developing since the previous year. Craig's report to the Pure Water Committee outlined two alternatives, one of which was the extension of the gravity pipeline and the construction of a second sedimentation reservoir, whereas the second was the extension of the gravity line and the addition of a filtration plant as recommended by James Child in 1912. Field also submitted a report to the Pure Water Committee that justified the continued preference for the Elbow as Calgary's water supply.[154] Comparative analysis of Bow and Elbow River water, he concluded, showed the Bow had a higher degree of pollution than the Elbow, which he attributed to the fact that the entire Elbow River basin above the water intake had a population of fewer than 500 people. The Bow River basin, on the other hand, had a population above the intake during the summer season in excess of 6,000. Added to the contamination from the resident population was that from the passengers and crews of the Canadian Pacific Railway trains, a continuous travelling population of 2,000. During the winter months, the "washings" from the trains' lavatories were deposited along the riverbanks for many miles above the intake, and with "the opening of spring, the rains wash the accumulated filth into the river from which is drawn into the supply mains of the city."[155] Pollution from such sources, warned Field, was particularly dangerous because the travellers were from many localities and thus "more dangerous in character than a resident population."[156] The city council chose to construct an additional reservoir adjacent to the existing one, but declined to extend the pipeline or construct a new intake to increase water pressure. By the spring of 1920, these improvements, according to the *Herald*, had eliminated discolouration of the water.

The high water years of 1915 and 1916 were followed by a drought from 1918 to 1922, which decreased the flood threat but increased water demand and emphasized the problems of distribution to areas such as North Hill. Superintendent Peter Breen responded to the problems of North Hill residents by accusing them of waste. "Some seem to have a mania for running water during the warm weather," said the superintendent, "and it not only does no good but deprives others of the use of it. There is no judgement used in this matter and it is a shame the way hoses are left running for no good reason. It must be put a stop to."[157]

After enduring years of drought, Calgarians greeted the spring rains of 1923 with relief and celebration. Freddie Johnston, president of the Turf Club, preferred the rain, even if it meant losing the spring horse races. H. W. Woods, president of the United Farmers of Alberta, was jubilant over the increased moisture. The rivers were not expected to cause problems because of the small amount of snow in the mountains. The first indication that the spring rains of 1923 would cause problems came on Sunday, May 28, when a deluge caused $1,000 in damage to the city's electrical system. Commissioner Arthur Graves regarded the damage as unimportant given the benefits that rain would bring to rural areas.

Joy turned to despair on June 1 when the Elbow River flooded. The *Herald* editorial on June 2 commented that it was not advantageous to make up for years of drought by having two or three days of torrential rain. In the newspaper's view, the weathermen of the province had gone to extremes, parching the populace until they longed for rain, and then flooding out homes, disconnecting the gas, and waterlogging the power plants. The *Herald* also raised the possibility that the rain was an answer to prayers since the city's businessmen had implored the ministerial alliance to pray for rain. Perhaps the alliance had prayed too hard, suggested the *Herald*. The residents along the Elbow who were impacted the most by the floods of 1923 might have been sympathetic to the farmers' need for rain, but they were justified in wishing that the need had been supplied over a longer period.

Figure 4.1 This view shows water dangerously close to the 25th Avenue Bridge between the Mission District and Earlton in June 1923.

Source: Glenbow Library and Archives, NA-1494–58

The damage to the waterworks system caused by the floods of 1923 brought about the revival of the pre–World War I plan to use the Elbow River for power generation. On June 19, Mayor George Webster contacted Charles Stewart, the Minister of the Interior and former premier of Alberta, asking for priority on the Elbow for the development of a combined water power and storage site. The request, noted Webster, grew out of the recent flood, which emphasized the need for the city to take steps to deal with flood control and future power and water supply. The site for the proposed development, which had already been considered in 1910 and 1914, was at Elbow Falls. The city, however, lacked the financial resources to undertake any of the work.

RECREATION ON THE ELBOW

Although Calgarians continued to heap scorn on the waters of the Elbow River for drinking purposes during spring breakup and the flood season from late May to early July, the river and its valley were objects of delight for the rest of the year. The Elbow River had been used for skating since 1883

Figures 4.2 and 4.3 Skating on the elbow of the Elbow River was popular until the completion of the Glenmore Dam in 1933. These views looking south show skaters on the Elbow just up from the Mission Bridge. Rideau Park is visible on the south shore of the river.

Source: Glenbow Library and Archives, NA-479–1 and NA-479–2

Figure 4.4 This is a view of skaters farther up the Elbow, possibly in the neighbourhood of Sandy Beach.
Source: Glenbow Library and Archives, NA-1280–6

when the first New Year's Day skating party was held. In 1914, the city's Parks Department provided dressing rooms and 1.5 miles (2.5 kilometres) of good ice. Lights for night skating were installed in 1915. The Parks Department maintained rinks at three locations on the Elbow River until 1917. Skating was not restricted to the section of the Elbow within the city limits, but extended at least as far as the Weaselhead. Broadcaster and historian Jack Peach recalled that between cold spells, the water of the Elbow River would rise above the ice and flow down in terraces over the rapids and form great, glassy sheets on the sweeping bends that would then freeze, leaving beautiful stretches of skating ice.[158] The skating parties would begin with an automobile trip to the Weaselhead, where a bonfire was made and snow boots were exchanged for heavy socks and skates. The skaters would then "set off down stream, the skates thunking down the ice terraces and scratching wide arcs across the flat stretchers of moonlit ice."[159]

The city's contribution to making the Elbow available for summer recreation was, however, a casualty of World War I. Parks superintendent William Reader lamented this fact, noting in his 1918 annual report that excellent boating and bathing could be had at St. George's Island and also on the

Elbow River in the vicinity of the Mission Bridge at comparatively small cost. The effort to promote swimming resumed with the end of the war, and in 1921, the city engineer, George Craig, proposed three possible swimming pool schemes. The first was for an indoor pool on St. George's Island, which was immediately rejected because of the $5,000 price tag. The second was for a pool on the Bow River at the Louise Bridge to be created by constructing a dam and adding two changing rooms for patrons. The third was for a similar type of development on the Elbow River near F. C. Lowes' residence. The city council adopted the last two proposals but was not prepared to fully fund these improvements, at least the one on the Elbow, from city revenue. It was suggested that Alderman Annie Gale encourage the various women's organizations in the city to raise funds by way of a tag day and that the city would match the amount raised dollar for dollar. The tag day campaign was either not organized or unsuccessful in raising the necessary funds, forcing the city to pay for the swimming pools. In 1922, the city provided $600 for the construction of a dressing station for the Elbow River pool, and a capacious dressing room was erected that year for the use of children visiting the swimming area.

Although the supporters of swimming pool development, including William Reader and Fire Chief James "Cappy" Smart, had achieved a small victory with the decision to build a bathhouse on the banks of the Elbow, it did not diminish their efforts to convince the city council and the ratepayers of the necessity of constructing swimming pools. In 1921, a bylaw for that purpose was defeated by the ratepayers, but in 1922, the idea was considered again, and a committee consisting of aldermen John Arnold, Alexander McTaggart, and James Garden was appointed to investigate the issue. In October of that year, a deputation led by Fire Chief Smart appeared before council to argue the merits of swimming pools. In December, Bylaw 2139 to raise $35,000 to construct a swimming pool in Victoria Park was defeated by a vote of 893 for and 4317 against. Although the next plebiscite would not be held until 1932, Reader, who was active in the Calgary Swimming Club, continued to investigate swimming and wading pools throughout North America during the 1920s and discovered that Edmonton had the most ambitious program. However, the fact that Edmonton had built three pools by 1929 did not spur the usual sense of competition between the two cities.

While Reader helped promote the idea of swimming pool construction, he continued to develop swimming in the Elbow River in cooperation with the YMCA and YWCA at the location near the Lowes' residence. Both institutions provided facilities and instructors for swimming lessons, though the only children allowed to participate were those who could not already swim. In 1926, the YMCA provided 49 boys with swimming lessons at its own pool and lessons for 49 boys and 49 girls at the Elbow River swimming area. By the late 1920s, a network of swimming holes had developed along both the Elbow and Bow Rivers.

Prosperity, Floods, and the Waterworks Question

By the late 1920s, prosperity had returned to Calgary as indicated by the value of building permits, which had reached $6,201,622 by 1928. The April 1929 issue of the *Western Canada Contractor* noted that Calgary was having another active building year, which was predicted to be better than 1928. The previous year's building total, it noted, was the highest since the boom days before the war. It was looked upon as evidence the city had reached a very definite stage in its development and an era of progress was at hand. Both the *Herald* and the *Albertan* published "prosperity issues" that extolled the anticipated era of progress. The December 28, 1929, issue of the *Herald* described how Calgary had reached the end of one of its most progressive years in history, with substantial increases in population, new building permits, bank clearings, and the income of all city departments. The march of progress, in the newspaper's view, had been steady throughout the year, and Calgary was poised to enter 1930 with the undisputed record of still being the largest city between Winnipeg and Vancouver. This prosperity prompted the administration to seriously consider major improvements to the city's waterworks infrastructure.

By June 1928, the idea of adding a filtration plant to the waterworks system was being evaluated. The city did not intend to construct a traditional water treatment plant as recommended in 1912 but instead opted for a less expensive and very unique approach compared to other western Canadian cities. The commissioners requested funds to proceed with experiments to overcome the muddy water problem by creating a natural infiltration chamber on the shores of the Bow River. These experiments involved the excavation of a trench along the banks of the Bow immediately north of the pumphouse. It was anticipated that as the water seeped through the sand and gravel of the river, it would be purified in a similar manner as if it were to go through a filtration plant constructed for the same purpose. The pure water would then be pumped into the water main system. It was a very ancient method of water purification that dated at least as far back as the Roman Empire.

The experimental infiltration basin was a great success. On November 29, Arthur Graves, the city commissioner, announced that Williams Island, which was located just upstream from the present-day Crowchild Trail Bridge, had been selected as the location of the new filtration system.[160] Graves was enthusiastic about this new addition to the Calgary waterworks system since it would reduce the city's dependence on Pumphouse No. 2. The city engineer, George Craig, anticipated the new facility would provide water to all the districts north of the Bow River. The city's plan to meet Calgary's water needs during this period of expansion also included the construction of new water mains to the North Hill area as well as the construction of a water tower.

The confidence of the city officials that they had effectively dealt with the waterworks question was shattered very soon thereafter. On May 31, 1929, a storm characterized by high precipitation and runoff occurred in the foothills and headwater areas of the Bow, Elbow, Highwood, and Red Deer Rivers. It caused a flood that covered Williams Island in silt, effectively destroying its capacity to provide filtered water. Given these circumstances, the city commissioners recommended a survey be made of the current waterworks situation as well as an assessment of the city's future needs. The Toronto firm of Gore, Nasmith & Storrie, the leading Canadian engineering consultants for municipal waterworks systems, was recommended for the task.

The firm was established in 1919, and William Gore, the senior partner, had come to Canada from England in about 1912. In England, he had been chief assistant to Sir Alexander Binnie, consulting engineer for the London Metropolitan Water Board. Gore had worked on several large-scale water schemes in the United Kingdom and abroad: in London costing $160,000; in Liverpool costing $2 million; in Birkenhead costing $7 million; in Merthyr Tydfil costing $7 million; and in Petrograd (St. Petersburg, Russia) costing

$50 million. He had written extensively on engineering subjects, including a treatise on reservoir design.

George Nasmith was a chemist and bacteriologist who for many years worked in public health laboratories for the Province of Ontario and the City of Toronto. He was a recognized authority on matters pertaining to water purification and sanitation.

William Storrie was a Scottish engineer who had worked on several water supply schemes. Upon arriving in Canada, he became resident engineer on the first Toronto water purification plant. Upon its completion, he became waterworks engineer for the City of Ottawa and then returned to Toronto to become chief engineer on the construction of its second water purification plant.

Following the decision to hire Gore, Nasmith & Storrie, G. A. Gaherty, president of Calgary Power, suggested a way of solving the flood threat posed by the Elbow.[161] He proposed that a low-lying dam be built on the Elbow River at a location close to the present-day Glenmore Dam and a cut be excavated through the banks of the Elbow between what is now the entrance to Heritage Park and the Glenmore Landing shopping centre. He anticipated that the floodwaters pushed by the dam into this backwater would then flow through the cut and continue southeast for a distance of 3 miles (5 kilometres) via a natural channel to join the Bow River south of the Ogden rail yards. Control gates located at the diversion would only be opened during a flood since the proposed system had the potential to drain the Elbow River dry east of the dam. Gaherty pointed out that it would not be advisable to dry up the Elbow within the city limits, though it would be possible to do. A few bridges would have to be built to accommodate the roads and the Macleod branch of the CPR, which were in the path of the diverted river. He thought that the Elbow River could be diverted to the Bow outside the city limits at a cost of about $500,000. The cost was considerably less than the damage that would be caused by a flood. The plan would also eliminate the flood threat to Calgary since the construction of the Ghost River Dam protected Calgary from flooding on the Bow River.

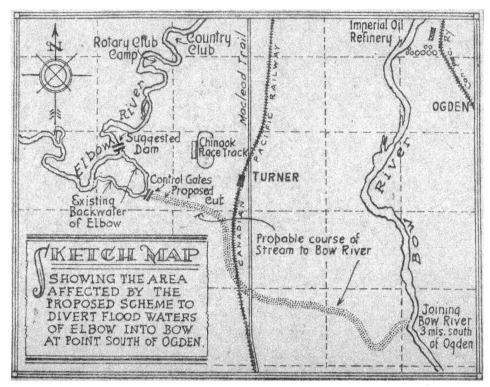

Figure 4.5 This map from the July 27, 1929, issue of the *Herald* illustrates the plan proposed by
G. A. Gaherty, president of Calgary Power, for controlling floods on the lower Elbow River. A similar plan
was proposed by Montreal Engineering in the early 1960s. The construction of this canal would have
reestablished one of the former routes of the Bow River. The embankment between Heritage Park and the
Glenmore Landing shopping centre was constructed to prevent water from following this course when the
Glenmore Reservoir was created.

CHAPTER FIVE

THE WATERWORKS QUESTION AND THE GREAT DEPRESSION

1929–1933

Between the retention of Gore, Nasmith & Storrie on June 10, 1929, to undertake a review of the Calgary water supply system and the approval by ratepayers of the firm's plan on November 20, yet another boom had become history. The official starting point for the Great Depression was the New York Wall Street crash on October 24. Calgary, and western Canada in general, however, did not immediately feel the economic effects. The December 28 issue of the *Herald* featured a series of articles dedicated to the prosperity of the previous year and the expectation that it would continue. Calgary, it noted, had reached the end of one of the most progressive and eventful years in its history, with substantial increases in population, new building permits, bank clearances, a street railway, electric lights, waterworks development, and tax revenues. The continued mood of optimism was also reflected in the January 1930 issue of the *Western Canada Contractor*, which noted the close of 1929 found the building industry in Canada enjoying the results of the busiest year ever recorded. In looking ahead to 1930, attention was drawn to the fact that conditions in the past 18 months had been vastly different from those in the United States where construction had fallen off from the peak of 1927–28. This was attributed to funds being diverted because of the Wall Street crash and high interest rates. It pointed to the opinions of a forecaster who argued the crash had not affected Canada in the same way since the event released money for building projects and lowered interest rates. As late as January 1931, the *Western Canada Contractor* remained optimistic that the increase in home construction would compensate for the cancellation of major commercial buildings such as the new 175-foot-high (53-metre-high) medical and dental building planned at the corner of 9th Avenue and 2nd Street West. With the closure of the Ogden shops in September 1931, which put 850 people out of work, the realities of the Great Depression had finally arrived in Calgary. The Glenmore Waterworks project would reflect this change as it went from a facility intended to meet Calgary's future expansion to being an immediate source of employment during the Depression. As Calgary's tax base declined and property tax rates rose, along with the cost of relief, the Glenmore project became a flashpoint in the growing tensions between the employed and unemployed, and between two strategies attempting to deal with the economic crisis.

THE GORE, NASMITH & STORRIE REPORT

The Gore, Nasmith & Storrie Report was released to the public on October 15, 1929, and considered at a special public meeting of the city council on October 17. It was tabled until October 21 pending the preparation of a draft bylaw by the city solicitor for submission to the ratepayers and its review by the Finance Committee. The report was one of several such documents prepared over the years by engineering consultants and city engineers on the waterworks question, beginning with the Keefer Report of 1887 and followed by the Ruttan Report of 1899, the Thorold Report of 1906, the Child and Mitchell Reports of 1907, which led to the construction of the gravity system, plus the Child Report of 1912, and the Craig Report of 1916 to the Pure Water Committee, which addressed the deficiencies of the gravity system.

Gore, Nasmith & Storrie's report began with a historical review provided by city commissioner Arthur Graves, who had an intimate knowledge of the waterworks question acquired first as a member of the city council and later as a city commissioner. Commissioner Graves' historical summary defined many of the problems the consultants had been hired to solve, which included the inadequate operation of the intake on the Elbow River. As Graves observed, the intake was located on a shallow stream with half a mile of river flats and gravel bars, across which the river channel roamed, increasing or decreasing in volume with the least provocation. On some days, the Elbow River ran in front of the intake, whereas on another day, it might be hundreds of yards away. Sometimes the Elbow was a quiet stream, but it could easily become a raging torrent, carrying trees and depositing gravel bars in front of the intake, with water the consistency of soup. When the flow of the river declined in the early winter, the intakes on the Bow and Elbow Rivers presented a new set of problems because they would become blocked by cakes of ice or "surcharged" with slushy frazil ice. The fall of 1928 was one of the most difficult and dangerous periods because both the Elbow and the Bow were simultaneously blocked with frazil ice. The sedimentation basin at the intake on the Elbow, which was intended to stop all the debris brought down by the spring floods, was only partially successful in collecting the heavier sands, and lighter deposits along with an assortment of fish were sent through the pipeline into the mains and on to the homes of Calgarians.

The rest of the report built on this historical summary. The firm of Gore, Nasmith & Storrie was instructed to prepare plans for a waterworks system to meet the needs of a city with a population of 200,000. This was a reasonable projection in June 1929 given the fact that Calgary's population had increased by 24,487 since 1926 to an estimated total of 90,000 in 1929, surpassing the population increases of the Greater Calgary era. The consulting firm shared the view of city planner and landscape architect Thomas Mawson as contained in his 1914 report on the economic development of Calgary that the city's population, even when it increased to 200,000, would be out of proportion to the incorporated area so there would be no need to annex additional land for many years to come.[162] The consultants did anticipate, however, that the Calgary waterworks system would be called upon to serve the needs of communities beyond the city's boundaries.

Calgary occupied a site that featured diverse topography transected by the deep valleys of the Bow River and its two tributaries, the Elbow River and Nose Creek, together with numerous small watercourses, or coulees. For Mawson, this landscape of river valleys and escarpments offered immense opportunities for park development, but to Gore, Nasmith & Storrie, the difference in altitude of approximately 575 feet (175 metres) between the lowest and the highest points was a challenge to their skills as hydraulic engineers. The occupation of the area had begun in the valleys of the Bow and Elbow Rivers and had started, particularly after 1906, to expand to the higher elevations. A total of 201.14 miles (323.7 kilometres) of water mains of various sizes had been laid to service the city's population. A water tank and two booster pumps had been installed to meet the needs of these higher areas such as North Hill. As Child had first observed in 1910, Gore, Nasmith & Storrie noted the excessive consumption of water by Calgarians. The system had delivered as much as 36 million gallons (164 million litres) per day over a short period, and the average monthly supply over a period of one month was 20 million gallons (90 million litres) per day. The consultants concluded that based on a population of 90,000 persons, this amounted to an average of 222 gallons (1009 litres) per person per day, which was greater than it should have been, even taking into account the dryness of the past season. By reducing water waste, they suggested the maximum monthly demand could be reduced to 200 gallons (909 litres) per person per day, or a future requirement for 200,000 persons of 40 million gallons (182 million litres) per day.

In their report, Gore, Nasmith & Storrie identified 11 principal deficiencies of the system, virtually all of which had been noted in the historical summary. These problems ranged from frazil ice, high turbidity in the spring, water pollution necessitating the excessive use of chlorine, the vulnerability of the gravity pipeline to damage from floods, and the inadequacy of the distribution system. This litany of problems ended with a discussion of the revenue from and the expenditures on the system, which provided Calgarians with the report's only good news. The system had produced a surplus since 1921, which ranged from a high of $68,924.05 in 1922 to a low of $3,869.32 in 1928. The overall trend, however, was a decrease in per capita revenue from $7.47 in 1921 to $6.31 in 1928.

The second part of the report, entitled "Time opportune for improved system," began with an endorsement of the view held by Graves that the system was being operated to the absolute limit of its capacity and was totally inadequate to meet any future increases in demand. Calgary, in the consultants' view, had been fortunate to avoid a major disaster. They paid tribute to the "extraordinary efforts" of the Waterworks Department in maintaining a supply of water without more inconvenience to the consumers than had taken place. They suggested Calgary may have waited too long to embark on the renewal of its waterworks system since there was a possibility the existing pumps would fail before the new scheme went into operation. Groundwater as a source of supply for the new system was immediately dismissed as inadequate for Calgary's growing population, leaving the two rivers as the only options. As in 1906 and 1907, the consultants considered the possibility of a gravity-based delivery system. Although both rivers came down from a sufficient height to provide water to neighbourhoods located above an elevation of 3800 feet (1160 metres), it would be necessary to go more than 50 miles (80 kilometres) up the Bow and 30 miles (50 kilometres) up the Elbow to achieve this result. Two pipelines were also considered necessary for safety reasons. Gore, Nasmith & Storrie concluded that the cost of such a system would tax the resources of the city, so they were forced to study less costly schemes nearer to the city that would require pumping in whole or in part. Their solution was the creation of a reservoir close to the city and the construction of a filtration plant. The reservoir would solve the problem of frazil ice and would aid in the water-purification process. Not only was the gravity idea as popularized by Child, Mitchell, and Watson in 1907 challenged, but so was the much-cherished view that such a pipeline would access a pure water supply somewhere on the upper reaches of the rivers that required no filtration before distribution. Since filtration, in the consultants' view, was necessary no matter how far upriver water was taken, the best scheme was the one that would secure the best results at the least cost to the city. They challenged the myth upon which the gravity pipeline had thus been built.

The disadvantages of using the Bow River as a city water supply were the prior rights on the river held by the Calgary Power Company, which had already built dams near Seebe and was about to initiate the Ghost River Dam project. Consistent with the view held since 1907, the consultants had also concluded that the Bow River was the more polluted of the two rivers since its banks were occupied by numerous population centres as well as the main transcontinental line of the Canadian Pacific Railway. Water tests made by the city bacteriologist supported this view, showing that almost without exception, the raw water of the Bow showed contamination, presumably of intestinal origin, that could be either human or animal, whereas only one-fourth of the samples taken at the Elbow River intake showed the same kind of contamination. The point that CPR passenger trains were a major source of contamination had been made years earlier by city chemist Fred Field in his September 28, 1916, report to the Pure Water Committee. The Elbow, in addition to being less affected by human settlement, also offered better locations for dam construction and the creation of a suitable reservoir close to the city, and also included the existing service reservoir in south Calgary. The lower flow rate of the Elbow was also an advantage since any dam had to be strong enough to allow the passage of the maximum level of floodwaters. The filtration process would be simpler and better results would be obtained from the Elbow than from the Bow.

Despite the report's early nod to the continued use of the Elbow River, Gore, Nasmith & Storrie presented the city with eleven possible schemes, six of which were on the Bow and five on the Elbow. The last scheme on the list and the one most highly recommended was the construction of a dam on the Elbow River at a site just upriver from a dam location that had been suggested by city engineer F. W. Thorold in 1906. The site, which they christened Chinook after the nearby Chinook racetrack, had a wide range of advantages, including its close proximity to the city and the service reservoir in south Calgary, thus minimizing the length of the pipelines required to connect it to the existing system. Concrete gravity dams of the type recommended by Gore, Nasmith & Storrie had been built since the early nineteenth century, by which time the correct profile for such a structure had been developed, along with successful methods of dealing with the uplift forces caused by water seeping through the dam and its foundations.[163] The first gravity dams were built in Alberta in 1911 and 1913 by Calgary Power at Seebe, while a third was being completed in 1929 just as the Glenmore project was under consideration.[164]

Evidence of bedrock along the banks and the riverbed offered the potential for a good dam foundation. The valley upstream from the dam site was either subject to floods or very steep and thus of little value for any use other than as a lake. The filters and pumping station needed to pump water to the existing service reservoir could be conveniently constructed near the proposed dam. The construction of a relatively short overflow dam 60 feet

(18 metres) high would provide a 90-day supply of water but would also allow for the passage of excessive flows during a flood event. A dam of that height could also be used to produce electricity to drive the pumps that moved the raw water to the filtration plant. Owing to the land's surface contours, there was very little drainage to the reservoir from the city, making it easy to prevent contamination. The only potential source of contamination was the military use of the Weaselhead area during the summer. This problem would be easily solved by the construction of an incinerator or an independent drainage system, which was under consideration. The proposed location also addressed the issue of water quality. According to the consultants, the raw water entering the reservoir would be the same purity as that of the existing gravity supply, but relatively long storage would improve its quality immensely. Both Thorold and the consultants from Gore, Nasmith & Storrie suggested the reservoir could be made a real beauty spot for use by the citizens. A road could be constructed around the reservoir as well as across the dam, which would create a lovely drive of approximately 10 miles (16 kilometres). The surrounding area was already attractive, and portions could be planted with trees to make the whole a desirable asset to the municipality. The final advantage to the proposed dam location was its estimated cost of $3,770,000, which was the lowest of all the potential sites. In the end, Gore, Nasmith & Storrie endorsed the decision that had been made in 1907 to rely on the Elbow River for Calgary's water supply but not for all the same reasons.

In addition to the construction of a dam and reservoir, as well as a filtration plant, significant upgrades to the water main system were also recommended in the form of 36-inch (91-centimetre) mains extending from the new water treatment plant along the south and east sides of the city that would connect it to the existing 24-inch (60-centimetre) mains wherever possible. The system would then be extended through the central core of the city and extended to the north side via an existing tunnel under the Bow River, where it would connect with 24-inch (61-centimetre) mains running west and north. A second 36-inch (91-centimetre) main would run along the west side of the city, connecting the service reservoir in south Calgary with Pumphouse No. 2. The main would also run under the Bow via the tunnel, where it would connect with the 36-inch (91-centimetre) main from the east side of the city. This system would ensure that the water supply to the entire city could not be interrupted by a single pipeline failure, as had been the case with the gravity system. Pumphouse No. 2 was to be converted into a continuously operating booster pumping station that would draw water from the system of ring mains at lower elevations and deliver it to the higher areas of the city. Lining the 20-million-gallon (91-million-litre) service reservoir with concrete was recommended since wave action on its gravel and earth banks caused turbidity in the water.

Gore, Nasmith & Storrie ended their report with a statement of confidence in the ability of the new system to solve Calgary's perpetual water crisis. The existing system could be totally dismantled without making a provision for a backup system since the Chinook reservoir would store enough water to provide a 90-day supply, and extensions made to the system could provide enough water for a city of 500,000. The water supplied to Calgary would be "pure, clear and attractive" and with sufficient pressure for all purposes, including fire suppression.

MERITS AND DEMERITS

At the October 21 meeting of the city council, the Finance Committee reported it had reviewed the necessity of the water system expenditure and recommended the preparation of a bylaw since it was within the financial capacity of the city. The first reading of Bylaw 2595 to raise $3,770,000 to construct the new waterworks system followed. The city council also decided to require a two-thirds majority for the November 20 plebiscite to determine public opinion on the proposed bylaw.

The debate that followed about the waterworks project raised many of the same concerns that had been under discussion since 1906. The first critics of the project were a group of doctors who were members of the Calgary Medical Association. They convened a special meeting on September 24 to bring their concerns to the attention of the rest of the medical community. This group included Dr. John Sinclair McEachern, who regarded the present system as inadequate because the water was taken from the Bow River, which was "sewage contaminated," and the filtration plant was worn out. He then offered his solution, which had already been tried with the construction of the gravity system between 1907 and 1909. Most cities, he pointed out, had to go a long distance for water, but Calgary had a good accessible supply in the unoccupied watersheds in the mountains, which were within a reasonable distance either up the Bow or the Elbow. He urged the civic authorities "to take immediate action and to go far enough into the unsettled mountain areas to obtain a suitable supply even if the cost seemed great."[165] Dr. H. W. McGill continued the critique of the present system by pointing out that much of the trouble was due to the Elbow River shifting its channel away from the intake and that the mains from the Elbow leaked. Dr. J. L. Allan asked whether the present supply was bacteriologically impure or whether it was simply a matter of taste and colour. A committee was struck to draw up a resolution urging the city council to take immediate steps to provide for "an adequate water supply for all purposes and that the sources of supply should be chosen to render it immune from human contamination for all time."[166]

The economic realities of tapping the pure water "El Dorado" located somewhere in the Rocky Mountains quickly brought about a change in what the "medicos" thought the city should do. At an emergency meeting of the Calgary Medical Association on October 21 to further consider the Chinook reservoir scheme, Dr. D. Gow reported that of the several schemes being considered, this was the only feasible one because of the high cost of piping a water supply from the mountains. He stated that freeing the water from organic matter by proper filtration then chlorination would result in a safe, pure supply of water and the present objectionable taste would not be evident. Presentations by Mayor Frederick Osborne and waterworks engineer W. J. Robinson at the medical association's November 13 meeting completed the doctors' acceptance of the plan. Osborne explained the need for an increased and better water supply, outlined the qualifications of the consultants, and described the Chinook reservoir plan in detail. Robinson pointed out the inadequacy of the alternatives, such as wells, the prohibitive cost of piping in water from a great distance, as demonstrated by cities in California and Oklahoma, and concluded with a description of how the water purification plan would work.

Opposition in the press came from the *West-Ender*, published by F. H. Newnham, which described itself as a little paper dedicated to the welfare of the community. The November 8 issue warned citizens not to be stampeded into any water scheme until they were sure it was something worthwhile and to remember that although the experts knew a lot more than they did—and the city council only knew what they were told—they would pay for any scheme, whether good or bad. The November 15 issue accused the consultants, the city officials, and the major daily newspapers of lying to the citizens about the need for the project and not having any respect for citizens' views. A case in point was the comments made by the mayor-elect, Andrew Davison, to a gathering of travelling men. According to the *West-Ender*, Davison told his audience that if the bylaw passed, Calgary would have clear, unfiltered water within 18 months, whereas the truth was that within 18 months, Calgary would have unfiltered water, but it would be more polluted than at present because the city would be getting its supply from lower down the river. The *West-Ender* wanted "absolute and ruthless candor . . . from city fathers [and not] bedtime stories."[167] It anticipated the proposed bylaw would fail since they knew the government had lost the confidence of the people. The ratepayers, in Newnham's view, wanted good, pure water and plenty of it, but they also wanted to be assured this proposed plan, or any other, was the best one and would serve the city for many years. The best source of large quantities of pure water, according to several old-timers, was wells, one of which was located in east Calgary, and there were "water systems used by the big stores."[168] Drilling a few test wells, in the *West-Ender*'s opinion, would not cost the city nearly $4 million and would deliver better results.

Another critic was Leonard H. Cooper, a local consulting technologist who responded to a *Herald* editorial in support of the project. He first outlined his qualifications, which included training as an analytical and consulting chemist by British chemist William J. Dibdin. Dibdin was considered one of the world's greatest authorities on water and sewage purification, and he had been the chief chemist to the Metropolitan Board of Works and the London County Council. After careful study of the Gore, Nasmith & Storrie Report, Cooper concluded that "Calgary will be supplied with a volume of water sufficient for the needs of 200,000 inhabitants, but we have no definite statement backed up by chemical and bacteriological figures that the quality will be any improvement on the water at the present moment coming through the mains."[169] The only analysis given in the report was about water samples taken from the Bow River on February 2, 1927, and the Elbow on March 23, 1929. Cooper regarded this as an inadequate testing of the water quality of the two rivers and that the limited amount of information provided indicated the Elbow was more polluted than the Bow. He also objected to the proposal that a road be built around the reservoir and to the suggestion that storing water in the Glenmore Reservoir would improve its quality since water would be constantly flowing in and out. The report also failed to explain the merits of the slow sand process of water purification or provide information to indicate it would work on Elbow River water. In an article in the *Herald* on November 18, Mayor Osborne responded by indicating that the fullest investigation into the conditions of the waters of the Bow and Elbow Rivers had been done. He also noted the report presented to the city council was not intended to be a highly technical document dealing with minute details such as those suggested by Cooper. If it had been, it would probably have run to at least 200 pages instead of 60 pages. As well, it would have dealt with many phases of the project only understood by professionals and at such length, would neither have been read nor understood by citizens. Osborne emphasized the fact that Gore, Nasmith & Storrie had consulted all the relevant documentation to make a decision. The article ended with Osborne stating his agreement with the consultants' judgement that the Elbow was the best source of pure water and that the project could be completed for $3,770,000.

A. Macleod Sinclair regarded Elbow Falls as the best site for a dam and suggested a way of paying for the extra costs of using this location.[170] James Moodie, in a letter to the editor of the *Herald*, agreed with Sinclair that the proposed Chinook site was the wrong location but for a different reason. He believed the dam would break during a severe flood, which was a possibility given the flood of 1929, and any scheme that had the potential to wipe out the lower part of the city, including the principal business centre, should not be considered for a moment. The dam, in Moodie's view, was also in the wrong location from the point of view of water quality since it was "pure water not a chlorinated emulsion that the parents of Calgary require and demand for their children."[171] He said that this objective could only be obtained by going far enough up the Elbow River to get beyond all possible sources of contamination and from which point the water could be brought by gravity to the city. In his opinion, such a place had been formed by nature at Elbow Falls approximately 35 miles (56 kilometres) from Calgary. A dam built into solid rock at the foot of the canyon would back water up between solid limestone walls for 4 or 5 miles (6.5 to 8 kilometres), and by adding to the height of the retaining walls, the capacity of the reservoir could be added to indefinitely and pipelines could be duplicated as required.

In the November 19, 1929, issue of the *Herald*, a citizen expressed fear that the reservoir would very quickly fill up with sediment. This view was based on personal knowledge of the Elbow River's flood sedimentation. Having observed that the Elbow River had deposited up to a foot of sediment on riverside lawns within a 24-hour period during previous floods, the individual anticipated that the accumulation would be even higher when the water was trapped behind a dam. Within 10 years, the person predicted, the accumulation of sediment would necessitate the dredging of the reservoir and asked, "Would this mean that for a couple of months we would be forced to drink muddy water while the sediment was being removed?" H. J. Duffield, an independent candidate for the city council, suggested that approval be given to the amount of money to be spent but that the actual details of the scheme be given further study.

Support for the proposal came from the Civic Government Association candidates in the November 20 civic election along with mayoralty candidate Andrew Davison, incumbent mayor Frederick E. Osborne, and the engineering staff of the city. The *Herald* and the *Albertan* were both strongly in favour of the project and responded directly to its critics. When fears were expressed that the dam would fail as one had in California, the *Herald* responded by pointing out that "modern, well-constructed dams rarely collapse."[172] The dam failure in California was the result of the failure of its builder to carry the base to solid rock. The site of the proposed dam was ideally suited for the purpose since it was a natural rocky gorge with an easily accessible, solid rock foundation. On the eve of the vote on the bylaw, the *Herald* urged its approval because Calgary's present water supply was totally inadequate to the needs of the population regarding both quality and quantity. Support was also recommended because the proposal had been investigated by the foremost waterworks engineers in Canada, approved by the health authorities of the province, and endorsed by intelligent scientific and engineering opinion in the city. The project was also supported by William Pearce, who argued that the consultants retained by the city were experts in hydraulic engineering and their views should be trusted.

Bylaw 2595 authorizing the borrowing of $3,770,000 to cover the estimated cost of construction was passed on November 20, 1929, with 4,272 votes for and 1,679 against, thus meeting the two-thirds majority of total votes required. With the approval of the waterworks bylaw, the city council selected Gore, Nasmith & Storrie to superintend the construction of the new water system through to putting it in operation.[173] The remaining members of the engineering team included city engineer A. S. Chapman, city waterworks engineer W. J. Robinson, and Dr. H. G. Acres, who was the engineer retained by the federal and provincial governments to review the plans and make periodic inspections of the work. P. J. Jennings was also involved as an inspection engineer, but his relationship to Acres is not entirely clear. The resident engineer on the project was Norman McDonald, who was an employee of Gore, Nasmith & Storrie. The first step in the detailed planning of the project was to drill 45 test holes at the dam site to determine soil conditions and the depth of the bedrock. The purpose was to determine the depth of a suitable foundation for the dam. The data was used by Gore, Nasmith & Storrie to complete the detailed plans for the dam through to the spring of 1930.

Council Preparations

While plans for the dam were in preparation in Toronto, the city council also undertook tasks in preparation for the start of construction. One of these tasks was to adopt a series of workers' rights provisions that would be incorporated into all the contracts. These included adopting wage scales consistent with the prevailing wages and hours of work in Calgary and area and specifying an eight-hour work day, with time-and-a-half to be paid thereafter and no piecework permitted. The city council would also give preference to Calgary-based contractors who were required to hire married men who had been Calgary residents for at least one year before the awarding of the contract.

Council chose a new name for the project when asked by William Storrie if it was the city's desire to retain the name "Chinook" on a permanent basis. Chinook had been chosen because the site was close to the Chinook racetrack, which had been built in 1914 by the Calgary Polo Club. Storrie suggested that if a new name were to be adopted, the decision should be

made soon since the continued use of a name on the plans and in the specifications was apt to be finally adopted as the name of the reservoir. The
special committee created for this purpose called for public input in newspaper advertisements in the *Herald* and *Albertan.* Some contributors were
inspired by the local history of the area and suggested Samuel Livingston,
the earliest resident of the area, and Glenmore, which was the name of the
school district and a further link to Livingston since it was the name of the
district where he came from in Ireland. The suggestion Sarcee recognized
the First Nation's association with the site. The history of Calgary and southern Alberta inspired the suggestions Colonel James Macleod, who had been
commissioner of the North-West Mounted Police, and George Alexander,
who had been a prominent businessman in early Calgary. One individual
suggested that the name Chinook be retained because more people knew
about the weather phenomenon than had ever heard of Sam Livingston.
Alberta sunsets may have inspired the suggestion Golden West. The names
Ypres and Earl Haigh commemorated the events of World War I. The potential cost of the project might have been the inspiration for the name Mon-
eymore. European associations were evident in the suggestions Caspian,
Emerald, Ulster, Ireland, Lough Neagh, Renfrew, Willington, Strand, Victoria, Kings, Millbank, Nelson, and Prince of Wales. One individual combined
the words *river* and *Alberta,* coming up with Riveralta, Rivalta, and Riverina,
which would give the project a Mediterranean tone.[174] The final choice was
Glenmore, which commemorated Sam Livingston's association with the site.

Transportation of workers to the construction site was also arranged by
the city council. After considering an extension of the street railway and
the purchase of businesses by the city for use in connecting the dam site to
the street railway, the decision was made to hire a private company to provide the transportation service. A call for tenders went out in July to supply
the service, but only the Brewster Transportation Company submitted a bid.
The company agreed to transport workers from 16th Street and 34th Avenue SE to the dam site at a cost of 10 cents each way and to maintain an
hourly service throughout the day. R. A. Brown, general superintendent of
the Electric Light and Street Railway Department, recommended the bid be
accepted despite the high cost because the city could not provide the service
any cheaper.

In March 1930, as these preparations were being concluded, Calgarians were reminded of the original reason why the project was begun when the city's water quality underwent its annual decline. The city council requested the commissioners investigate the current state of Calgary's water supply and explore the idea of drilling wells to obtain a pure water supply pending the completion of the Glenmore project. Gore, Nasmith & Storrie rejected the idea as well as Alderman Russell's suggestion that an early start be made on the North Hill water tower and Alderman Ross's suggestion that two units of the new filtration plant be built on the Bow River. In William Storrie's view, these were expensive short-term solutions that would only interfere with the plan to build an adequate system. There was no alternative for Calgarians but to endure two more years of bad water in the spring. The old system, including the infiltration basin on Williams Island, had to be kept going. The infiltration basin went back into operation, but the flooding that spring ended its capacity to deliver filtered water. The city administration was satisfied with the results being obtained from the infiltration basin because it was helping to ensure the entire city had water. Mayor Davison did, however, concede that the citizens were not getting filtered water, which they would have had if the flood of 1929 had not occurred or if the drought conditions had not required the basin to be used on a continuous basis. "The infiltration scheme," in his view, had "absolutely proven its value from every viewpoint from which an unprejudiced citizen could view the project and will continue to do so increasingly until the new source of supply is delivering water."[175]

During the winter of 1929–30, the city council was also under pressure to commence construction work as soon as possible. The necessity of hiring local labour and starting work immediately was brought home to the council by numerous letters and presentations. These began as early as November 23, 1929, when the Calgary Trades and Labour Council requested the city make an immediate start on the project by hiring workers to clear the reservoir site as an unemployment relief measure. As pressure mounted on the city council to deal with the unemployment issue, it in turn reminded Gore, Nasmith & Storrie that Calgary had an unemployment problem and that they should help mitigate it by speeding up the preparation of the plans. William Storrie acknowledged the anxieties of Mayor Davison regarding the make-work value of the project but indicated that the drafting of the plans was being done as quickly as possible.

CONSTRUCTION BEGINS

In July 1930, a call for tenders on the first of 14 contracts to build the Glenmore Waterworks complex went out, with the first contract (Contract 1) being for the construction of the Glenmore Reservoir.[176] The initial eight tenders were opened on July 16, with the lowest bid being submitted by the Winnipeg firm of George B. Wood & Company for $727,647.80. The next lowest bid was by the Calgary firm Bennett & White for $781,209.60. The only other Calgary company to submit a bid was Stewart, Grant & Mannix, which bid $1,131,947.20. Gore, Nasmith & Storrie recommended Bennett & White be awarded the contract based on the view that the firm had the engineering skills to meet the needs of the project and was also a Calgary-based company. The Finance Committee and the city council agreed, and on July 21, they awarded the contract to Bennett & White pending its agreement to the implementation of an eight-hour day. The city's policy of hiring local contractors had clearly worked to the advantage of Bennett & White. This decision was particularly satisfying because George B. Wood & Company had won the contract for the Calgary post office on the basis of a lower bid than Bennett & White in November 1929.[177]

Even before the city council meeting that chose Bennett & White, A. B. MacKay, on behalf of George B. Wood & Company, protested the decision and requested an opportunity to appear before the city council. The request was filed. When George B. Wood & Company was officially informed of the decision, the firm responded by saying the city should have withheld the final awarding of the contract until it had the opportunity to produce its engineer, who had vast experience in that class of work and would have been able to dispose of William Storrie's criticisms of its bid. The decision to award the contract to Bennett & White was supported by the General Contractors Association.

The principals of the Bennett & White construction company were Joseph Garnet Bennett, who was born in England in 1882, came to Calgary in 1910, and formed a construction firm in partnership with William White in 1916. It was incorporated as Bennett & White Construction Ltd. in 1925. When

White retired in 1932, Bennett's sons bought his shares, and in 1936, they took over active control of the company from their father. By the time the company bid on the Glenmore project, it had several major projects to its credit, including Spillers mill in Calgary, a grain elevator in Medicine Hat, the Department of Chemistry building at the University of Saskatchewan, the Medicine Hat Courthouse, a warehouse in Calgary for Crane Limited, a reinforced concrete bridge in Swift Current, and the Famous Players Theatre in Calgary. The company had never built a dam, but it recruited V. G. Hindmarsh, an engineer from San Francisco, to direct operations at the dam site.

The groundbreaking ceremony was held at 9:45 a.m. on July 26, 1930, under grey skies and drizzling rain, which did not prevent a large crowd of citizens from gathering to observe the proceedings. Mayor Davison turned the first sod with a gilded spade and then presented J. G. Bennett with the plans, specifications, contract, and the first order to commence work. He was in turn presented with a miniature of the spade with which he had broken the ground. Construction started immediately, and a "steam shovel began to rumble a few yards down the hill and ten minutes later a deep trench was lengthening out and big trucks were plying up and down the slope carrying away the dirt."[178] Bennett & White's construction office, the storage yard for the construction materials, and the concrete-mixing plant were all located where the water treatment plant is today. Towers were constructed on both sides of the valley to permit the operation of a skyline to deliver concrete from the batching plant. The hauling of sand and gravel to the site was subcontracted to the Commercial Cartage Company, the predecessor of what is today the Standard Construction Company. The gravel for construction was obtained from several sites that included the Elbow River itself, a pit in Manchester, and what was called the "brewery pit," which was located on the Bow River at the brewery in Inglewood. The gravel at that site was excavated by a bucket attached to a pulley strung between the two banks of the river.

By August, the Elbow River had been diverted to the south side of the valley and a cofferdam constructed to allow the dewatering of the riverbed. The construction site was divided into 16 units extending from one side of the valley to the other. The construction of each of these units began with the excavation of a cutoff trench about 10 feet (3 metres) wide and several feet below the lowest point or seam in the bedrock through which water was

Figure 5.1 Site preparation, August 7, 1930
Source: Glenbow Library and Archives, ND-10–56

leaking or to a maximum depth of 30 feet (9 metres) below the riverbed. The excavation of these trenches revealed that the layers of sandstone and shale were irregular, necessitating the removal of more material than was first thought necessary to reach a firm foundation based on the soil tests made in 1929. This required extra work on the part of Bennett & White, which was not included in its original contract, raising the cost of the project.

The cutoff trench was located at the point where the upstream face of the dam met the ground surface. The purpose of the trench was to reduce the possibility of water flowing underneath the structure and exerting upward pressure on the dam, which would be identical to the buoyant force on an object submerged in water. Minimizing this pressure was fundamental to ensuring the stability of the dam. Further precautions to reduce the upward force of water, referred to as hydrostatic pressure, included the installation of drainage pipes 2 inches (5 centimetres) in diameter and 5 feet (1.5 metres) apart that connected the rock under the cutoff wall to a drainage channel incorporated into the dam. At certain intervals, holes were drilled into the bedrock below the drainage pipes to a maximum depth of 20 feet (6 metres) to permit the passages in the rock to be sealed by pressure grouting with cement. As a result of the precautions taken during construction, tests made in 1933 showed the total drainage or leakage into the tunnel from all sources was only 3 gallons (13.5 litres), with the result that no grouting of the foundation was necessary.[179]

Once a watertight seal had been made between the base of the dam and the bedrock, the surface of the cutoff trench was brushed with a wire brush and filled with Class A concrete with a weight of 3,000 pounds per square inch (20,000 kilopascals). Successive layers of Class B concrete with a weight of 1,500 pounds per square inch (10,000 kilopascals) were then added to form the familiar rectangular profile of the dam. Additional amounts of Class A concrete were used to add a 12-inch (30-centimetre) facing on the dam, as well as to build the bridge. The concrete was placed in 5-foot (1.5 metre) layers, with each layer thoroughly tamped using a mechanical vibrator. The surface of each lift was sloped upward one foot (30 centimetres) in a downstream direction and left fairly irregular to ensure a good bond with the next lift. Several keys, which were grooves in the concrete about 12 inches (30 centimetres) deep, were created to increase the resistance against horizontal shearing stress. Immediately after being laid, each concrete layer was protected from extreme temperatures and kept wet for a period of 14 days. To permit the pouring of concrete in freezing temperatures, the aggregates and the water were heated by steam, and immediately after they were placed into the structure, the section was enclosed in canvas and a minimum temperature of 45 degrees Fahrenheit (7 degrees Celsius) was maintained for a period of at least three days. The pouring of lifts of only 5 feet (1.5 metres) in depth permitted the dissipation of the heat that was generated as the cement hardened.

Concrete pouring began on October 13, 1930, at construction unit 9D. Three shifts worked from Monday to Saturday, with generally no work on Sunday. A team of inspectors monitored the work of Bennett & White, checking the quality of the cement, the aggregate, and the concrete, and whether it was being properly covered and heated. The pouring of cement continued at construction units 6D, 7D, and 8D through to mid-December, when a decision had to be made as to when construction would be stopped. This decision had to balance the need to get the work done against sound engineering. Dr. Acres was not satisfied the cement could be safely poured during freezing weather and was fearful the safety of the dam might be imperiled if the cement were to be chilled by frost. The city council also received advice from labour groups, which were of the opposite opinion. Bennett & White advised the city that it had three options, one of which was to shut the project down until March 15, 1931, which had been anticipated in the terms of its contract. A second option was to run the job during moderately mild weather, which would add $24,750 to the cost of the project. The third option of continuing construction despite the weather conditions would add an additional $45,000 to the final cost.[180] Bennett & White was willing to allow work to proceed during the winter as a means of assisting the unemployment situation as long as the company was protected against loss. The city could not afford to pay the additional costs, which resulted in construction coming to an end on December 30. The unemployed not only benefited during the fall of 1930 from working on the dam, but also from the decision made on November 27 to allow them to cut trees in the reservoir area for sale as Christmas trees.

Concrete pouring resumed in early April 1931, with the same procedures being followed. During the spring and summer of 1931, Gore, Nasmith & Storrie's resident engineer, Norman McDonald, became particularly concerned about the quality of the concrete being made by Bennett & White and the manner in which it was being poured. In letters to Bennett & White during this period, McDonald noted the use of dirty aggregate and the inadequate construction of forms and tamping of the concrete, which left a honeycomb appearance. If McDonald's team of inspectors detected inadequate work, he required that it be redone at the contractor's expense. He refused to allow any bulging forms or honeycombed concrete. If any portions of the surface appeared porous, the entire section had to be chiseled out to form a key to ensure the permanence of the patch that was then applied. The whole area of the patched surface had to be cleaned up and rubbed down with a carborundum brick to eliminate, as far as possible, the unsightliness of the repair work. In a letter dated April 17, McDonald expressed his disappointment with the work being done and feared that "unless a very great change is made immediately, this structure will be such that we will all be ashamed to show our friends."[181] He was confident the appearance of the structure was of sufficient importance to Bennett & White that "the utmost care will be taken from now on to produce a structure which will have a satisfactory appearance and one which will receive favourable comments from those who are technically informed as well as the general public who know nothing of the nature of the work other than its general appearance."[182] Bennett & White rose to the occasion, and McDonald had high praise for the work when the project was complete.

As construction of the dam proceeded, Bennett & White also fabricated the components for the bridge across the top of the structure, which included railings. The bridge's reinforced arches and deck were completed in the summer and fall of 1931. It was the fourth reinforced concrete arch bridge built in Calgary, the first having been completed in 1915 in the Mission District. The dam and the bridge were completed in October 1931.

In December 1930, the city council, ever-conscious of the need for employment, authorized the commissioners to call for tenders for the two 36-inch (91-centimetre) pipelines that were to connect the Glenmore Waterworks complex to the distribution system, and Gore, Nasmith & Storrie was asked to have the plans for the filtration plant prepared as soon as possible. On January 5, 1931, the second project contract (Contract 2) was awarded, this one for the manufacture and installation of the 36-inch (91-centimetre) pipeline, to the Canada Lock Joint Pipe Company from Saint John, New Brunswick.[183] The pipe was made up of 12-foot (3.6-metre) lengths of welded steel cylinders lined on the inside by a 1.5-inch (4-centimetre) layer of concrete and on the outside by a 2.5-inch (6.4-centimetre) layer of concrete. The western arm of the pipeline extended from the north end of the dam north along 16th Street West to Pumphouse No. 2 on the Bow River, with a branch along 35th and 36th Streets to the reservoir in south Calgary. The eastern arm extended from the southern end of the dam east to 8th Street East, north along 8th Street East to 50th Avenue, east along 50th Avenue to Macleod Trail, and then along Macleod Trail and Spiller Road into the Ramsay District at 17th Avenue SE. The excavation of the trench for the pipeline was carried out by day labour provided by the city and paid for by the federal government as an unemployment relief project, so every effort was made to reduce the use of machinery and increase the amount of human labour required. The contract was extended in June to include the construction of two 48-inch

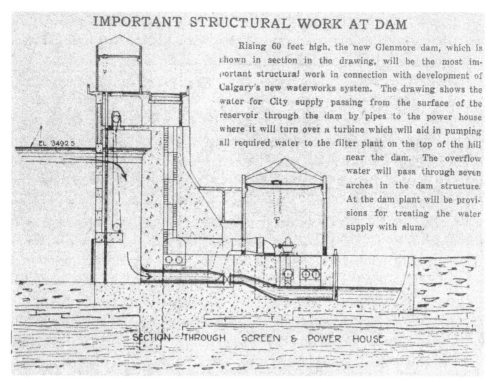

IMPORTANT STRUCTURAL WORK AT DAM

Rising 60 feet high, the new Glenmore dam, which is shown in section in the drawing, will be the most important structural work in connection with development of Calgary's new waterworks system. The drawing shows the water for City supply passing from the surface of the reservoir through the dam by pipes to the power house where it will turn over a turbine which will aid in pumping all required water to the filter plant on the top of the hill near the dam. The overflow water will pass through seven arches in the dam structure. At the dam plant will be provisions for treating the water supply with alum.

SECTION THROUGH SCREEN & POWER HOUSE

Figure 5.2 Article and diagram from the May 10, 1930, issue of the *Albertan*

(122-centimetre) pipelines of similar design to connect the pumphouse to the water purification plant. One pipeline was intended to deliver water from the reservoir for processing, while the other was to convey treated water back to the pumphouse for delivery to the city via the 36-inch (91-centimetre) main system. The valves for the pipeline were supplied under Contract 3, which had been awarded to Victaulic Company of Canada.[184]

The construction and equipping of the filtration plant, the construction of which was also initiated in the spring of 1931, was divided into three contracts.[185] Contract 4 for the substructure was advertised in March. Before the bids were opened, Bennett & White proposed the normal tendering process be suspended and it immediately be awarded the contract on a cost-plus basis. The initial reaction of the city council was to agree, but the decision was immediately reversed pending input from the engineering consults and the receipt of proposals from other contractors on the same basis.

Contract 5, which was for the superstructure, was awarded on September 11 to J. McDiarmid Construction. Provisions in the contract, which would later become an issue, included the use of Tyndall stone, brass for the doors, and marble for the floors, walls, ceilings, and wainscoting. Contract 6, covering the equipment for the purification plant, was awarded on the same day.

On October 26, Contract 7 was awarded to Fred Mannix for the construction of the embankment on the properties of Osborne Brown and Dr. Mackid. Its location today is between the entrance to Heritage Park and the Glenmore Landing shopping centre. Mannix's bid of $35,400 was the lowest, with other bids being submitted by the Commercial Cartage Company, which was already supplying the aggregate for the concrete being used in the dam, for $39,000, and J. E. Jefferies for $50,400. The embankment would be built across a former channel of the Bow River and without it, the reservoir created by the Glenmore Dam would have partially drained through the present-day subdivisions of Haysboro and Ogden to the Bow River. The topsoil was removed from the area on which the dam was built and a cutoff trench was excavated in the middle. The fill material was procured near the site and consisted of sandy clay. It was hauled to the job in large caterpillar wagons by gasoline tractors and deposited in layers. The traffic of the heavy equipment over the fill was very effective in consolidating it.

In mid-December, Gore, Nasmith & Storrie submitted a year-end report that noted the progress made on the first seven contracts and compared the expenditures to date to the original estimates made in October 1929. Contract 1 for the construction of the Glenmore Dam was over the original estimate by $294,790.40. The final cost of the 36-inch (91-centimetre) pipeline estimated at $572,000 was $40,000 under budget, while the cost of the valves for the pipeline was on budget. The filtration plant was under budget by $330,000. The construction of the embankment by Fred Mannix was on budget at $35,400. The most significant disparity between the estimated cost and the actual cost was for the construction of the dam, and Gore, Nasmith & Storrie made a special effort to explain the results. The cost increase was noted in the December 16 issue of the *Herald*, but the newspaper drew no conclusions about the way the project was being managed.

Gore, Nasmith & Storrie's year-end reports for 1931 also included a report on the elevated tank to be erected at 10th Street and 21st Avenue NW to improve water service to the long-suffering residents of North Hill. The contract for the tank's construction was awarded to Dominion Bridge and funded through the Dominion Government Relief scheme. Another report addressed the issue of modifications to the dam to mitigate floods, which had not been a consideration when the project was first planned. The report noted there had been flood conditions on the Elbow River for some months during the spring and summer freshets. The largest flood for which there is a record occurred in June 1929, which gave a maximum flow in the river of 15,300 cubic feet per second (430 cubic metres per second). The engineers recommended the installation of two conduits and valves of enough capacity to make use of the storage reservoir to reduce the flood flows downstream.

The construction of the pipelines, filtration plant, embankment, and water tank on North Hill was also completed in 1932. Contracts 8 to 12 were awarded in the spring of 1932 for the construction and equipping of the screen house, pumping station, and chemical building. The screen house was located on the upstream side of the dam and removed floating debris from the water. The pumphouse located on the downstream side of the dam moved raw water to the filtration plant via a 48-inch (122-centimetre) pipeline and then to the city via a 36-inch (91-centimetre) pipeline. The chemical building located between the dam and the filtration plant added alum and chlorine to the water.

The preparations made in December 1931 for a flood proved useful in late May and early June 1932. Portents of a flood were first recorded in the engineer's journal on May 26 when he noted the water level in the river was down, but it was raining heavily and work on the penstock was being pushed ahead. The rainfall increased, with a total of 3.54 inches (90 millimetres) falling between May 31 and June 3. During the evening of June 1, the rising river made it dangerous to work in the section of the construction site that Bennett & White was within days of completing. That evening, the cofferdams went out. The journal entries for June 2 and 3 recorded the passage of the crest of the flood. The June 2 entry recorded that water in the river was continuing rise, and at noon on June 2, it was 18 feet (5.5 metres) below the crest. Bennett & White rescued as much lumber as possible that morning, and the boom of the crane being used on the dam bridge was let down. The flood forced the relocation of Bennett & White's blacksmith shop. The shed of Dominion Bridge could not be rescued and was caught in the flood. By midnight, the water was 5.5 feet (1.7 metres) below the crest and still rising. The next day, reports from Bragg Creek indicated the water was going down, having reached its crest about noon. Gore and McDonald estimated that during the evening of June 2, the flow into the reservoir during the evening was in the neighbourhood of 25,000 cubic feet per second (700 cubic metres per second). A decision was made to increase the height of the embankment because of fears it would be breached. All the staff were working, and one man was on duty all night to watch developments. A huge crowd of people came out to observe.

The consequences of the flood of 1932, as with every flood since 1909, were extensive, with damage to the gravity system and yet another water supply crisis for Calgary. The *Herald* headline for June 4 described the gravity-line collapse and announced the city was facing "the most acute water shortage in its history."

The gravity line that fed the city reservoir collapsed under the terrific pressure imposed by the heavy rains, and at noon on Saturday, June 4, the city commissioners announced that no water of any kind was coming through the line. With only a four-day water supply available in the reservoir, repairs to the gravity line were rushed. Following the cleanup of the site after the flood, Contract 13 was awarded to the Simplex Value & Meter Company, and Contract 14 for the supply of alum feed machines was awarded to the E. Dean Wilkes Company. The filter sand for the filtration plant was supplied under contract by M. J. Couch and prepared and placed by city crews. The filter gravel was supplied and placed by J. N. Jeffries from his plant on the Bow River, thus combining the resources of the two rivers.

The Glenmore project was completed with only two accidents on the construction site. An unidentified individual died from injuries sustained from a fall while working on the filtration plant in the fall of 1931, and on August 26, 1932, the *Herald* described the death of H. P. Jensen, who drowned after falling into the reservoir. He swam about 30 feet (9 metres) after the fall but was unable to hold on to a rope thrown to him in a rescue effort. He let go of the line, and the current carried him downstream where other employees later recovered his body.

Figure 5.3 Construction progress to October 1, 1930
Source: Glenbow Library and Archives, ND-10–60

Figure 5.4 A portion of the cutoff trench that was excavated to a depth that ensured the dam was securely attached to the bedrock and that water was excluded from the area below the dam. Water seeping under the dam would exert upward pressure on the structure, which had the potential to cause it to fail.
Source: Glenbow Library and Archives, NA-2597–57

Figure 5.5 The washing and mixing plant that supplied the aggregate for the production of the concrete (1930)

Source: Glenbow Library and Archives, NA-2597–49

Figure 5.6 Construction progress to October 30, 1930

Source: Glenbow Library and Archives, NA-2597–60

Figure 5.7 Construction progress to November 1, 1930
Source: Glenbow Library and Archives, ND-10–64

Figure 5.8 Construction progress to December 2, 1930
Source: Glenbow Library and Archives, ND-10–68

Figure 5.9 Construction progress to December 23, 1930

Source: Glenbow Library and Archives, ND-10–69

Figure 5.10 Construction progress to January 8, 1931

Source: Glenbow Library and Archives, PA 3163

Figure 5.11 Construction progress to April 7, 1931

Source: Glenbow Library and Archives, ND-10–73

Figure 5.12 Construction progress to May 1, 1931

Source: Glenbow Library and Archives, ND-10–74

Figure 5.13 Construction progress to June 1, 1931
Source: Glenbow Library and Archives, ND-10–84

Figure 5.14 Construction progress to June 18, 1931
Source: Glenbow Library and Archives, NA-2063–2

Figure 5.15 Construction progress to July 2, 1931

Source: Glenbow Library and Archives, ND-10–86

Figure 5.16 Construction progress to August 3, 1931

Source: Glenbow Library and Archives, ND-10–91

Figure 5.17 Construction progress to September 2, 1931

Source: Glenbow Library and Archives, ND-10–96

Figure 5.18 Construction progress to September 30, 1931

Source: Glenbow Library and Archives, NA-2597–63

Figure 5.19 Construction progress to September 30, 1931

Source: Glenbow Library and Archives, NA-2597–64

Figure 5.20 Construction progress to October 2, 1931

Source: Glenbow Library and Archives, ND-10–98

Figure 5.21 Construction progress to October 15, 1931

Source: Glenbow Library and Archives, ND-10–99

Figure 5.22 By June 5, 1932, construction on the dam had progressed to the point where the dam was able to mitigate the worst flood to occur on the Elbow River.

Source: Glenbow Library and Archives, NA-2063–3

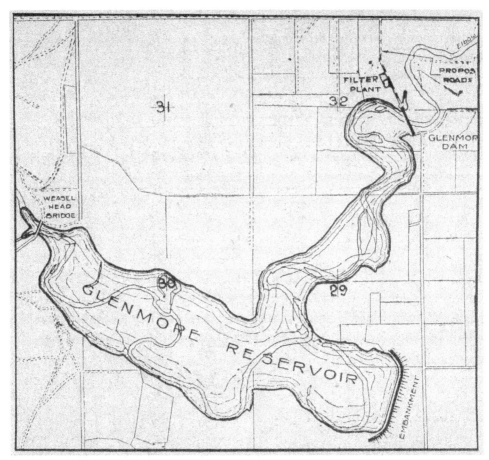

Figure 5.23 This map from the May 30, 1930, issue of the *Albertan* shows the relationship between the channel of the Elbow River and the Glenmore Reservoir. The buildings constructed by Sam Livingston and occupied by Osborne Brown at the time the Glenmore Dam was created were saved for posterity and eventually ended up in Heritage Park. The only other building relocated before the flooding of the valley was a Rotary Club building, which was moved to the Earl Grey Golf Club to serve as its first clubhouse.

RESERVOIR LAND ACQUISITION

As the dam was being built in the fall of 1929, the city acquired the land to store the water impounded by its construction. Gore, Nasmith & Storrie originally estimated that 900 acres (364 hectares) would be covered by water and that 600 acres (243 hectares) of additional land was required for a shoreline. After some inquiry, the engineers fixed a flat price of $100 per acre ($250 per hectare), for an estimated total cost of $150,000. Mayor Osborne took the opportunity to investigate land prices at that location in advance of the city's land acquisition scheme becoming public. Real estate agent W. D. Milner was hired by the mayor and dispatched on a clandestine mission to interview the owners of various properties and ascertain what price they were willing to accept for their land without knowing it was to be included in the Glenmore project. Milner was instructed to act without disclosing the name of the proposed purchaser and to report back to the mayor. Milner interviewed various landowners, including Archdeacon Arthur J. B. Dewdney. Dewdney had made several improvements to his land, which was located on the east side of the Elbow River, close to where the Foothills Hospital is today. Other property owned by his wife and daughter extended across the Elbow Valley onto the highland to the west of the Elbow River, which is now occupied in part by the Earl Grey Golf Club. The Dewdney residence overlooked the Elbow Valley and consisted of "a large residence with well-appointed stables and other buildings. All were neat and well kept."[186] The house was served by gas from the Calgary gas pipeline from Turner Valley, and a septic tank sewerage system had been installed. It was, in the view of Fred Filteau, the author of a 1932 report on the city's land acquisition process, "the best suburban residential property in southern Alberta."[187] By 1929, Dewdney and his family had moved to Victoria and had already put their property up for sale before being approached by Milner. The entire Dewdney property holdings were at the time listed with real estate agents Mapson & Durrell for $70,000. Milner reported his findings to the mayor, who instructed him to procure an option from Archdeacon Dewdney on 387.12 acres (157 hectares) for $70,000 without telling him the purpose for which the purchase was being made. Milner tried unsuccessfully to have the price reduced. Upon hearing about the intended use of the land, Archdeacon Dewdney was later reported to have said that he would have given the land to the city free of charge.[188]

Any hope Mayor Osborne had of acquiring more land in a similar manner ended on October 17 when both the *Herald* and the *Albertan* published an aerial photograph of the Elbow Valley indicating the location of the dam and the land required for the reservoir. The mayor and the city council now had to acquire 2,010 additional acres (813 hectares) from landowners who, unlike the Dewdneys, were anxious to retain the ownership of their land as permanent residences. The city council first passed an amendment to the city charter that gave the city the legal power to expropriate the required land, even though the land was outside the city limits. However, on the advice of valuators E. B. Nowers and H. S. Jones, the city would use expropriation as a last resort. The valuators suggested that, based on their experience, arbitration boards typically got higher prices than those obtained by private negotiation. The city council also engaged the services of valuators Mowers, Jones, & Milner, whose duties were to negotiate with owners to obtain offers to sell at prices that appeared to the valuators to be fair and reasonable.

In February 1930, the city council established the Lands Committee, to which the valuators reported and in whose hands rested the final decision to purchase. This committee consisted of Peter Turner Bone, Mayor Andrew Davison, Commissioner Arthur Graves, and aldermen Eneas McCormick, Ralph Patterson, Frederick White, Robert Weir, Joseph Ross, and Robert Parkyn. When Wilmot Milner was elected to council in 1930, he retired from the board of valuators, and together with Alderman Lloyd Fenerty, joined the Lands Committee. J. C. Leslie was added to the board of valuators to replace Milner. On March 24, 1930, the city council approved the commissioners' request that they be authorized to consummate transactions for the purchase of land required for water purposes with the approval of the Lands Committee and with the further proviso that prices to be paid were recommended by the board of valuators. The city council, however, became involved in several of the more contentious land purchases.

With the necessary machinery established, protracted negotiations with the various landowners took place from March 1930 to November 1931, when the last property was acquired. In his final report, E. B. Nowers noted that the total cost of his services, along with those of Jones, Milner, and Leslie totalled $6,850. In anticipation of criticism of the amount paid, he pointed out that in practically every case, they had long, drawn-out negotiations and numerous interviews with owners and their solicitors. He noted that "fancy" prices were asked, in fact far higher proportionally than that paid for the Dewdney property.[189] The purchase of the Dewdney property, high as the price had been, and no doubt justified under the circumstances, nevertheless set a standard for all subsequent land purchases.

The group with the oldest claim to the land was the Tsuu T'ina Nation, with whom negotiations were conducted through to October 1931. It was the second time the city had taken an interest in acquiring their land; the first time was an effort to obtain land for a park just before World War I. An account of the final stage in these negotiations was described in an article entitled "City and Sarcee Seal Land Pact at Colourful Pow-Wow" by the *Herald* in its October 24 issue. A total of 593.5 acres (240 hectares) of land was purchased at $50 per acre for a total of $30,046.80.[190] This became what is now the Weaselhead delta, which came into existence because of the creation of the reservoir.

The 80 acres (32 hectares) of land purchased from Osborne Brown was located in what is now the southern portion of Heritage Park and the boat launch lagoon. The buildings were originally built by Sam Livingston. Brown had purchased some of the Livingston land as well as the buildings, which dated from the 1880s. He had lived on part of the old Livingston place for more than 40 years. Two or three years before the interest in his land for reservoir purposes, he had remodelled the old house, spending $4,300 on the residence, along with several thousands of dollars on other improvements to the property. "Mr. Brown," noted Mowers in his final report to the city council, "is no longer a young man who felt keenly the giving up of his home with its old associations."[191] Following the purchase, Brown bought 10 acres (4 hectares) immediately across what is now 14th Avenue from the old property. The city paid him $12,945 for his land, with $600 added to cover improvements, $490 to cover land that had been broken, and $9,465 for his residence.

The land located east of Weaselhead Flats, which is now the middle of the reservoir and North Glenmore Park, was part of the Robinson Ranch, which dated back to the Sam Livingston era in the 1880s. The city purchased 720 acres (290 hectares) of the 1,600 acres (647 hectares), for which it paid $68,480, or $95 per acre ($237.50 per hectare). Added to the cost of the land was $1,320 to cover wells and fencing and $200 for broken land. A further $10,000 was added to cover the cost of severance.

The land of Dr. L. S. Mackid was located south and east of the Brown property, which today is the southern portion of the reservoir and the land between Heritage Park and the Glenmore Landing shopping centre. As with

Brown, the construction of the Glenmore Waterworks interrupted Mackid's plans to retire on his land. Under the terms of his agreement with the city, the city agreed to lease back a portion of the land to Mackid, allowing him to continue living there and the city to proceed with the Glenmore development. He was paid a total of $59,618.40 for 195.38 acres (79 hectares) to which was added $18,881.60 for buildings. He was paid $305 per acre ($762.50 per hectare), the highest cost of land for the project.

The Rotary Club held a 21-year lease dating from June 13, 1928, on a portion of Elbow Valley located north of where Heritage Park is today. The city agreed on August 12, 1930, to purchase the unexpended portion of the lease and compensate the club for the improvements it had made.

The property of B. F. Elmore and M. H. Ford consisted of a portion of the Elbow Valley and the highland, which is now part of Heritage Park. The city purchased 139.7 acres (57 hectares) for $13,000. J. B. Durrel owned 29.2 acres (12 hectares) of land, which today would be in the centre of Heritage Park. He purchased his property in 1928 for $120 per acre and had already made improvements and was planning to construct a new house. The City of Calgary also acquired the properties of George N. Bull, Franc A. Rose, Charles W. Hague, John R. Loomis, William Roper Hull, and Emma B. Davis in a rural residential subdivision called Mayfair. This subdivision consisted of a large island in the Elbow River, along with land in the river flats and a portion of the highland located west of the Glenmore Causeway. The William Ross estate sold the city 143.64 acres (58 hectares) of unimproved land, which was located where the water filtration plant and athletic field are today, for $21,546.

The city acquired a total of 2,397 acres (970 hectares) for $347,866.82, which cost $197 per acre ($492.50 per hectare) and was 866.82 acres (350 hectares) more land than was estimated when the project began. The purchase of additional land was the result of engineering needs and the fact that if the city expropriated or purchased the greater part of a property, including the land on which buildings were situated and any land bordering the river, the owner did not want to retain the remainder of the property, so the city had to buy it as well. The cost overruns on the construction of the Glenmore Waterworks and the purchase of land were capitalized, which meant the city could issue debentures for the amount.[192]

In addition to the 12.5 acres (5 hectares) leased to Dr. Mackid, the city also leased land to the Earl Grey Golf Club. The club had been established in 1919 on land on the brow of the escarpment between 7th and 8th Avenues surrounding Earl Grey School. By 1924, a small clubhouse had been built on the south side of Hillcrest Avenue, and the club had 271 members but lacked an adequate course. The first three holes were located on the school grounds, so members couldn't play until after school was out. Prairie grass was a main feature of the rest of the course, which was divided by city streets, thus providing yet more hazards. In May 1925, the city commissioners expressed the view that "protection must be assured for the city against damage claims where golf clubs within the city limits make a practice of driving across streets."[193] The commissioners were willing to consider an application from the club to continue the practice if the club was willing to assume liability for any damage claims that might be made in the case of accidents. In 1929, residential development pushed the club south to the area between Premier Way and 38th Avenue SW. In May 1932, the club applied to lease 107 acres (43 hectares) of land that had been part of the Dewdney property on the north side of the Glenmore Reservoir. The city Lands Committee's recommendation that the property be leased for $500 per year was approved by the city council. The clubhouse at the new site was originally part of the Rotary Club camp located in the Elbow Valley below the golf course.

The need to clear trees below the anticipated shoreline of the reservoir was seen by the city as a chance to provide an opportunity for the unemployed. At its November 24, 1930, meeting, the city council decided to let the unemployed cut the trees below the future waterline and sell them as Christmas trees. The engineers discouraged the cutting of trees above the shoreline.

HEY, YOU "DEFICIT DEALERS"!

The critics of the Glenmore Waterworks project faded away following its approval on November 20, 1929, as it became a major source of jobs in the midst of a worsening employment crisis. However, cost overruns and the use of certain types of construction materials would rekindle fears that something was wrong with the Glenmore project. The city's program of counter-cyclical budgeting as a strategy to deal with the Depression began in the summer of 1930 when the city council and the commissioners considered additional projects that, like the Glenmore Dam and Reservoir, served the long-term needs of the city, as well as addressing the immediate need to create jobs. The creation of public works programs was spurred on by news that the federal government intended to pass relief legislation to provide partial funding for construction projects. The most ambitious public works program, suggested by Alderman Samuel Savage, recommended $800,000 in projects, including building more swimming pools.[194] Savage also wanted to take steps to improve the city's parks and boulevards. The Calgary Municipal Street Railway was also included in the list of improvements, as was a subway under the CPR tracks at 4th Street West.

Commissioner Arthur Graves made suggestions that included spending $55,000 to gravel all the city lanes during the winter of 1930–31. Not only would this provide work, but it would alleviate the great inconvenience caused to motorcar owners every spring when lanes became veritable quagmires after the ground thawed. The engineer's office was also asked to create a list of storm and sanitary sewers that needed to be built. Graves favoured projects such as laying sewers since they had maximum labour creation potential because the trenches could be dug by hand. Graves also suggested paving all the roads within the city limits that led to the main highways. He had arrived at the need to do this work after taking a drive around the city and after receiving many complaints about the condition of the roads. The city council also expressed the view that something should be done before another year rolled around, and a particular type of pavement could be used on the roadways to reduce the cost. These various suggestions were compiled by Graves in a special list Mayor Davison submitted to the provincial government in the fall of 1930 as part of the procedure to obtain federal government relief funds.

A letter from Mayor Davison to Premier John Brownlee dated October 16 prefaced the list of capital projects with a plea for swift action on the request. Because there were many married men in Calgary who had very little employment that year, and who were now destitute, some of the work had to be commenced immediately; otherwise the city would be forced to hand out large sums of money for direct relief. The final list included two projects that related to the Glenmore Waterworks, namely clearing 200 acres

(81 hectares) of land in the reservoir and laying the 20-inch (51-centimetre) and 36-inch (91-centimetre) water mains. The other projects included gravelling the streets and lanes, building a new bridge at 25th Avenue SW on the Elbow River as well as four swimming pools, repairing the Sunnyside slope, extending the sewer system, and doing other sundry jobs. The total cost of the work was $580,574, of which Calgary would pay half, with the remainder coming from the federal and provincial governments. Davison ended his letter by returning to the theme of the impact of the Depression on Calgary, noting that "at this writing, more than 900 married men are registered with us for city work." The options for Davison were to pay people to do useful work or to pay them to be unemployed.

The federal government's program to deal with the Depression, which was made public on September 26, 1930, provided $4 million to partially fund municipal public works for the unemployed. On October 9, Davison returned from Ottawa having successfully obtained a commitment from the federal government to provide $200,000 and a commitment from the provincial government to provide $150,000 for public works. Married men who had lived in Calgary for one year were to be given preference when hiring. The city council, however, was not content to limit its expenditures to the mayor's list and added several other projects it considered to be in the public interest. These included a nurse's residence, park improvements, and three more swimming pools. At the October 23 city council meeting, Mayor Davison warned that the city could not afford the additional expenses. The citizens of Calgary agreed with Davison, and the plebiscites for these additional projects were defeated during a civic election on November 19.

While the City of Calgary was designating funds for capital projects to meet the need for employment, it also had to deal with the ever-increasing cost of providing relief to the unemployed. The city had made an effort to deal with its destitute citizens as early as 1895, but the circumstances of the early 1930s created unprecedented levels of demand for financial aid that quickly overwhelmed the resources of many municipal governments, including Calgary. Increasingly, the unemployed were driven to riding the rails in search of work and relief. In August 1930, George Thompson, superintendent of the Relief Department, reported to Mayor Davison that it had cost the city $500 more that month to feed the unfortunate than in July 1929. By the end of October 1930, more than 3,000 people were listed at the Alberta Employment Service as unemployed in Calgary, which was an increase of more than 600 from the previous week. This was over 1,000 more than were registered in Edmonton and over 300 more than the combined number of unemployed men listed in Edmonton, Lethbridge, Medicine Hat, and Drumheller.

By November 1930, Calgary was taking steps to protect itself from the army of unemployed drifters by instituting a registration system to determine who was eligible for relief. There was no possibility of drifters taking part in the city's relief scheme for single unemployed men because tickets were not issued to anyone who had not registered before October 31 and who had not lived in the city since August 1. By April 1931, a report to Mayor Davison from the Relief Department indicated that between November 20, 1930, and April 15, 1931, the cost of caring for the single unemployed had reached $50,440.95 for the three levels of government, and during that period, more than 192,000 bed-and-board tickets had been issued. By June 1931, Calgary, in the view of the *Herald*, had become the "sucker city of the West" as the army of drifters continued to arrive en masse in the community.[195] The June 24 issue of the newspaper described how "by freight train, blind baggage, and on foot, wandering transients were flocking into Calgary daily by the score for the purpose of registering under the latest unemployment scheme, and at noon no less than 1,550 had registered since the office opened at 9 o'clock Tuesday."[196] Interviews with some of these transients conducted by the *Herald* confirmed that Calgary was the place to be if you were unemployed.

In 1929 and 1930, the City of Calgary was in a position to meet these demands. The September 13, 1930, issue of the *Herald* reported that the city's tax revenue was higher than in 1929, and the city was well pleased because local property owners had paid their taxes. Financial conditions had not been the best, but in spite of this, citizens had rallied, and the majority had made every effort to pay their taxes on time. The October 20 issue of the *Herald* described a booming economy, and in the same issue, the newspaper reported that the city's expenditures had increased as work was provided. On November 12, 1930, the *Herald* reported that the city's revenues were ahead of the 1929 figures.

In 1931, the city's financial position began to change dramatically as the nonpayment of taxes created a deficit in the city's operations. As tax revenue went down, property taxes went up. The mill rate went from 44.5 mills in 1929 to 52 mills in 1932. The *Herald* for September 17, 1931, reported the city had been forced to borrow $450,000 to keep operating. Fall-off in general revenue and large relief expenditures were blamed. According to Commissioner Graves, because the city had been forced to borrow from the bank to make up for a big drop in general revenue and exceedingly large expenditures for unemployment relief, it had reached the stage where it had to curtail expenditures in every department if a serious financial situation were to be avoided at the end of the year.

By the spring of 1932, Calgary taxpayers who still had jobs were growing increasingly anxious about the conduct of the civic government, including some of the decisions about the Glenmore Waterworks. This mood was evident in the April 14, 1932, issue of the *Mention*, the reincarnation of the *West-Ender*, which published an article suggesting the Beauharnois Dam scandal in Quebec had its parallel in Calgary's Glenmore project. The Beauharnois scandal revolved around the charge that the Beauharnois Power Company had given $700,000 to the Liberal Party of Canada in exchange for the right to dam the Beauharnois River for electricity. The *Mention* article reminded readers of its comments in 1929 about the Glenmore project being unnecessary and overhyped by Mayor Davison. In the view of the publisher, F. H. Newnham, the events since the project's approval had proven him correct since the dam and reservoir had not yet been completed after two and a half years and the waterworks system was still not in operation. The article repeated what had been said in 1929, which was that the large daily newspapers were not giving citizens the facts. Events since 1929 had also provided Newnham with new reasons to be critical of the project. These included the use of marble in the construction of the filtration plant and the process by which land had been purchased. As a solution to the situation, the newspaper recommended the creation of a "taxpayers protective association." Other cities had organized similar organizations, and a tax revolt in Chicago became a topic of discussion in Edmonton. He insisted that Calgary had to join this movement because if "we must do the paying, let's do a little saying."[197]

Figure 5.24 This editorial cartoon from the June 16, 1932, issue of the *Herald* encapsulates the sense of impending disaster felt by the members of the Taxpayers' Research Bureau.

In early May 1932, both the *Herald* and the *Albertan* once again reported an increase in the costs to build the dam and to purchase land for the reservoir. On this occasion, however, the *Herald* took the opportunity to raise some questions about the way the project was being managed. In an editorial entitled "Taxpayers receive another shock," the paper pointed out that even if allowance was made for unanticipated costs, "it must be admitted that the enormous disparity between the actual cost and the engineer's estimates leaves something to be explained."[198] The city's failure to anticipate the extra costs for both the dam and the land was seen by the *Herald* as the result of too much haste on all sides in getting the project underway. It suggested that had additional funds been provided to cover these contingencies when the project began, the current financial problems would have been avoided.

This call for action was first met by a May 4, 1932, petition for the recall of the entire city council as well as Commissioner Graves. Six reasons were cited as the basis for this action, the first being inefficiency and lack of ability. The second was the condonation of reckless expenditure in connection with the construction of the Glenmore Dam and the purchase of property for the reservoir. The third reason was the condonation of reckless expenditures on the Sunnyside slope. The fourth was the condonation of political patronage among civic employees. The fifth was the lack of a courageous and competent relief policy to decrease taxes and yet give greater unemployment relief. The sixth and final reason was the failure to follow a policy of rigid economy and to spend civic monies where they would do the most good.[199] The petition was received by the city clerk but was rejected.

The failure of the petition was followed by the creation of the Taxpayers' Research Bureau on June 3, 1932. Neither political nor partisan in its aims, the Taxpayers' Research Bureau appealed to all citizens regardless of political affiliation to lend support to a new movement designed to ease the almost intolerable load of taxation. The time had come, its sponsors believed, that no one political unit had enough power to cope with the mounting bill of taxes and government expenditures. Members of the bureau included former alderman Frank Freeze, sitting alderman Harold Riley, and former city solicitor David Moffat. Freeze had served on the city council from 1918 to 1921 and from 1926 to 1929. He was a strong advocate of operating the city on sound business principles, including exercising tight fiscal control, and had been active in the formation of the Civic Government Association. Harold W. H. Riley had moved with his family to Calgary in 1888 when he was 11, settling on a farm in what is now West Hillhurst. In 1905, with the creation of the Province of Alberta, he was appointed Provincial Secretary and Registrar of Companies. In 1907, he was appointed honourary secretary of the newly established University of Alberta, and in 1910, he went into business, organizing and becoming president of Riley's Limited. His role in Alberta politics began with his election as alderman in 1911, followed by his election in 1912 as the member for the constituency of Gleichen. Following service in World War I, he returned to Calgary, where he resumed his role in the economic and political life of the community. Riley played an important part in the creation and operation of the Calgary Stock Exchange and served on the city council between 1932 and 1935. He served as the chairman of the Special Council Committee on Relief.

The Taxpayers' Research Bureau sent letters demanding the city operate on the basis of a balanced budget. Its first opportunity to enter the debate about the expenditures on public works as a solution to the municipality's economic problems was the plebiscite on the proposed subway under the CPR tracks at 4th Street West that was held on June 29, 1932. The operation of the Relief Department was another target of the Taxpayers' Research Bureau.

The Taxpayers' Research Bureau became involved in the growing concern about the Glenmore Dam and Reservoir at a general meeting held on October 6, 1932. A resolution from the floor was passed directing the bureau's executive to request a public inquiry into the Glenmore project. The executive included this request in a letter to the mayor, the commissioners, and the city council, which included other suggestions for improvements. The bureau recommended that all existing wage agreements between the city and its employees be terminated as of December 31, 1932, and new ones negotiated regardless of the existing collective bargaining agreements. A second recommendation was that the auditors of the city be changed and that in the future, no auditing firm be retained for longer than five years. The city council was also requested to undertake a public inquiry into all the costs relative to the construction of the Glenmore Dam, with particular reference to the price paid for all the land acquired for the project and the cost of all works whether undertaken by contract or carried out by the city under the supervision of its own engineers.

For the city commissioners, Mayor Davison, and the majority of the city council, the letter was the last straw in what had become a public whispering campaign. The commissioners reacted by "declaring that they were tired of attacks being directed against civic employees, former mayors, present aldermen and former aldermen, landowners and any person that had anything to do with the purchase of the Glenmore Dam site and the construction of the dam itself."[200] They requested that city solicitor Leonard Brockington prepare a report for the Tuesday, October 11 meeting of the city council as to the procedures to follow to conduct a judicial investigation. On Monday, October 10, Mayor Davison announced this decision and indicated that every person who had anything to do with the big project would be subpoenaed as a witness, and any person who wished to make charges of any kind would be invited to appear before the tribunal. "We are going to get this matter cleared up for good and all," the mayor declared. The city council endorsed the idea of a judicial inquiry, with only Alderman Jean Romeo Miquelon opposed because he regarded it as a waste of money. On October 13, 1932, the city council advised the Taxpayers' Research Bureau that the decision had been made to undertake a judicial investigation under Section 155 of the city charter. The bureau was requested to give input but made no response.

The October 18 issue of the *Herald* reported that the Taxpayers' Research Bureau had decided not to participate in the city's investigation and declined the opportunity to make its criticism clear. Its position was explained in a letter from Riley, who indicated the bureau was satisfied with the terms of the investigation. At the meeting on October 18, 1932, the city council formally requested a judicial investigation be undertaken and conducted by Justice Albert Ewing of the Alberta Supreme Court. One-time critic of the location of the project, A. Macleod Sinclair, was chosen as commission counsel. The city initially decided it would not require legal counsel during the investigation, but when Justice Ewing was advised of that decision, he advised the city that although it had the right to refuse counsel, it was not a good idea. Ewing stressed that the municipality had a vested interest in having representation because the city had more complete information on the subject than outsiders. Facts might be given in evidence that, he suggested, could lead to an incorrect inference, but which a slight explanation would correct. If no city official were present to provide clarification, a serious wrong might be done to someone connected with the city. John S. Mavor was subsequently appointed counsel for the city. David Moffat acted for a group of unidentified taxpayers, which was as close as the Taxpayers' Research Bureau came to actually participating in the inquiry.

The inquiry was organized by October 26, and everyone waited for the filing of charges with the commission. When it became known that no charges had yet been filed, commission counsel A. Macleod Sinclair once again issued another invitation for any person who had knowledge that might be of interest to the inquiry to come forward. Despite the lack of formal charges being filed, the city officials intended to proceed anyway. One mayor, one former mayor, 21 aldermen and former aldermen, and at least a dozen city officials were included in the list of 55 witnesses the city intended to summon to give evidence.

The faceoff between the administration and its critics began on November 7 with testimony by former mayor Fred Osborne, who explained the process by which land had been purchased, stressing how strict secrecy on the part of city officials prevented land values from jumping sky high. This was illustrated by the manner in which he had approached Calgary real estate agent W. D. Milner and "without telling him much, asked him to secure an option for an unknown client on land in the general area upon which the dam was built." Milner informed Osborne shortly afterward that he was able to secure an option on the property of Archdeacon Dewdney by virtue of a deposit of $1,000 and a total purchase price of $70,000 plus interest. The option was approved by the city, except that considerable savings were had by making the sum $70,000 without interest. Once Archdeacon Dewdney became aware of who had purchased the land, he said in a letter to Mayor Osborne that he would have offered to give the land to the city for free. He also indicated that the city had not undertaken to pay Milner a commission since that fee would be paid by the landowner. Osborne ended his testimony on the land purchase with a declaration that he had no personal interest in the land the city bought for the dam nor did any of his relatives and denied that he had been offered any bribes in connection with the project. Moving on to the question of the dam, Osborne outlined the reasons why it had been built and the decision of the city council to require a two-thirds majority on the bylaw approving the Glenmore project rather than a simple majority. He also denied that Bennett & White had any influence over the city's decision to hire engineering firm Gore, Nasmith & Storrie.

Other city administration witnesses included Mayor Davison, who repeated Osborne's view that the project was necessary and denied any collusion between Bennett & White and city officials to inflate the cost of the project.[201] He also testified to the fairness of the land purchase procedures and denied that he had been offered any bribes in connection with the project and that neither he nor any members of his family were involved in the land purchase. Davison continued to testify the following day, dealing with his denial of any collusion between the firm of Gore, Nasmith & Storrie and the Bennett & White construction company with regard to the awarding of the dam contract. According to Moffat, collusion was suspected because there was only about $334 difference between the engineers' estimate of the cost of the dam and the amount of the tender submitted by Bennett & White. In Davison's view, this merely showed Bennett & White was a good bidder.

Davison was then questioned by F. H. Newnham, publisher of the *Mention*, who subjected him to "a grueling cross-examination" in which he charged the mayor with boosting the Glenmore project to an unwarranted extent during an address to a commercial travellers' luncheon. Newnham also referred to the marble staircase and the bronze fittings in the Glenmore filtration plant. He illustrated his view that such expensive fittings were inappropriate in such a building with the fact that the courthouse where the inquiry was being conducted lacked similar appointments. Davison pointed out that solid marble had not been used and that Tyndall stone was more suitable since it was harder and thus had a much longer life than brick.

William Gore outlined the advantages of the dam, which included flood prevention and the fact it would save the city about $45,000 in pumping charges annually while at the same time providing an adequate water supply for 200,000 people.[202] City solicitor Brockington testified to the integrity of the land purchase process and that the city had obtained the land at the best possible prices.[203] He had advised against the use of expropriation since, in his view, such an approach would have inflated land prices. City waterworks engineer Robinson provided evidence in support of the necessity of the project.

The first critic to appear as a witness was Hugh Duffield, a civil engineer, a member of the executive of the Taxpayers' Research Bureau, and an unsuccessful independent candidate in the 1929 municipal election. He admitted he had never suspected at any time that there was any malfeasance or breach of trust on the part of any city official or engineer in connection with the construction of the Glenmore Dam. He admitted he had never seen the dam or the site until July 1932 and that the whole structure as it now stood was beyond reproach from an engineering point of view. William Storrie immediately jumped on this statement to further emphasize the lack of credibility on the part of the project's critics. When asked to "crystallize" his objections to the new dam, Duffield's response was that it was too near the city, the reservoir was subject to contamination, and it was too large and expensive. He preferred that water be pumped from the Bow River into a reservoir in the city. When reminded by J. S. Mavor, counsel for the city, that many sites had been evaluated, he only indicated that further study of Bow River sites should have been made. Commission counsel Sinclair also asked Duffield about the numerous negative letters written to the newspapers about the project, one of which Duffield had penned. Duffield replied that he could not remember sending the letter. During his two days of testimony, Duffield made statements about the project but could not actually provide the court with details of how he came by his information. A case in point was his statement that the city had paid the Calgary Golf and Country Club $12,000 for an easement over its property when the club would have provided it free of charge. When asked by Mayor Davison who had provided the information, he said he could not remember and had just heard it mentioned somewhere. In the view of the administration, Duffield's most outrageous suggestion was that the city water supply had been deliberately "polluted" by the Waterworks Department with excessive amounts of chlorine while the voting on the bylaw was being carried out, thus influencing a favourable vote. Duffield, however, denied he had actually made that accusation and that the administration was free to make whatever inferences it wished about his testimony. City waterworks engineers submitted documents to the inquiry showing that the charge about polluting the water was totally false.

In addition to the testimony of various witnesses, Ewing also requested that commission counsel Sinclair obtain the services of a competent independent land valuator whose findings might provide guidance to the commission. Sinclair retained Fred Filteau to make a very careful and comprehensive report. In his report, Filteau explained how he evaluated the land. He divided the land into river flats, rises and low-lying flats, and top land, which was or had the capacity to be brought under cultivation. He considered river flats to be the least valuable since such land was cut up by old river channels and was difficult to access. Its scenic value was relatively high, but only because it was associated with a highland area. Standing on the uplands, Filteau observed that "one looks out over the valley of the Elbow and then on towards the Mountains."[204]

Justice Ewing submitted his report at the end of November 1932. It dealt with two questions, the first of which was whether any official of the city or any contractor or landowner had been guilty of malfeasance, breach of trust, or other misconduct in connection with the construction of the Glenmore Dam or any contract in connection with the purchase of land. The second question was whether the expenditures in connection with the construction of the dam were justified. With regard to the first question, he was unable to discern any single act that had not been done in good faith, and he was unable to name any individual who should be subject to censure. He came to a similar conclusion with respect to the purchase of the land. Although the Ewing Commission exonerated everyone involved in the Glenmore project, the atmosphere of suspicion that led to the inquiry had one victim. The lone casualty of the inquiry was Arthur Graves, who lost the municipal election in 1932 when he should have had the honour of being in office upon the completion of the project.

FINANCING THE GLENMORE WATERWORKS

The construction of the Glenmore Waterworks was to be paid for by the sale of debentures, as had been the case for all major public works projects undertaken by the City of Calgary since 1884. In a June 25 report to the city council, city treasurer F. S. Buchan reported that in April 1930, the Bank of Montreal had approved a $1.5 million line of credit to cover the initial phase of construction under a pledge by the City of Calgary to the bank for the debentures. These bonds were authorized and sold without difficulty and payment received in December 1930. The proceeds fully discharged the city's obligations to the Bank of Montreal in the amount of $685,000. City treasurer Buchan had other good news about the financial position of the city as of May 1, including the fact that the amount collected for taxes for 1931 was more than in 1930. This tax amount meant not only could the city fulfill its obligations to the Bank of Montreal, but also that other obligations including school board grants and sundry accounts payable were paid almost in full.

The initial arrangements to finance the project had been made with the passage of Bylaw 2636 to authorize the issuing of debentures for $1.5 million. No problems were encountered in the disposal of these bonds. By June 1930, the entire proceeds of the 1930 debenture issue had been spent, and it was necessary to arrange for the financing of the remaining amount, estimated at $2.27 million, required to complete the project. By July 1931, however, the bond market had suffered a sudden collapse, which made further funding through the traditional route of issuing debentures not immediately possible. City treasurer Buchan recommended the city request a $2 million line of credit from the Bank of Montreal with debentures totalling $2.27 million pledged as security. He anticipated these debentures would be issued and sold in the spring of 1932, by which time it was hoped the bond market would improve. The city council followed the recommendation and authorized the borrowing of funds from the Bank of Montreal.[205]

By December 1931, as anticipated, the city had not sold the waterworks debentures that had been pledged as security for the $2 million line of credit obtained in July. This amount was carried forward when the city requested additional credit from the Bank of Montreal in December 1931, bringing the total indebtedness of the city to the Bank of Montreal to $4.5 million. The bank agreed to lend the City of Calgary additional funds based on a commitment that the city control its debt. The various debts were not to exceed a total of $3.85 million at any one time.[206] As well, the city was to concentrate on the disposal of its unsold debentures to cover the loan from the bank rather than making further capital expenditures. The waterworks debentures and other capital outlays were to be offered at a price that would make them attractive to investors, and the city was to confirm that the federal and provincial governments would pay for public works undertaken as relief projects. The bank stated that the manager of the main branch of the Bank of Montreal, N. C. Frances, was "not opposed to relief work being carried as long as it was paid for out of current revenue or by advances from the Dominion Governments while it has on hand the large amount of un-marketed Debentures against which the bank has made advances."[207] The city was required to budget for and levy its full estimated debt requirements plus any deficits that might carry over from the previous year and not include any unrealizable surpluses or projections of future revenue.

The city agreed to actively pursue the sale of the waterworks debentures but only if it could obtain a reasonable price at a reasonable rate of interest. The city, at the suggestion of Mayor Davison, also agreed to revise its charter to permit it to issue five-year treasury bills that could be used to pay off its loan to the bank, thus avoiding the immediate necessity of issuing debentures at a high interest rate. Issuing treasury bills rather than debentures also avoided the necessity of the city having to make payments to the Sinking Fund, which had been established to deal with long-term capital expenditures. The treasury bills were to be secured by the waterworks debentures that would be held by the bank but not immediately sold. In March 1932, the Alberta Legislature passed revisions to the Calgary city charter empowering it to issue treasury bills to a total of $2.27 million without a vote by ratepayers but subject to the approval of the Board of Public Utilities. The city was also empowered to pledge any outstanding debentures as security for the treasury bills. The proceeds of the treasury bills were to be used to pay off the line of credit extended by the Bank of Montreal for the construction of the Glenmore Waterworks project. In March, the bank was part of a syndicate organized to sell the treasury bills.

While the City of Calgary struggled with the task of financing the Glenmore Waterworks project, it was also having problems retiring old debts dating back to the pre–World War I boom as a result of the devaluation of the Canadian dollar relative to the American dollar.[208] The city council solved the problem in December 1932 by making the decision not to pay the exchange on debentures redeemable in New York. This decision immediately created a crisis in the already strained relationship between the Bank of Montreal and the City of Calgary because of the loan issue. The local manager of the Bank of Montreal immediately reacted by requesting the newly elected council of 1933 to reverse the decision. For a couple of hours on January 4, 1933, the bank suspended the credit of the City of Calgary with the result that it could not cash the paycheques of engineering staff on the Glenmore project.[209]

The City of Calgary and the Bank of Montreal were able to re-establish a working relationship by mid-January, when the city followed through with the plan drafted in 1932 of giving the bank debentures to cover the Glenmore Waterworks loan. The city had been hesitant to pass these securities on to the bank, fearing they would be sold to the disadvantage of the city. Following the transfer, city officials met with W. McDonnell, the manager of the main branch of the Bank of Montreal, to determine the bank's intentions with respect to the unsold waterworks debentures, which were the only security the bank had for its $2 million loan. The manager advised the city there was no danger the bank would sell the bonds because the city had done a very effective job of destroying any market for Calgary securities. As McDonnell advised the mayor in January, as a consequence of the city's decision with respect to certain maturing debentures, there was at that time no market for the sale of City of Calgary securities. Even when the city's standing had been re-established and city securities could be sold, public financing could not be arranged on favourable terms while the large issue on the waterworks account remained. In March 1933, Bylaw 2859 was passed authorizing the issue and sale of $2.27 million worth of debentures bearing interest at the rate of six percent. At the same time, Bylaw 2860 was passed authorizing the sale of treasury bills in an equal amount and to pledge the debentures authorized by Bylaw 2859 to the Bank of Montreal as collateral for the payment of the treasury bills issued under Bylaw 2860. This attempt to liquidate the debt to the bank also failed and the $2 million line of credit was converted into a permanent loan with interest payable at 6 percent, which was later dropped to 4.5 percent.[210]

Paying for the construction of the Glenmore Waterworks project continued to create financial problems for the city for the rest of 1933 as a result of holdbacks, extra expenses, and wage claims. The contracts for the construction of the various phases of the project allowed the City of Calgary to hold back 15 percent of a contract for a two-year period following the issue of the completion certificate. This time allowed for the detection of any deficiencies in workmanship and their mitigation, the cost of which would be deducted from the amount of the holdback. The city was required to start paying the holdbacks in May 1933 when Riverside Iron Works was eligible to received $735.[211] Eleven other contractors, along with Gore, Nasmith & Storrie, were entitled to receive holdback payments totalling $407,969.48. The largest single payment of $168,143.44 was due to Bennett & White in November. Early in the year, Mayor Davison had begun negotiating with the various contractors to arrange for the payment of the various amounts in installments and with the Bank of Montreal, as well as with the federal and provincial governments to obtain the funds required. By October, the contractors who needed to be paid had agreed to accept a two-thirds payment with the balance owing deferred for one year from their respective due dates. On this basis, the city had to pay $246,421.93 by December 31, 1933, which included accrued interest of four percent.[212] The agreement with Bennett & White required the city to deliver a promissory note in the amount of $63,412.91 with interest at the rate of seven percent per annum before and after the maturity date of December 20, 1933, with payment for the amount owing on the holdback account due by December 23, 1934. The city, however, failed to deliver the required documents by the due date, resulting in its receipt of a letter from Bennett & White's lawyers that gave the city an ultimatum. S. J. Helman, the lawyer for Bennett & White, advised the City of Calgary that if it failed to deliver the promissory note by 11 o'clock on Saturday, December 30, Bennett & White would demand full payment of the holdback in cash. A special meeting of the city council was called, and an emergency loan was acquired from the federal government in the amount of $300,000 to finance the holdback payments.

The city was also called upon to pay invoices from Bennett & White and other contractors for work not covered by the original contract but which the resident engineer had requested. Although the city did not have the funds set aside to pay these bills, they were ultimately reviewed in great detail by the council and paid upon the submission of the appropriate documentation. Extra wage claims were also made based on the "workmen's rights" provision of the project contract. Lawyer G. W. Edmunds filed claims against Bennett & White for Contract 1 on behalf of 125 individuals. Claims for truck hours were also submitted by H. H. Gilchrist and were adjudicated by the senior engineers on the project. One of the points made during the review was that workers feared for their jobs so delayed their efforts to obtain what they regarded as additional pay until the project was completed.

COMMISSIONING

Construction of the new Glenmore Waterworks officially came to an end on December 14, 1932, when the system was transferred to the city and testing in preparation for putting it into full operation began. Testing the system, supervising its first months of operation, and training staff to operate the plant were the responsibility of the engineering firm of Gore, Nasmith & Storrie under the terms of its 1929 contract. This transition took place just as the old system suffered yet another failure, which began on December 5 when the gravity pipeline was "blocked by a small mountain of frazil ice" and water was supplied by the reservoir in south Calgary. Pumphouse No. 2 on the Bow River was also working at full capacity. According to city waterworks engineer Robinson, the Dominion Bridge Company had been asked to work 24 hours a day if necessary to complete the tie-in of the new system. An emergency arose between the new plant and the city water main system. As had been done since 1909, city waterworks crews worked day and night to deal with the crisis. By December 9, the failure of the old system was complete when Pumphouse No. 2 and the infiltration plant on Williams Island were put out of operation because of ice on the Bow. Damage to the infiltration plant and the Bow River intake left North Hill residents in the familiar position of being without water but in the unfamiliar position of hoping it would be the last time. Desperate efforts were underway to connect the new plant to the water main system and to clear the debris from the pumphouse. This latter task came close to costing the lives of waterworks employees who were nearly drowned when the ice jam on the Bow River collapsed.

On January 10, filtered water was pumped to the city for the first time, and by January 19, 1933, 5 million gallons (22.7 million litres) were being pumped daily and both the western and eastern connections had been completed to the city's system of 24-inch (61-centimetre) mains. Much to the annoyance of the *Herald*, the gravity line remained in operation until early February. By February 16, the gravity line capacity was reduced to one million gallons (4.5 million litres) per day, and the Glenmore Waterworks operated at 20 million gallons (91 million litres) per day.

The Glenmore Waterworks went into operation amid an atmosphere of crisis as the possibility of the Bank of Montreal not extending further credit was producing newspaper headlines that predicted the imminent financial collapse of the city. Despite this mood, community interest in the completion of the project rapidly mounted in the new year. The January 8, 1933, issue of the *Daily Journal* recorded the arrival of an ever-increasing number of visitors who toured the filtration plant. On January 12, a delegation of members and officers of the Alberta Federation of Labour toured the facility. On January 22, an open house was attended by thousands of Calgary citizens. They came via two city buses, which carried 35 loads of visitors, as well as by thousands of private cars. The entire staff was on the job, guiding and explaining how the plant worked and how the filters were washed numerous times during the process. Visitors continued to come to the site until August and apparently walked about unsupervised, causing some minor problems, which was noted in the *Daily Journal*. The *Daily Journal* issue for January 29 noted that "someone had tampered with a wash value in the filter building while someone shut the alum feed machine and flooded about 2 inches of water onto the floor. This tampering was done while an employee was looking after the chlorine machine." The dam also became an attraction for young people who wanted to swim. The August 12 issue of the *Daily Journal* noted that several young people had found the cushion pool of the dam to be a very good swimming hole.

By May 25, the operation of the system had settled into a routine, with the *Daily Journal* noting the amount of alum and/or chorine used in the water treatment process. The routine was enlivened by some interesting visitors, including Sky Pilot Young, who dropped by on July 1 looking for one of his sheep, and Caribou Bill and his pals who came by on the evening of September 8.

With the Glenmore Waterworks in operation, the infiltration plant on Williams Island was closed and the island transferred to the jurisdiction of the Parks Department, which in turn leased it to the Calgary Archery Club in 1934 for five years.[213] The large rectangular dugout in the middle of the island that had collected the water filtered by the Bow River gravels was used as a swimming pool.

CHAPTER SIX

Community Use and
Exclusion on the Elbow

1930–1946

The post-construction relationship between Calgary and the Elbow River was a contrast between intensive use below the dam and a policy of exclusion of people from the Glenmore Reservoir itself. Fear that human-borne diseases would contaminate Calgary's pure water supply and fear that during World War II, saboteurs would deliberately pollute the water or try to blow up the dam justified the policy. Preventing Calgarians from using the reservoir beginning in 1933 was the first time any restriction had been imposed on their access to the Elbow River since the Chipman Ranch Company had placed a notice in the June 17, 1887, issue of the *Tribune* stating that no picnics were allowed on its land without permission. The Elbow River below the dam became a summertime rather than a year-round recreational area as it had been before 1932. The opportunity to skate from the Bow River to Weaselhead Flats, which was fondly remembered by many people, including Jack Peach, now belonged to an earlier chapter in Calgary's relationship with the Elbow River.

NO BODIES IN THE RESERVOIR

The issue of pollution was of far greater concern to the city than it had been to the engineers of Gore, Nasmith & Storrie. The Glenmore Reservoir was closed to the general public with the exception of members of the Earl Grey Golf Club and their guests. The necessity of this closure to protect Calgary's water supply was first suggested by Calgary's Medical Officer of Health, Dr. William H. Hill, when the Earl Grey Golf Club lease was under debate. Even if the city desired to create a park during the early 1930s, such an undertaking was well beyond its resources. The city lacked the means to develop all the available parkland within the city limits, let alone land beyond its borders.

Since the use of the reservoir as a park was perceived, at least by some city officials, as a threat rather than a benefit to the city, its administration was transferred to the Waterworks Department by the city council in May 1934. This decision was made at the recommendation of the city commissioners who advised the city council that in the "interests of affording every protection necessary to a pure water supply . . . it would be advisable to place these properties entirely in the charge of the Waterworks Superintendent for control and operation under the direction of the Commissioner."[214] The city's authority and responsibility to protect the water supply from contamination had been extended to the entire watershed by the 1930 revisions to the city charter. This policy was also consistent with the administration of the reservoir in south Calgary around which Reservoir Park had been created in 1910. Trees and grass were planted to reduce dirt from being blown into the reservoir, and no public access was permitted. It was, however, listed as one of the parks in the Calgary Parks system. Despite these regulations, the Glenmore Reservoir became a favoured but somewhat clandestine destination for many Calgarians.

Between 1939 and 1941, the issue of security at the waterworks was redefined when war in Europe and Asia created new potential threats to Calgary's water supply. The start of World War II in Europe in September 1939 did not immediately prompt a sense of emergency on the part of the city council. This was evident in its response to a letter received from the City of Brandon in October 1939. The letter advised of the need for municipalities to take steps to protect their infrastructure.[215] The city commissioners were advised to keep the issue in mind, and the letter was filed.

The mood changed with the fall of France in June 1940, at which time the city council approved a policy excluding people born in Germany from employment by the city and approving the firing of any employee who expressed pro-enemy sympathies.[216] The city council also took steps to protect the Glenmore Dam from fifth-column activities. A wire fence was constructed around the buildings, a commissionaire patrolled the grounds, and the waterworks staff were instructed to be increasingly alert to trespassers. A boom was constructed above the Glenmore Dam to protect it from floating objects and explosives. These measures were considered drastic by the city commissioners but necessary in view of the fact that the country was at war with a brutal and unscrupulous foe. The commissioners did not want to see a repeat in Calgary of events that had occurred in other countries and believed it was time to take appropriate action.

In 1940, citizens also took the initiative to protect the Glenmore Waterworks complex through the creation of the Calgary Special Constabulary. The creation of the force developed out of a meeting of the Urban Municipalities Association held in Calgary on June 8, 1940. The constabulary's first parade was held on June 25, 1940.[217] The force was created as a civilian arm of the City of Calgary police to aid in the maintenance and/or restoration of order and "civil morals" and the alleviation of distress resulting from emergencies such as earthquakes or sabotage. The constabulary conducted regular patrols around the perimeter of the Glenmore Reservoir.

In 1941, the city council became increasingly concerned about the potential of air raids. The air raid danger to Calgary's utility systems in general and the waterworks in particular were of great concern to Alderman Frank Roy Freeze. In a January 20 memorandum to Mayor Andrew Davison and the city council, he identified nine action items to reduce the possibility of sabotage or destruction of the waterworks system. His suggestions involved various ways to undo all the work done in the building of the Glenmore Waterworks system. These included finding an alternate location in "natural high areas" in which to store Calgary's water supply rather than in the reservoir created by the dam on the Elbow River, as well as the old idea of drilling wells as an alternative to the present system. All the alternative water system plans suggested by Gore, Nasmith & Storrie in its report were to be reviewed and possibly implemented. The restoration of the gravity system was also put forth, as was draining the reservoir to remove it as a landmark in the hope of confusing enemy bombers. Alternatively, Freeze suggested the Glenmore and Ghost River Dams be used to store the water of the Bow and Elbow Rivers, thus camouflaging the locations of the rivers and thereby confusing any bomber pilot trying to find Calgary. Other ideas included reducing the amount of water in the reservoir and the establishment of an alarm system to warn residents to evacuate. In the event that the dam was breached, he suggested that plans be outlined for residents to cope with the consequences. For example, would Rideau and Elbow Park Schools be suitable places of refuge against the wall of water that would move down the Elbow River? What else could be done to ease people's minds through safety operations? The report of the Air Raid Preparations Committee presented to the city council on March 2, 1942, however, made no reference to the Glenmore Waterworks. In fact, it assumed the system would be unaffected by an air raid and suggested that residents attach a garden hose to the tap inside or outside their basements, presumably so homeowners could put out any fires caused by the raid.[218]

By 1943, the Air Raid Preparations Committee was directing most of the civil defence activities and the Sabotage Committee had disappeared. At the request of the city commissioners and the police commission, responsibility to protect the reservoir was transferred to the regular city police force as provided for in Bylaw 3488. The authority to control the use of the Glenmore Reservoir was based on section 287 of the city charter. This provision gave the city administration the power to protect the reservoir site by police or other guardianship from damage and trespass, and the reservoir and the water and sources thereof from contamination. Bylaw 3488 listed various prohibitions with respect to the reservoir that included entering the reservoir site without authorization; damaging any fence or sign around the reservoir; dumping any filth, rubbish, or refuse of any kind; bathing, wading, or washing in the water; sailing, paddling, or rowing a boat or using a boat propelled by motor power on the water of the reservoir except by an authorized person; fishing by any means whatsoever from the water of the reservoir except when it was deemed necessary by the waterworks engineer;

skating or sliding on any ice on the reservoir or engaging in the sport of ice boating on the ice; and throwing, laying, placing, or depositing on any ice on the reservoir sticks, stones, gravel, sand, ashes, or any other article, substance, or thing. Any person who failed to comply with the provisions of the bylaw would be guilty of an offence and liable to conviction or penalties specified in the city charter. Despite the bylaw, people made frequent use of the site since the police department lacked the resources to prevent it.

THE LIDO OF CALGARY

By January 1931, progress on the construction of the Glenmore Dam had eliminated the opportunity to skate from Weaselhead Flats to the Bow River, but skating on the lower Elbow remained possible and very popular through to Christmas 1932. According to William Reader, "as many as five thousand people had been counted on this area at one time." The end of skating on the Elbow came between Christmas and New Year's of that year when the Waterworks Department found it necessary to release a large quantity of water from the dam. "This has," lamented Reader, "unfortunately ruined all further prospect of skating on the Elbow River for this season and has deprived this department of some hundred dollars of revenue."[219]

Figure 6.1 The Elbow River played a significant role in providing swimming facilities before the city council and the majority of citizens could be convinced of their value. Most of the swimming holes were located on the Elbow River. This is a view (left to right) of Marjorie Lumb, Edith "Phoebe" Sanders, and Constance Sanders swimming in the Elbow in 1915.
Source: Glenbow Library and Archives, NA-2788–73

Figure 6.2 Swimming was one of the sports actively promoted by William Reader after World War I as part of his efforts to develop a recreation program for the Parks Department, which he valued highly for its contribution to the development of youth. This picture from the 1920s shows Ken Ford about to dive into the Elbow River at an unidentified location.

Source: Glenbow Library and Archives, NA-1290–3

Figure 6.3 This is a view of the Elbow Park swimming pool, the development of which began in the early 1920s. It was more commonly referred to as "Lowes' pool," since F. C. Lowes' house was located immediately to the west. The project included the construction of a bathhouse, which served as both a changing room and a first aid station. It was located along Elbow Drive at 29th Avenue SW.

Source: Glenbow Library and Archives, NA-4099–11

Figure 6.4 This is a scene from the mid-1940s at Lowes' swimming hole showing the boom across the Elbow River, which was placed to reduce the potential risks to children while swimming. The west end of Mission Island can be seen across the river.

Source: Glenbow Library and Archives, PA-3538–20

Figure 6.5 This is a view of the Elbow Park swimming pool taken in the 1940s from the west. It includes the 1923 bathhouse as well as the oversized checkerboard in the foreground.

Source: Glenbow Library and Archives, PA-3538–21

The construction of the Glenmore Dam, however, had a positive effect on the recreational value of the lower Elbow River by enhancing its use for swimming. Local resident Leslie Sara and others commented that the temperature of the water had increased. Swimming on the Elbow became so popular that it motivated Sara, in one of his articles, to invoke the image of Lido Island near Venice in describing its popularity. The value of swimming came into prominence beginning in 1933, when the Parks Department's partnership with the YMCA and YWCA to provide swimming lessons was expanded and competitive swimming was added to its recreation program. The Parks Department also placed the swimming holes on the Bow and Elbow under the supervision of qualified swimmers. Several these supervisors were unemployed and were trained as swimming instructors by the YMCA, which then organized swimming lessons at the individual pools on the rivers. In 1933, arrangements were made to hold a swimming gala on the Elbow River, with handpicked swimmers from the playgrounds and swimming holes to meet in "friendly competition." Mr. A. Baxter, the owner of the Crystal Pool, allowed the city to use his facility to run the competition when weather conditions prevented the use of the Elbow. On September 7, Commissioner Thomas Riley opened the gala in front of a crowd that filled the spectators' space around the pool to capacity. There were 144 entries in the 10 events, which were broken into age groups for boys and girls 14 years old and younger, 18 years old and younger, 18 years of age and older, and a novelty event open to boys of any age. Every playground and swimming hole group was represented, with each entering its full quota in the events. All competitors were under the direction of their supervisors, who were aided by older lads who could not qualify for entry. The St. George's Island, Victoria, Elbow Bend, CNR, Elbow Park, and 24th Avenue swimming holes were represented in the competition, along with the regular playgrounds. The Rotary Park team placed first, while the 24th Avenue swimming hole squad under Mr. Fyfe came second, and the Victoria Park swimming hole team came third.

In 1934, a watchman was kept on duty throughout the bathing season and various improvements were made to the Elbow Park swimming pool that included the addition of a comfort station, covering the changing room floors with rubberoid, and providing a drinking fountain. Several big boulders were removed from the riverbed, and booms and rafts were added for the use of the bathers. The next swimming gala was another great success, with teams from the swimming holes at Millican and Bonnybrook participating. Bowness Park hosted the event, with the Street Railway Department giving all the winners certificates. Fifty-seven prizes were distributed to the winners in 17 events. The events were organized by age group and included a 25-yard dash for boys and girls younger than 12 years of age. Boys and girls younger than 14 years of age could enter a 25-yard dash, a 100-yard relay, and a diving competition. Boys and girls between the ages of 14 and 18 could enter a 50-yard dash, a 100-yard dash, and a diving competition. The same events were open to boy and girls 18 years of age and older. "One quarter" races were arranged for men and ladies. There was a quarter-mile canoe race for girls in pairs and a similar distance open to any competitor, and a 50-yard balloon race for boys and girls of any age completed the competitive portion of the program. A lifesaving exhibition given by members of the YMCA Leisure Time Club and a diving exhibition by Miss Maie Sharkey rounded out the day's events.

The Elbow River proved to be popular for bathing again in the summer of 1935, with the area "again thronged with both children and adults throughout the summer season."[220] More than 1,500 boys and girls took swimming lessons, which were given one day a week by the YMCA and YWCA. The Parks Department placed booms across the river to create a swimming area, but as Reader observed, these were ignored by the great majority of the bathers who "use every part of the Elbow from the dam to the Ninth Avenue Bridge"; however, the booms did "provide a safe bathing place for the very small children."[221] The grounds around the changing room at the Elbow Park swimming pool were kept clean and tidy, and the necessary pruning, cultivating, and grass cutting was done by the lifeguards. The lifeguards provided first aid to 70 individuals, with most of the injuries being the result of broken glass in the bed of the Elbow River. The 1935 swimming gala was held on August 9 at Bowness Park, which once again showcased the valuable contribution of the YMCA and YWCA in making their pools available for swimming classes. The list of events was expanded to include younger children, with a 15-yard dash for first-year swimmers and events for boys and girls aged 14 to 16.

The 1936 bathing season was highlighted by the addition of a giant checkerboard to the Elbow Park swimming pool, which proved immensely popular with children and adults alike. The squares consisted of concrete tiles, and the board was 15 feet (4.5 metres) square and 1.75 inches (4.5 centimetres) thick. The black tiles were made of Portland cement, sand, and lamp black, and the white tiles were made of Atlas white cement and white sand. The board was slightly tilted to drain water. The playing pieces consisted of couplings of 4-inch (10-centimetre) wooden water pipes, with one set painted green and the other set painted red. There were chessmen that were 5 inches (12.7 centimetres) high, with 8-inch (20-centimetre) kings. An iron hook was provided to move the pieces around the board. It was surrounded by a fence, with one row of benches inside the fence. This was the final year the swimming gala took place since no funds could be obtained for prizes.

The popularity of Calgary's river for recreational purposes through to the mid-1930s did not stop the campaign to construct swimming pools. Efforts to achieve this goal had continued since 1929 by the Young Men's Section of the Calgary Board of Trade. In October, the group urged that a bylaw be placed before the ratepayers to provide $100,000 for the construction of three swimming pools. The majority of the members of the 1929 city council expressed support but decided that other proposals for capital expenditures were more urgent. In May 1930, the Young Men's Section resubmitted its proposal to the city council, with the request that it be put before the ratepayers at the fall election. In making the submission for the second time, the Young Men's Section reviewed the need, civic responsibility for, and cost of such a program. It pointed out the obvious fact that the boys and girls of Calgary depended on the rivers for their summer swimming. The cold water and the swift currents made the rivers extremely dangerous, with the result that several drowning fatalities had occurred in past years. In addition, it pointed out that swimming was one of the healthiest exercises since it developed the whole body and gave children confidence. Swimming pools would enable all the children of the city to learn to swim, thus allowing them to take care of themselves when boating and visiting summer resorts. The swimming pool at Bowness Park was too far away to make it available to the majority of children since the cost was prohibitive. Children had to pay for streetcar tickets and 25 cents to swim, even if they provided their own bathing suits and towels. Examples of cities that paid for children's swimming included Edmonton, where there were three pools, as well as Saskatoon, Drumheller, and Fernie.

The final section of the proposal outlined a plan that explained the construction of a self-supporting project in terms of construction costs and ongoing maintenance. The pools in Edmonton earned sufficient revenue to cover their operating costs. This financial success had been achieved despite the fact that Edmonton had a larger foreign-born population and the three pools were not conveniently located. In Calgary, the three swimming pools could be built for $100,000, which would be repaid in 20 years, with total interest charges of $8,500. The potential annual income for a swimming pool in Calgary based on the experience of Edmonton, where there were 135,000 swimmers, was 7 cents per person, so if the cost was raised to 20 cents, those 135,000 swimmers would generate sufficient funds to pay for both the capital and operating costs of the facility. The delegation from the Young Men's Section further suggested it would not be a burden for the City of Calgary to carry the capital costs of the project since it would represent a minimal charge to the average householder. In 1938, another attempt to construct swimming pools in Calgary was made and came narrowly close to success. A plebiscite in 1941 was finally successful, and the first swimming pool to be built by the City of Calgary went into operation in Mewata Park.

PARKS AND PLAYGROUNDS

Although the Elbow Park swimming pool continued to be the focus of the Parks Department's activities in the Elbow Valley during the 1930s, the Depression provided the city and the Parks Department superintendent, William Reader, with an opportunity to continue the same polices that had been implemented during the 1920s. More land was added to the parks system because the city appropriated land for the nonpayment of taxes, which increased the size of Roxboro Park and added portions of Mission Hill above Mission Road to the designated park space.[222] Reader's plan for the development of the land around Roxboro included the designation of all land south and west of Mission Road to 34th Avenue East and the escarpment as Mission Park. The former location of the oxbow lake, which F. C. Lowes & Company had tried to fill in before World War I, was designated as Roxboro Park. The area above Roxboro Park to the west was to be landscaped as part of an extension of St. Mary's Cemetery south to 33rd Avenue East. The two blocks of land south of 30th Avenue and east of 2nd Street East were to be developed into recreational areas, which would provide a football field, baseball diamond, and basketball and volleyball courts.

Stanley Park was increased in size with the addition of land along the Elbow River. Reader did not develop a master plan for Stanley Park with the exception of laying out a road at the eastern edge of the park area along the escarpment, which he designated as Parkhill Boulevard Drive. Lacking the resources to undertake any actual development, the city renewed the lease of that land to the Calgary Auto Club for another five years in 1938.[223]

Reader also continued appropriating small plots of vacant city land not officially designated as park space and small plots of city land that had no other potential use, such as traffic circles, boulevards, and corner lots, as well as land that was undeveloped or generally neglected by its owners. One such appropriation was the Mission Bridge Islands, which remained the property of the CPR although the railway company appeared to have forgotten the fact. Building on the efforts of the 10th Boy Scout Troop, he designated the Mission Bridge Islands as the Rideau Bird Sanctuary, and in 1930, planted 100 trees provided by Mrs. Pearce in memory of William Pearce.

The portion of the former Britannia subdivision located in the Elbow Valley but beyond the boundaries of the city was also coveted by Reader as a future park site. The only thing he could do during the 1930s was to arrange for an unemployed person to operate a concession stand at the location in an attempt to reduce the vandalism Jack Leslie had been drawing the city's attention to since 1928.

Reader broached the idea of developing a river valley trail system in 1933, when a pathway was developed along the bank of the Elbow River from 5th Street West to the swimming pool grounds. He anticipated limited opportunities for further extensions because much of the riverbank was private property.[224] Although Reader had initially regarded the future development of a trail system impossible for that reason, by 1932, he had decided that the time had come to develop a scenic driveway system with boulevards to link up the various parts of the trail system. In his view, "the time was opportune because it could be undertaken at the present time with practically no additional expense by the utilization of the relief labour presently available."[225]

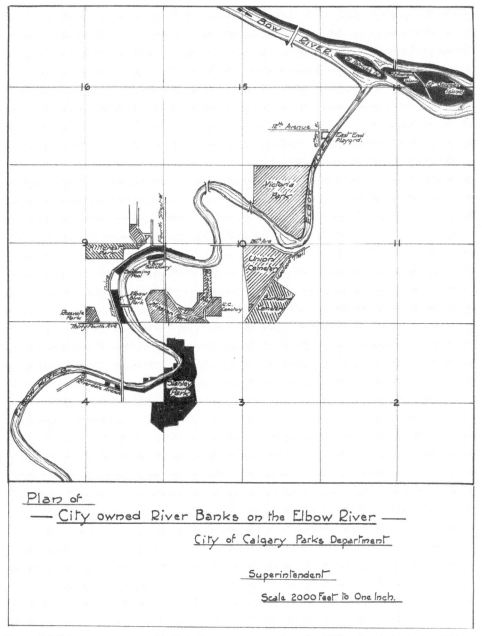

Figure 6.6 This map was prepared by Parks Department superintendent William Reader in the late 1930s to show the land owned by the City of Calgary in the Elbow Valley that he intended to use in the development of a parks system. It consisted largely of land obtained by the city because of the non-payment of taxes.

Source: City of Calgary Corporate Records Archives, Parks and Recreation Department Fonds

CHAPTER SEVEN

POST-WAR CALGARY
AND THE ELBOW RIVER

1947–2017

After 1947, the city that had been prophesied during the pre–World War I boom actually came into existence. This development brought continuity and change to the role of the Elbow River in the life of Calgary. Residential and recreational land use expanded along the Elbow, and the pre-war subdivisions of Elbow Park, Elboya, Rideau Park, Mission, Victoria Park, and Erlton became fully occupied inner city communities. Suburbia invaded the shores of the Glenmore Reservoir with the creation of Bel-Aire, Mayfair, Eagle Ridge, Bayview, Oakridge Estates, and Lakeview Village. The recreational uses of the Elbow Valley were expanded by the ongoing development of Stampede Park, the replacement of the original Canadian Northern Railway Company yards by Lindsay Park and the Repsol Sport Centre, and the waterway's incorporation into the river valley trail system and park development, the most significant being North and South Glenmore Parks. Even before Calgary's post-war expansion, the policy of keeping swimmers, fishers, and other intruders out of the reservoir in the interests of water purity had proven impossible to enforce. Incorporating the Glenmore Reservoir into post-war Calgary was resolved by 1963 in a manner that dealt with both water-quality issues and the demand for recreational space. The use of the Elbow River below the Glenmore Dam as a formal recreational venue, which had been a highlight of the years before 1936, was eliminated. Water from the Elbow was not, however, able to sustain the new, expanded City of Calgary on its own. In 1973, it began to share that responsibility with the Bow River with the construction of the Bearspaw Water Treatment Plant.

Significantly absent from the history of the Elbow River through to 2013 were spring floods of the severity that had occurred before 1932. This problem, while largely forgotten by the general public, re-emerged in the 1960s, at least in the imaginations of the engineers in the City of Calgary and the Province of Alberta Water Resources Branch. Their anxieties would be realized in 2005 and 2013.

The Water Supply Limits of the Elbow River

The renewed growth of Calgary in the late 1940s revived the waterworks question. In 1949, city waterworks engineer W. E. Robinson investigated the age-old questions of Calgary's future water requirements, the use and abuse of its water supply, future sources of supply, and the ability of the system to deliver quality water at the right pressure. In an October report, Robinson pointed out that the Glenmore filtration plant had been designed to deliver 200 gallons (909 litres) per capita per day to a city with a population of up to 200,000. The Glenmore Reservoir had been designed to provide a 90-day supply of water based on a consumption rate of 40 million gallons (182 million litres) per day as long as the flow of water in the Elbow was above the levels recorded in 1922–23. Since 1933, however, there had been periods during which the flow of water in the Elbow River had been below the lowest level indicated in the hydrographic data available to the dam designers in 1929. These instances of low water levels occurred between 1933 and 1936 and in 1948. Robinson expected these low levels to continue through to 1950. During these periods, the water level in the reservoir could not be maintained, reducing the ability of the turbine-driven pumps to deliver raw water to the filtration plant. Its ability to work at full capacity was reduced in turn. The Glenmore Waterworks was also not designed to accommodate the increase in per capita water consumption, which had gone from 198 gallons (900 litres) per person per day in 1933 to 215 gallons (977 litres) in

Figure 7.1 This is a view of the Glenmore Waterworks and the reservoir area on the eve of its transformation into a suburban region of Calgary.

Source: Glenbow Library and Archives, NA-2864–462g

1949. Robinson attributed the increase to the excess lawn watering and the habit of letting taps run to prevent water lines from freezing. He regarded the high level of water use excessive since statistics from other cities indicated that 200 gallons (910 litres) per person per day was adequate to meet domestic and lawn watering needs. In his view, Calgary's water consumption was abnormal and every means should be employed to bring it in line with actual requirements. The problems created by unanticipated low flows in the Elbow River and higher per capita use were compounded by water loss caused by leaking reservoirs, water mains, and plumbing fixtures, which had been evident since before World War I and had been noted in Gore, Nasmith & Storrie's 1929 report.

Given this analysis, Robinson recommended minimal changes to the diversion and water treatment facilities and major changes to the distribution system. The installation of two new electrical pumps to increase the amount of raw water delivered to the water treatment plant during dry years was the only change suggested for the water treatment facilities. Construction of a 300-million-gallon (1,364-million-litre) covered filtered-water reservoir to replace the old reservoir in south Calgary, a new 4-million-gallon (18-million-litre) reservoir on North Hill, a survey of the main system to detect leaks, and the replacement of leaking mains were his recommended changes to the distribution system. He recommended, in effect, that the city bring the standard of the distribution system up to that of the diversion and water treatment facilities. Water conservation measures included metering water use, which had been first suggested as early as 1910. Edmonton, Winnipeg, and Vancouver had demonstrated their ability to reduce consumption by up to 65 percent. The proposed modifications were considered adequate to address the water supply question since Robinson anticipated that Calgary's population would only reach 150,000 by 1960.

The city commissioners and the city council agreed with Robinson that new electrical pumps were required but felt an independent consultant should review his other recommendations. The resident engineer during the original construction of the Glenmore Waterworks, Norman McDonald of Gore & Storrie, was retained for this purpose. Since 1933, he had become a principal member of the firm, which had been renamed Gore & Storrie with the passing of George Nasmith in 1937. McDonald agreed with Robinson's emphasis on conservation measures and the need to plug the leaks in the system rather than making changes to the Glenmore Waterworks complex beyond the purchase of two new electric pumps.[226] He disagreed, however, on the urgency of the main replacement program and the population projections suggested by Robinson. He regarded the projected 1960 population of 150,000 for Calgary as too optimistic. His recommendations were approved, and the firm of Gore & Storrie was engaged to supervise the construction of two new reservoirs and the installation of new pumps with Norman McDonald once again serving as resident engineer.[227]

By 1955, the measures taken to reduce water leaks and encourage conservation had successfully reduced per capita water consumption to 133 gallons (605 litres) per day. With no further reductions in water consumption anticipated, Gore & Storrie was again retained to report on the need for expansion of the Glenmore Waterworks plant and the availability of underground sources of supply. The consultants recommended the filtration plant be doubled in size and the conservation efforts be continued. The possible use of wells as sources of water was rejected.

In 1961, Gore & Storrie was commissioned for the last time to undertake a study of the Glenmore facility and Calgary's water needs. In the consultants' report, McDonald indicated that with further modifications to the Glenmore Waterworks, the system could support a population of 600,000 with an ample supply at all times, but that if population growth continued, new sources of supply would have to be found within 10 years.[228] The construction of a new filtered-water pumping station and the conversion of the existing pumping station at the dam to a station for the pumping of raw water only were carried out in 1964.

By the early 1960s, population growth led Calgary to consider ways it could take additional water from the Elbow River as well as draw upon other sources of supply. In 1961, R. T. Hollies examined the possibility of additional dam construction on the Elbow that could serve the needs of Calgary regarding water and flood control. He came to the conclusion that this option was too expensive.[229] Another suggestion, which went back to 1907, was that a pipeline be constructed to access the reservoir of "pure water" located in the upper reaches of the Elbow River watershed. In 1961, planning began for the utilization of the Bow River on a permanent basis rather than as a supplement to the supply from the Elbow, which had been the case since 1907. In 1966, the firm Underwood McLellan & Associates was retained to undertake a study of the water supply from the Bearspaw Dam. The new Bearspaw Water Treatment Plant went into operation in 1973.

Parks

The post–World War II and post–William Reader era in parks development began in 1948 when a subcommittee of the city's Lands Committee was struck to prepare a list of the parks to be retained in the parks system. The 1948 list eliminated many of the park areas Reader had envisaged in the 1920s and 1930s for the Elbow Valley, including the Mission Hill area, the Mission Bridge Islands, which were no longer designated as a bird sanctuary, and the innumerable small plots of land such as the Elbow Drive plot. Elbow

Swimming Pool, Elbow Boulevard Park (renamed Woods Memorial Park in honour of C. H. Woods, who provided funds in the 1920s for its development), and Roxboro Park (formerly Roxborough Park) survived the review. The Parks Department's interest in using the Elbow River for organized swimming programs came to an end as the department's emphasis shifted to constructing swimming pools and developing a park around the reservoir. The revision of the bylaw forbidding swimming in park areas symbolized the changing relationship of Calgarians to the rivers. The recreational use of the Elbow River below the Glenmore Dam became an individual matter, with drifting down the river by a variety of means being the popular choice.

One of the new parks included on the list was Sandy Beach, which compensated to a degree for the loss of other parks along the Elbow River in the 1948 review. Sandy Beach had an informal history as a recreational area dating back to the turn of the century.[230] Landscape architect and town planner Thomas Mawson, who was particularly impressed with the valley escarpment, was the first person to suggest the area had potential as a park. The opportunity to establish a park came when the collapse of the pre–World War I real estate boom forced F. C. Lowes to abandon his plan to create a river valley community called Britannia, and the land was acquired by the city for non-payment of taxes. From the 1920s through to the 1940s, the area continued to be a popular spot for excursions since access was possible via the streetcar to Sifton Boulevard and a ford across the Elbow River at the end of Riverdale Avenue. The informal use of the area resulted in considerable vandalism, which prompted Jack Leslie to renew his request that some effort be made by the city to protect the area. In September 1945, he suggested the city put up signs prohibiting the lighting of fires based on the idea that if fires became illegal, the cutting of trees for fuel would cease.[231] Leslie was advised by the commissioners that the city did not have the authority to prevent the starting of fires in the city. City workers did, however, erect signs reading "Fires must be extinguished before leaving." Leslie regarded this as counterproductive since he felt it would encourage the very activity he was trying to stop. He suggested the signs instead read "No fires permitted in this area." He also suggested the area be declared a park since that would give the city police the authority to prevent fires. Leslie also noted the problem of sanitation, given the fact there were many small groups of people using the area at all times. On holidays, however, "there [are] generally a few big picnics with as many as five hundred to one thousand people and no water or toilet arrangements of any kind. In hot weather, the flies and stench is horrible. A shallow well equipped with a hand pump ought to overcome the water situation but toilet arrangements will probably be more of a problem."[232]

The city council was persuaded that the area should be considered as a possible location for a park and in October 1945, referred this suggestion to the Parks and Playgrounds Committee. While the committee was pondering the question, Alderman Robert Thomas Alderman in July 1946 suggested the city might consider building summer homes in the area because "there were good bathing facilities in the river and it would help the city's reputation as a centre for providing amusements for its citizens."[233] In September 1946, the Parks and Playgrounds Committee recommended that the portion of the quarter-section of land lying in the flat below the hill and fronting the river be designated as a park. With this decision, planning for its use as an athletics grounds began. The creation of a detailed plan for the park in terms of functions and its actual size was delayed by the need to complete the planning of the subdivisions of Altadore and Britannia above the valley to the west and east.

One of the owners of land on the upland area to the west of Sandy Beach was Eric Harvie. In November 1952, Harvie, in a meeting with Mayor Donald Mackay, suggested the Altadore subdivision be modified to provide for the expansion of Sandy Beach into a park extending west to 14th Street. In return for the city donating land to the expansion plan, he promised to donate 5 acres (2 hectares) of his own land, negotiate for the purchase of other private land in the area, and donate a substantial sum for the development of the entire area. Since World War II, Harvie had acquired a significant personal fortune as a result of the oil boom, a portion of which he wanted to use to benefit Calgary. Based on statements later made by Mayor Mackay, Harvie was motivated by the lack of adequate parks in Calgary compared to other cities in the world.

Harvie's suggestion was referred to the Special Lands Committee for review. In its August 1953 report to the city council, the committee recommended a large area south of 50th Avenue SW as being suitable for a park in addition to the area in the Elbow Valley already dedicated to park use, so there was no need for the expansion of Sandy Beach. At the city council's August 24 meeting, the recommendation of the Special Lands Committee was narrowly defeated seven to six in a vote, and Harvie's park proposal was referred to the city commissioners for a report. Although Harvie's proposal was not popular with the Special Lands Committee, it was supported by the residents of Altadore, who organized a petition in September signed by 210 residents. By November 1953, the commissioners, with input from Alex Munro, the superintendent of Parks and Recreation, had arrived at a compromise that was satisfactory to both the city and Eric Harvie, who had agreed to donate $100,000 toward the development of what was referred to as River Park. His contribution of land was reduced to 2.5 acres (1 hectare). The city council then approved the plan and directed the Special Lands Committee to draft an agreement between the City of Calgary and Eric Harvie.

After nearly two years of further negotiations, the Special Lands Committee, chaired by Alderman Paul Brecken, submitted the city's agreement with Eric Harvie to the city council for approval at its October 11, 1955, meeting. This agreement, which incorporated the compromise of 1953 with respect to the amount of land to be included in the park to the west of the Elbow Valley, provided for the creation of a park "for rest and relaxation in a natural setting."[234] This objective was to be achieved by a landscaping plan to "enhance the natural features of the land" through the planting of grass, trees, and shrubs at appropriate locations, excluding ornamental flowerbeds or manicured lawns, along with the development of a system of foot and bicycle paths connecting informal play areas, picnic sites, lounging areas, and lookouts.[235] Bridle paths separated from the pedestrian routes were also to be included. Automobile access and commercial concessions were to be restricted to further maintain the natural setting.

The city council, however, tabled the proposed agreement and decided to ask Eric Harvie to contribute his $100,000 to the development of Glenmore Park, which had been approved earlier that year. The vote on the motion to abandon the 1953 plan endorsed by the city council to create River Park was passed by a vote of eight to five with aldermen Reginald Smith, Frederick Parker, Kennett Lyle, and Paul Brecken, as well as Mayor Mackay voting nay. A meeting followed between Harvie and the Special Lands Committee at which time Harvie rejected the request to revise the agreement to accommodate the city's plans for a park around the Glenmore Reservoir. Given Harvie's refusal to revise the original agreement, it was brought back to the city council for approval or rejection on January 23, 1956. Harvie's rejection of the city's request angered Alderman Brecken, who became a strong opponent of the Harvie plan along with aldermen Donald McIntosh and Peter Morrison.

At this meeting, an attempt to kill the Harvie plan and return to the original plan of 1948, thus foregoing any of the benefits offered in the agreement with Harvie, was lost on a tie vote. A second motion, however, passed, and the agreement was referred back to the Special Lands Committee for further consideration. Opponents of the scheme felt there was sufficient parkland in the area without entering a restrictive arrangement with Harvie. They argued that some of the proposed parkland could be sold for building lots to finance the large Glenmore Reservoir Park. Alderman McIntosh referred to the cash offer from Harvie as a "lousy $100,000, which would force the city to go to Mr. Harvie's corporation every time they wanted to do something in the area."[236] Those in favour welcomed the offer of 2.5 acres (1 hectare) and $100,000 toward park development in part to encourage Harvie's willingness to assist with the development of other parks, particularly a children's zoo on either St. George's or St. Patrick's Island. Mayor Mackay, by arguing in support of the Harvie plan Harvie realized his chance to assist with park development in the downtown area had passed and an expanded river park could serve to mitigate this lost opportunity. Alderman Lyle agreed with Harvie and Mayor Mackay that Calgary needed more parks and rejected the idea of measuring their worth in dollars. In his view, the critics of the Harvie offer were "going to murder this park before it is born by putting a dollar value on it."[237] He concluded if the city did not reserve large areas for parks now, it never would. Alderman Parker agreed with Lyle, saying the best thing the city could do would be to acquire as much parkland as possible. "Sometimes I think our land department is money mad," he said. "They will do anything at times to get money, money, money."[238]

The editors of the *Albertan* and the *Herald* were appalled at the conduct of Brecken, McIntosh, and Morrison, as were many citizens, who made their opinions known in letters to the newspapers. The *Albertan*, in an editorial entitled "Tomorrow's Calgary," noted that the chief merit of the Harvie proposal was not the cash and the land, but the attention it focused on the need for more and better parks in the city.[239] In a January 25, 1956, editorial entitled "Naturally They'd Prefer Ugliness," the *Herald* castigated the Morrison–McIntosh crowd for their disgraceful treatment of Harvie's efforts to improve the city. In its view, the park situation in Calgary was "deplorable, considering the opportunities which have come and gone. Calgary has not one single, large, natural park of the kind Mr. Harvie wanted to help create. It is to be wondered, really, how many people in positions of authority around City Hall actually know what a real park is."[240]

The Special Lands Committee, which was chaired by Alderman Brecken when it met on February 1, reversed its position on the agreement and recommended the Harvie offer of $100,000 be rejected and the 75 acres (30 hectares) sold for development. Aldermen Morrison and McIntosh were unrepentant and explained their position in an open letter published in the February 2 issue of the *Herald*. They were opposed because it would mean the city would have to forgo the income from the sale of the 75 acres (30 hectares) and the ongoing collection of taxes. Going forward with the agreement would mean the city would be subsidizing one area of Calgary with a lump sum of nearly half a million dollars when many sections of Calgary were doing without parks. The second point made was that the city now had 1,450 acres (587 hectares) of parks and the additional 75 acres (30 hectares) was not needed. Their third and most important objection was that the proposed recreational area was not going to be a park for all Calgary citizens, but an exclusive park planned for and used by only a few people. Its character would be ensured by the exclusion of automobiles. "How many families," he asked, "would enjoy St. George's Island on a Sunday if they had to park their car half a mile away and walk in carrying their children?" Even if families did make the effort to come, the children would not be happy because no pop, ice cream, or hot dogs would be permitted. The activities permitted in the park would cater to the elitist interests and activities of the well-heeled residents of southwest Calgary. To them, the regulations "will keep the average Calgarian out of the park and it will become the exclusive preserve of people with sufficient wealth to maintain a stable of horses. Practically every provision of the agreement demanded an exclusive park for the privileged few but paid for by all the citizens of Calgary."[241]

The *Herald* editorial staff responded in the same issue by systematically refuting each of the committee's points. It maintained that no other area in Calgary was better suited for a park than River Park and that land dedicated to park use in the downtown core was being subsidized to a far greater extent. It made the point that the committee's view on access was ridiculous since the park could be reached by the South Calgary bus route and was closer than Bowness Park and much more easily reachable than Glenmore. In the *Herald*'s opinion, the committee preferred to have cars roaring around and ice cream and pop stands, showing that it did not have the "faintest glimmer of an idea what a park really [was]."[242] Does the whole vision of aldermen Morrison and McIntosh, asked the *Herald*, "stop at hot dogs?" Accusing Harvie of trying to benefit Calgary's elite and keep the average Calgarian out of the park was, in the *Herald*'s view, "an attempt to make River Park into a class issue at the lowest level of cheap politics."[243] A letter to the editor from Mrs. Agnes Spensley also challenged the committee's knowledge of actual park development and use in Altadore. Having lived in Calgary for nearly 13 years, she recalled having spent 10 of them trudging more than a mile to South Calgary Park because there were no buses. When parks were created in Altadore, they consisted of 2 acres (0.8 hectares) at 16th Street and 37th and 38th Avenues SW; 2 acres (0.8 hectares) at 17th Street and 47th and 48th Avenues SW; and 1 acre (0.4 hectares) between 15th and 16th Streets on Acton Avenue SW. She scoffed at the idea that the 1,450 acres (587 hectares) extending south of 50th Avenue and west to Weaselhead Flats was in easy reach of the community. "Have a nice hike, Altadore," she concluded. "You can't get there by car unless you hit Spring Bank municipality and Sarcee Road."[244] Harvie, the individual at the centre of this debate, made no public statement, but his lawyer publicly accused the Special Lands Committee of a double-cross.

The recommendation of the Special Lands Committee set the stage for another stormy city council meeting on February 6. At the meeting, a motion passed with Mayor Mackay casting the deciding vote to accept with thanks the original offer by Eric Harvie of $100,000 and 2.5 acres (1 hectare) and proceed with the development of River Park up to the sum of $100,000. Despite the view that the Harvie plan had been saved, the battle over defining the area to be included in River Park continued at the February 27 meeting when a bylaw authorizing execution of the agreement with Glenbow Investments received third reading. Glenbow Investments was owned by Harvie, and he used it to manage his various business interests.

STANLEY PARK

Some of the land designated as parks in the 1920s and 1930s, but not included in the 1948 list, was rescued for that purpose by community action. In January 1951, Elboya residents John McCormick and J. G. St. Denis requested the Special Parks and Recreation Committee consider the beautification and retention for park use of the riverbank between Elboya Bridge and 4th Street SW. In its view, it should be retained as a natural park site so the riverfront could continue to be used for swimming. It also requested the triangular piece of property used as a skating rink in winter be developed into a floral park. This land along the Elbow River had been designated as parkland by the city council in May 1934 for future development as part of Stanley Park, but it had never been transferred to the administration of the Parks Department. Parks superintendent Alex Munro indicated the department would use the land for a park if requested to do so but anticipated delays in carrying out the plan. In March, another portion of what was intended to be part of Stanley Park was threatened by an offer to purchase the land occupied by the AMA auto campsite. W. D. Hulbert, president of the Elboya Community Association, immediately organized a petition that was signed by 91 ratepayers. The petition protested the proposed sale of the old AMA campsite in the Elboya area for an auto camp or for any other commercial purpose. It noted "the original intention of the parties who opened up this subdivision was that the area now occupied by the Tourist Camp should be a park area and it was for this reason that it was not subdivided into lots when the original survey was made."[245] The petition was referred to the Planning Department, which indicated the area had been identified under the comprehensive city plan as a future park and playground site and recommended against the sale of the land. The city council agreed and on April 16, for the third time, it designated the land as a park pending the end of the lease.

In December 1955, the holders of the AMA lease made a second attempt to purchase the land, which on this occasion was opposed by the Parkhill–Stanley Park Community Association. The association reminded the city council of the commitment made in 1951 and recommended the natural park area be set aside for future park development. At its meeting December 12, 1955, the city council, for the fourth time, dedicated the area for parks purposes. The development of the city's master plan was completed in 1959.[246] By the time development began, the oxbow lake, the preservation of which had been part of the plan as suggested by the city engineer in 1912 and by William Reader in 1924, had disappeared.

GLENMORE PARK

The second new park developed after World War II in the Elbow Valley was created around Glenmore Reservoir. With the exception of the Earl Grey Golf Club, people were excluded from the reservoir by virtue of Bylaw 3488. The reversal of that policy began on August 19, 1946, when the city council approved a motion by Alderman Frank Freeze to make the bridge across the Glenmore Dam part of a scenic drive around the reservoir. Such a structure had originally been suggested by the Town Planning Commission in 1934 but never acted upon. At the same meeting, the city council also asked Waterworks Department engineer William Robinson to report on the use of the Elbow River immediately below the dam. Dr. W. H. Hill, Calgary's Medical Officer of Health, was also asked to report on how the use of the reservoir and the Elbow River immediately above the reservoir for boating, swimming, and other diversions would affect Calgary's water supply as long as a boom was used to protect the dam from being hit. Robinson warned against any use of the reservoir, "particularly the Weaselhead area, which was purchased to provide a natural settling pond in flood season thereby preventing the major portion of the gravel and silt carried by a flood being deposited in the reservoir itself."[247] The ability of the Weaselhead to perform this function, according to Robinson, was attributable to a dense growth of willow and scrub, which prevented the reservoir from being filled with gravel and silt. Any opening of this land for picnics would, in his view, "most likely result in this area being denuded by fires, thereby defeating the object [for which] it was purchased."[248] To allow swimming would interfere with the ability of the entire reservoir to purify the water. Bacteriological surveys made from the dam to above Elbow Falls indicated water quality in the reservoir was much better than anywhere else on the river, thus proving the reservoir was performing its function. A second issue was the cost of providing adequate supervision for any recreational activities, the lack of which could result in fatalities. In Robinson's opinion, other parks below the dam would provide greater benefit to more people. The lack of beaches, which limited the reservoir area's recreational value, was also noted. Dr. Hill, in a series of letters to the city council, further developed the theme that swimming would interfere with the role of the reservoir as a means of purifying the polluted water flowing into it. Any use of the reservoir would remove the "advantage of the great sanitary safeguard of storage."[249] Like Robinson, he endorsed downstream use of the Elbow. As a result of Robinson's and Hill's comments, Bylaw 3488 was revised on November 12 to provide for the use of the area below the dam as a park and the development of a scenic highway that would circle the reservoir via the bridge across the dam.

Calgarians, however, were not willing to limit their swimming activities to the pool below the dam, and illegal use of the reservoir continued. In August 1952, according to the *Herald*, the city commissioners requested the police withdraw charges against two people caught swimming in the Glenmore Reservoir until the administration had time to consider possible further revision of the bylaw. A committee of council members consisting of Alderman Walter Boote, Dr. Ross Upton, and Les Hill, to which was added Calgary's Medical Officer of Health, Dr. W. H. Hill, was created to hear submissions related to the use of Glenmore Dam property for picnicking, fishing, boating, and swimming.

The city's intention to review its policy on the Glenmore area was immediately endorsed by the Calgary Fish and Game Association. Fishing under proper supervision, it argued, would not affect water quality.[250] In support of its case, endorsements were obtained from Clarence Pautzke, chief of the Fishery Management Division, Washington State Department of Game, and R. B. Miller of the Department of Zoology at the University of Alberta. Miller stressed the need to regulate the picnicking activities and the use of motorboats on the reservoir and suggested that even if it remained closed, natural contamination was occurring because of the number of dead fish and vegetation. The very small additional contamination resulting from fishing would be, in his view, "a drop in the bucket and would certainly not change the picture."[251] The *Herald* lent its support in an editorial entitled "1,300 Acres of Undeveloped Real Estate," arguing that the citizens of Calgary were "getting sick and tired of looking at this vast, disused piece of civic real estate which had cost the city $347,928.82 in 1931, and in that 21 years, nothing had been done to develop the land around the reservoir."[252]

The willingness of the commissioners, some members of the city council, and the *Herald* to contemplate making use of the recreational potential of the Glenmore Reservoir was totally unacceptable to recently retired city solicitor David Moffat. In an August 20 letter to Mayor Mackay, he attacked the commissioners for their decision to request that charges be withdrawn against the two people caught swimming. Their action, he argued, had nullified the bylaw protecting the reservoir, thus giving the pressure groups a complete victory without giving the city council and the citizens of Calgary any voice in the matter. Moffat also pointed out that the city council had no authority to allow the use of the reservoir for any purpose other than as a water supply. He repeated this in a letter to the editor of the *Herald* and, like Hill and Robinson, claimed the purity of the water in the reservoir was under threat from the selfish interests of a few people. He argued that the construction of boathouses, bathhouses, and toilets to permit boating and swimming on the reservoir would "result in the pouring into the drinking water of much human excreta from people who may be suffering from or [be] carriers of dangerous diseases."[253] This condition could only be dealt with by chlorination. He likened the use of chlorinated water from the reservoir in which swimming was permitted to the use of treated sewer water in other cities. "You will have difficulty," he advised the *Herald*, "in convincing our citizens to substitute purified sewer water for the clear mountain water of the Elbow River which can be protected from pollution to its source."[254] He concluded by contrasting the interests of 135,000 people in the purity and cleanliness of their drinking water with the "desire of a few to gratify their own pleasures who have all the facilities for this purpose elsewhere." Between September 10 and 30, several letters to the editor appeared in the *Herald* in favour of either opening the reservoir or keeping it closed.

While the *Herald* editorial board, David Moffat, and various *Herald* readers debated the relative purity of Elbow River water and the implications of the use of the Glenmore Reservoir, a committee of council members that had been created to investigate the recreational use of the reservoir submitted an interim report. An inspection of the reservoir indicated to the committee that it had beaches that could be used by swimmers and that the Alberta Board of Health and the Board of Public Utilities had the legal authority to change the use of the reservoir. Provincial involvement in the decision as to the future of the Glenmore Reservoir was particularly important to both sides in the debate since each expected the province to uphold their view. Provincial involvement was also desirable from the point of view of David Moffat's successor as city solicitor, Edward Bredin. As Bredin explained in a memo to Alderman Walter Boote, the city council had full power over the Glenmore Dam and could authorize any use whatever, while the local Board of Health had the power to stop any use that it felt might reasonably endanger the water supply of the city.[255] Dr. Hill, as well as Bredin and Moffat, all sent letters to the Alberta Board of Health and the Board of Public Utilities to clarify the issue of jurisdiction. The response to all cases was that both boards supported the recreational use of the reservoir but would not make that decision on the city's behalf, creating the situation Bredin had noted in his memorandum to Alderman Upton.[256]

Following the presentation of its interim report, the committee held a public meeting on September 25, 1952, to gauge public opinion on the matter. Not surprisingly, the leading opponent to the use of the reservoir was David Moffat, who was supported by W. Carter, who suggested that such use would simply add more garbage to the area. Supporters for opening the reservoir, in addition to those individuals and organizations that had already spoken, included G. F. Batch of the Alberta Light Horse Association, who was in favour of the creation of bridle paths. The committee also received letters in support of both sides, with the most interesting one coming from David Milne, who wanted to use a tract of land adjacent to the reservoir for a duck farm, with the waters of the dam to serve as a free range for the waterfowl. He pointed out that the paddling of the ducks would add oxygen to the drinking water and the "sight of four thousand ducks sailing majestically

Figure 7.2 This editorial cartoon from the August 26, 1952, issue of the *Herald* illustrates the newspaper's view that the Glenmore Reservoir was a natural recreational area for Calgarians.

on the placid surface of our reservoir at twilight will create a beautiful panorama, and the sight of fifty-thousand white duck feathers floating on the surface of the water will so closely resemble water-lilies that we will have no need for the real thing."[257] He did suggest there might be some objection to the natural fertilizer being added to the water by the ducks, but that would be removed by chlorination, and whatever got through would be useful for watering lawns, gardens, flowerpots, and window boxes. As compensation for this concession, he promised to give the city every duck egg found floating on the reservoir and one free duck to every member of the city council at Christmas.

Based on this input, useful or otherwise, the committee recommended the policy of forbidding swimming in the reservoir and picnicking around the reservoir be continued and strictly enforced. It also recommended the land lying between the west boundary of the Earl Grey Golf Club be developed as a golf course. The construction of a scenic drive at a suitable distance from the shoreline was endorsed, as was the use of the reservoir for fishing and sailing, with powerboats prohibited. The committee suggested that regulation of the use of boats could be delegated to a yacht or boating club. Dr. Hill endorsed the report based on the strict prohibition against swimming.

The city council did not take the obvious step of pursuing the compromise policy with the Calgary Board of Health that was suggested in the report despite its endorsement by Dr. Hill, who was a member of the board. Instead, the city council referred the report to the city commissioners. The city council was reluctant to implement the report's recommendations because of Moffat's and Bredin's opinion that it did not have the authority to make that decision. The spectre of diseased people polluting an otherwise pure water supply, as suggested by Moffat, and the expectation the Calgary Board of Health would override any decision in favour of opening the reservoir to swimming as suggested by Bredin led to a stalemate.

In September 1953, Alderman Edward Watson attempted to break the stalemate by suggesting the land between the filtration plant and 50th Avenue SW be turned over to the Parks Department. The possible use of this land by the Waterworks Department and the unresolved issue of River Park led to the idea being abandoned. Alderman Watson's actions prompted the Property Owners Association to suggest that the future use of the Glenmore Reservoir be settled by a plebiscite to be held during the 1954 civic election. In December 1953, David Moffat advised the city council that he also endorsed the idea of a plebiscite. The city council and the commissioners agreed with this approach, and from March to October 1954, Bredin drafted a ballot in consultation with Moffat. On the eve of the civic election on October 13, the city council decided not to submit the issue to a plebiscite because of the continuing concern it did not have the authority to do so.

In May 1955, the city council finally took the obvious step of consulting the Calgary Board of Health.[258] A motion was passed calling for the Glenmore Dam area to be opened as a recreational park for fishing and boating and as restricted picnic grounds, subject to the approval of the city and provincial Boards of Health and subject to them having the right to do so under provincial licence. The Calgary Board of Health responded on June 2 and indicated its support for the recommendations of the Special Lands Committee as contained in its report tabled in September 1953 forbidding swimming and the use of motorboats. It also noted the "psychological effect on the citizens" if bodies of drowning victims could not be recovered. In its view, Calgarians were uncomfortable with corpses in their water supply. It also noted the implications of Calgary deriving its water from an impounding reservoir that also impounded pollution. The letter removed the impediment to the city taking action, and at the July 18, 1955, meeting, the city council unanimously passed a motion that the Glenmore Reservoir be reserved as a future park site.

Having decided to make use of the reservoir with the caveat that actual human contact with the water be minimized, the city's Planning Department began making decisions regarding the use of the land around it. The department's approach to land use around the Glenmore Reservoir was a complete reversal of the spirit of the 1953 Special Lands Committee's report that emphasized the need to minimize human impact in the interests of water quality. Its plan, as submitted to the city council on December 17, 1956, provided for a protected swimming area, picnic areas, and an "Indian Village" where the Weaselhead Flats environmental reserve is today, along with an aquarium, solarium, museum, outdoor theatre, and band shell in what would become North Glenmore Park. A new Parks Department administrative building, a parks superintendent's residence, botanical gardens, winter gardens, and a conservatory were proposed for the area north of the Earl Grey Golf Course. A riding academy and golf course were to be located at the present locations of the Rockyview Hospital and Heritage Park.[259] The Planning Department also anticipated that community groups would undertake the development of some of these activities, such as the riding academy and sailing. The precedent for this approach had been established in 1932 when land was leased to the Earl Grey Golf Club. The plan was approved with only aldermen Grant MacEwan and Donald McIntosh attempting to reduce the impact the plan had on the area's natural beauty. The *Herald*, which feared the city council would not create a park, commended the plan but expressed some concern for what it called the "brush off" it gave to MacEwan's motion to preserve the natural beauty of the area. While the paper conceded that area's use as a recreational facility would affect its natural features, the city council was advised to ensure there was no unnecessary tampering with the area's "natural beauties and contours." Calgarians, it argued, "had seen a great lack of consideration for the value of natural contours and other features in laying out of new subdivisions where slopes, hills, valleys and even isolated trees were ruthlessly eliminated by the blades of a fleet of bull-dozers."[260] Glenmore Park should be planned with the land's natural character in mind.

Having approved a plan for the use of the Glenmore Reservoir that was a complete repudiation of the terms upon which the reservoir was to be opened for use, various community organizations, the city council, and the Planning and Parks Departments, along with the city commissioners, collectively worked toward a more detailed allocation of activities and uses in the area. In June 1957, the Alberta Light Horse Association applied for permission to construct a bridle path. The city council approval was given on the basis the path would be open for public use, the association would construct the necessary fences and gates at its own expense and protect the city against liability for injuries, and the association would provide any policing required.[261] This use continued the tradition established by the World War II mounted patrol. Following the bridal path's completion, the Alberta Light Horse Association, along with several like-minded individuals representing the Calgary branch of the Canadian Pony Club and the Calgary Stampede, proposed to the city commissioners that land be reserved for the creation of the Glenmore Park Riding Academy. Its purpose would be to promote horse riding "in all its phases," as well as educate particularly young people in horse breeding, training, and care. The proposal was prompted by the association's need to find a new home to replace the Chinook Stables built in 1914 by the Calgary Polo Club and located east of the reservoir, which were being torn down to make way for the development of the Haysboro subdivision. In May 1958, the Calgary Western Riders also made an application for the reservation of land. To the great joy of fishers and boating enthusiasts, the city council also opened the reservoir to boat use.[262]

At the May 26, 1958, meeting, the city commissioners brought their plan to the city council for approval. They wanted to develop the Glenmore Reservoir area by leasing land to various community groups. The majority of the city council members accused the commissioners of having ignored its directions to preserve the natural character of the area and regarded the leasing of various portions as unacceptable. The majority of the city council members wanted the administration to take more direct control. The plan was referred back to the commissioners until such time as they were prepared to present a comprehensive scheme for the entire park.

The promoters of the yacht club, which was now formally incorporated as the Glenmore Yacht Club, were not deterred and returned to the city council with a proposal to develop land for use as a club. Despite the city council's decision on May 26 to defer any decisions on park development until a suitable master plan had been presented and its rejection of leasing land to private organizations, it voted on August 4 to approve the Glenmore Yacht Club's proposal in principle. Aldermen MacEwan and Watson were the only members of the city council whose votes were in any way consistent with the way they had voted in May. The decision was a call to action for the Calgary Fish and Game Association, which had already advised the city in June of its objections to the city leasing land around the reservoir. It made its view known in newspaper advertisements and in a presentation to the city council. The Glenmore Yacht Club responded to the efforts of the Calgary Fish and Game Association by attempting to derail its plan by also speaking to the city council. On June 8, 1959, Bylaw 5264 approving the yacht club lease was passed. Following this decision, the Calgary Fish and Game Association launched a successful legal challenge to the bylaw. The yacht club offered the services of its lawyer free of charge to the city to appeal the case. The city accepted the offer, but Justice Clinton Ford of the Appellate Division of the Supreme Court of Alberta upheld the decision.

The Glenmore Yacht Club lease controversy effectively stopped the administration's plans, which had received some support in the city council to develop sports facilities in Glenmore Park by means of leasing land to private clubs. Land for the creation of riding academies by the Calgary Western Riders Association and the Alberta Light Horse Association was never provided. The city did, however, allow the Alberta Light Horse Association to build a bridle path, which was provided for in a bylaw passed in August 1957. Curling, archery, football, and snowmobile clubs were all denied land leases in the area.

The yacht club controversy and the lack of a master plan did not, however, preclude the city from reserving land around the reservoir for community use. In May 1960, 21 acres (8.5 hectares) on the east side were reserved for a hospital at the request of the Chronic Hospital Board. A second proposal regarding the use of the land around the Glenmore Reservoir that also met with strong support from the commissioners, the Planning Department, and the city council was the creation of a park for special needs children. The Calgary chapter of the Active Club of Canada suggested the park in the fall of 1960, and by January 1961, a 9.95-acre (4-hectare) site at 14th Street and 50th Avenue SW had been selected for what the club called Happy Land. Its proposal was to combine a summer camp for handicapped children with the second school for developmentally delayed children in Calgary, as well as western Canada's first combination swimming and therapeutic whirlpool.

In the spring of 1961, the commissioners presented a new master plan to the city council that incorporated community input, both welcome and unwelcome, the concerns of the Chronic Hospital Board, and the need for a gravel supply located on city-owned land south of the Bow River.[263] The plan proposed a five-year capital expenditure budget for Glenmore, which was designated as a regional park along with St. George's Island and Bowness. The land at the west end of the reservoir where Weaselhead Flats is today was to become a natural park. The area on the north side of the reservoir and south of Lakeview was to become a picnic area and beaches with access roads. The area north of the causeway was designated for use as a golf course, and the land to the south and east of the causeway was designated for use as an auxiliary hospital. A children's farm and picnic area was to be located where Heritage Park is today. The entire south side of the reservoir was to be future beach and picnic areas.

The city council first debated the revised plan on April 3, at which time Alderman MacEwan attempted to infuse the city council members with a greater concern for the preservation of the natural environment around the reservoir, which he had first tried to do in 1956 and again in 1958. At the request of the majority of the city council, however, he withdrew his motion until the next meeting on April 17, pending receipt of further information from the commissioners. At that meeting, the city council approved a motion that attempted to combine MacEwan's interest in the preservation of the natural character of the Glenmore area and the scaled-down development plans of the administration with the decision, at the same meeting, to approve the construction of a causeway across the reservoir as part of the southern freeway system later christened Glenmore Trail. The motion directed the administration to develop the area south of the causeway with "distinctiveness marked by retention of its natural character" and to restrict development between the causeway and the dam to "docking facilities, trails, picnic ground facilities, a lot of tree planting and a comfort station." The intent of the motion was immediately compromised by the city council's acceptance of the commissioners' recommendations to exclude the Weaselhead area from the park, thus allowing for its future use as a gravel pit, and to exclude the area designated for hospital use southwest of the future site of the Glenmore Trail and 14th Street SW interchange, as well as designate an area for a children's farm.

Although the city council minutes and the newspaper coverage of the meeting indicated little concern over the intention to allow swimming in the reservoir, the issue was subsequently raised by Alderman David Russell, who requested a report from Dr. Leslie Allan, Dr. Hill's successor as Calgary's Medical Officer of Health. The doctor's report repeated the same concerns first raised by Dr. Hill, reminding the commissioners that the reservoir without swimming provided a pure water supply. Given the contents of the letter, Alderman Russell, at the May 1 city council meeting, specifically asked the commissioners if swimming was to be allowed, a reasonable assumption given the fact that the master plan included two beaches. Commissioner Steele replied that at the moment, swimming was not envisaged.

Despite the apparent confusion over some of the details of the Glenmore master plan, the commissioners felt the city council's decision of April 17 regarding the plan gave them sufficient direction to proceed with the preparation of a new, comprehensive bylaw, and thus bring to conclusion the debate that had begun in 1946 as to the future development of the Glenmore Reservoir. In drafting the new bylaw, the Law Department was guided by the city's legal responsibility to protect Calgary's water supply. Related to that responsibility was its acceptance of the view first stated in 1932 by Dr. Hill that swimming in the reservoir would compromise water quality.

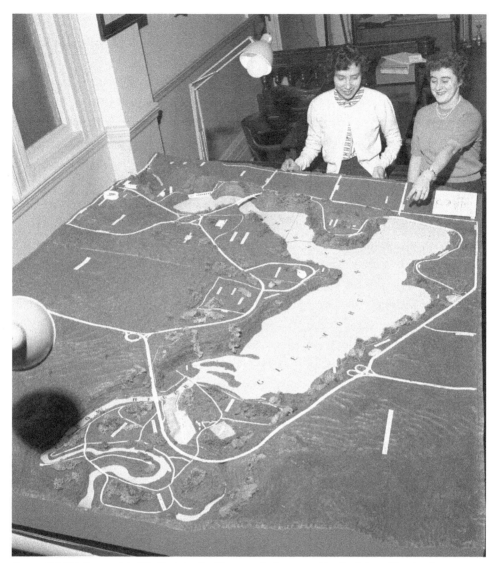

Figure 7.3 This is a model of the first plan for Glenmore Park prepared by the Calgary Planning Department in December 1956, which was on display at City Hall. The plan featured a protected swimming area, picnic areas, and an "Indian Village" where the Weaselhead Flats environmental reserve is today. What is now North Glenmore Park was to be the location of an aquarium, solarium, museum, outdoor theatre, and band shell. A new Parks Department administrative building, a parks superintendent's residence, botanical gardens, winter gardens, and a conservatory were proposed for the area north of the Earl Grey Golf Course. A riding academy and golf course were to be located at the present locations of Rockyview Hospital and Heritage Park. A road was proposed to cross the Weaselhead environmental reserve at 37th Avenue SW. This plan was endorsed by the city council but later rejected in 1958.

Source: Glenbow Library and Archives, NA-5600–8138a

The Law Department was also concerned that the bylaw be drafted to ensure there would be no repeat of the successful court challenge that had struck down the Glenmore Yacht Club bylaw in 1960. The judgement in the case of Shaddock v. the City was also a concern since the passage of a bylaw establishing the Glenmore area as a park would provide an additional basis on which an application could be made for an injunction that prevented the city from exercising its control of the area in a way that adversely affected public interest in the park. It wanted to ensure it did not lay the basis for a legal challenge to the bylaw.

The result was the drafting of two bylaws to replace the one passed in 1943 that separated the water supply use of the Glenmore Reservoir from its use as a recreational facility, with the dividing line between the two areas being the new Glenmore Causeway. The first readings of the Glenmore Waterworks Bylaw 6039 and Glenmore Park Bylaw 6040 were given on April 16, 1963. The most significant feature of Bylaw 6040 was its prohibition against swimming, bringing the use of the reservoir in line with the 1953 Special Lands Committee report. Revisions were incorporated into the bylaw before its second reading on May 27 that extended the boundary of the park area to the west, incorporating the Weaselhead area. Between the second and third readings, further revisions were made regarding the Eagle Ridge subdivision. Following the approval of Bylaws 6039 and 6040, the yacht club made a revised proposal to the city, which was accepted and not challenged.[264] In 1974, the use of the reservoir for dragon boat races was permitted.

Land originally purchased by the city but excluded from administration under Bylaws 6039 and 6040 included the area for Happy Land on 50th Avenue SW, land designated for hospital use on the south side of the reservoir, land for the Eagle Ridge subdivision south of the hospital site, and the children's farm located south of Eagle Ridge. The residents of 50th Avenue SW opposed the Active Club's proposal for Happy Land with the result that the city reversed its decision to grant the club a lease. The transformation of the children's farm into Heritage Park began in May 1961 when Eric Harvie notified the city commissioners of his interest in creating an "old-time village" that could house his collection of historic artifacts. He suggested the village could contain a traditional blacksmith's shop, carpenter's shop, and tin shop, all complete with tools and equipment, as well as a homesteader's house and a flour mill.[265] The city was interested in Harvie's idea of a heritage village since it had already acquired Sam Livingston's residence, which was in need of a new location.[266] Given this encouragement, Harvie arranged for the participation of the Woods Foundation in providing funding for the development of the children's farm. In November 1962, approval was given for the development of what was then referred to as Story Book Farm, and in December 1963, the name was changed to Heritage Park. The only opposition to the plan came from Alderman MacEwan and P. A. McVicar, a private citizen. MacEwan argued that the land was better suited for development of a native arboretum.

The last battle over land use around the reservoir began in 1963 when the city council refused an application to reclassify the land located between what is now Heritage Park and Glenmore Landing to permit the construction of seven 16-storey towers and 50,000 square feet (15,240 square metres) of commercial space.[267] However, the city Land Department failed to purchase the property as directed, and in 1974, a second development was proposed and successfully stopped by community action. In 1976, the Campeau Corporation began a third attempt to develop the property, which it wanted to develop as townhouses and low-rise apartments to accommodate approximately 1,900 people. The communities in the area rallied again to resist or at least modify the development, with the newly created Grant MacEwan Park Fund Association spearheading the effort. The choice of the association's name took advantage of MacEwan's well-established reputation as a defender of the natural character of the Glenmore Reservoir area, which he had earned as a Calgary alderman. The July 5 public hearing on the Campeau proposal included a well-organized presentation by the association that featured a personal appearance by MacEwan. The *Herald* reported that "a woman in the audience wept as Mr. MacEwan described the wildlife that still lives on the shores of the Glenmore." The group was able to stall the Campeau proposal and convince the majority of the city council that the land should be purchased as a park. The association suggested various strategies to acquire the land, including a special tax and a land swap. In September 1976, the Parks and Recreation Department recommended against its purchase as a park. The recommendation was rejected by the city council, which encouraged instead that communities in the association try to raise the money to purchase the land. In January 1977, when the Campeau Corporation submitted a second development application, the association had changed its objective from preserving the natural character of the area to developing the land by raising it to the level of the dike and then constructing a boat launch and storage area, as well as a clubhouse, museum, nursing home, tennis courts, and extensive picnic and parking areas. The proposal preserved public access to the Glenmore Reservoir, which had been an issue since the late 1940s, but abandoned any effort to preserve the natural character of the area.

CATASTROPHIC FLOODS: A REAL OR IMAGINED THREAT?

The flood threat to Calgary after 1932 was confined to winter inundations of communities along the Bow River caused by ice jams. The completion of the Bearspaw Dam and other measures had solved this problem by the early 1960s. Spring floods, at least in the minds of the public, were a fading memory. The "floods" of 1942, 1948, 1951, 1953, and 1963 were mild affairs compared to those of 1915, 1923, 1929, and 1932 in terms of the disruption of the community and the destruction of public and private property. No dramatic rescues of citizens stranded by a sudden rise in the river levels had been required, and the city had not been cut off from the rest of the world because of damage to its network of bridges. Although the Elbow continued to be perceived during these events as a sinister presence in the community intent on causing harm, residents were confident the river had been restrained within its banks, which only needed to be reinforced by sandbags at strategic locations. Their sense of security was illustrated by an article in the June 5, 1953, issue of the *Albertan* that described how the "angry waters of the Elbow" were "gnawing away" at the riverbank while citizens enjoyed the Stampede in Victoria Park.

The lack of concern on the part of the public for the potentially damaging effects of spring floods was in sharp contrast to the recognition of the threat on the part of city and provincial government officials. Their concerns were first expressed in October 1951 by the city's waterworks engineer, W. E. Robinson. He pointed out that a measure of flood control had been incorporated into the Glenmore Dam but that changes in the Elbow River channel below the dam had reduced its effectiveness. The flood-control measures consisted of two steel penstocks controlled by two 12-foot

(3.7-metre) Dow valves that passed between 9,000 and 10,000 cubic feet per second (283 cubic metres per second). When the dam was first constructed, a flow of water below the dam up to 8,000 cubic feet per second (226 cubic metres per second) did not create any flood problems. Since 1932, however, the channel of the Elbow River had silted up and gravel bars had formed to such an extent that people complained when a flow of 5,000 cubic feet per second (142 cubic metres per second) was passed downstream.

To determine what should be done to maintain the carrying capacity of the Elbow, Robinson recommended that a traverse survey be made to locate the top of the riverbank and ascertain its relationship to all the existing sub-division surveys so that future encroachments of the riverbank by landowners along the Elbow River could be prevented. The problem was a legacy of the way the floodplain adjacent to the Elbow River had been subdivided before World War I. The edge of the Elbow River had been used as a boundary in the city's development plans. Fluctuations in the water level and the natural process of erosion and accretion had the potential to change the location of this boundary. The size of backyards could increase or decrease depending on the actions of the river. Some landowners, and even the City of Calgary, had taken advantage of this situation to extend the riverbank boundary, which restricted the capacity of the channel to carry water and increased the potential for damage during floods. Along with the survey, Robinson also suggested specific locations along the river that were in need of flood protection. These included the bend in Victoria Park, as well as the gravel bars above and below the Mission and 25th Avenue Bridges. Dikes were required on the west bank from the 25th Avenue Bridge to 1st Street and west from 38th Avenue SW to about 5th Street West. The Park Hill slope had to be stabilized and Dr. Obourne's house on 26th Avenue SW relocated.

City engineer Ivor Strong endorsed Robinson's recommendations but did not think there was sufficient time left in 1951 to undertake the survey and the specific tasks outlined. His immediate priority was the construction of a dike to protect the houses on low-lying land near the 25th Avenue Bridge. The dike would not, however, solve the groundwater problem, so he endorsed the removal of Dr. Obourne's house on 26th Avenue. He anticipated a complete survey could be done during the winter and an estimate made of the actual quantities of gravel to be removed and how the task could be accomplished. The necessary permission from the Alberta government to conduct dredging operations was requested in 1952 but not pursued, and neither was the survey to establish the relationship between the Elbow River and the adjacent subdivided land.

The implications of the Elbow River's declining ability to carry water flows in excess of 5,000 cubic feet per second (142 cubic metres per second) without causing floods became increasingly urgent in the following decade. In 1961, concern on the part of the province about flooding in the Erlton district prompted J. L. Reid of the Department of Water Resources to request flow data from E. P. Collier, the district engineer for the Department of Northern Affairs and National Resources.[268] Collier supplied Reid with four historical photographs taken during the floods of 1915 and 1929 by staff from the Department of the Interior. Photograph No. 7049 was particularly revealing since it had been taken as the peak of the flood passed the Canadian National Railway Bridge at 4:15 p.m. on June 26, 1915. Based on Geological Survey of Canada data and the elevation of a manhole cover featured in the photograph, he estimated the height of the water to be about 7 feet (2.1 metres). He also passed on data recorded at the former gauging station located a little below the Holy Cross Hospital and the 12th Avenue Bridge for 1915, 1923, 1929, and 1932. The data indicated the flood of 1932 had been the highest of the four floods, but that the peak in that year in the area of Erlton was lower than for the other three years because of the effect of water storage in the Glenmore Reservoir. He doubted the reservoir would have a similar modifying effect on a future flood of equivalent size and shape. His general conclusion was that a recurrence of the 1932 flood could produce water levels in Erlton similar to those experienced in 1915, 1923, and 1929. He emphasized the fact that the water level in the Glenmore Reservoir before the flood and the control procedures adopted at the Glenmore Dam during the flood would have considerable bearing on water levels in the Elbow River below the dam. If no modifications were made to the dam, a future flood of the 1932 magnitude would result in water levels as much as 4.5 feet (1.4 metres) higher than what had previously occurred in the Erlton neighbourhood. Collier's photographs were not only records of the past, but portents of things to come.

Collier's concerns were echoed by Calgary city engineer A. H. Nicolson in a September 28, 1961, letter to E. B. Newcombe of the Manufacturers Life Insurance Company. He indicated that the Glenmore Dam, having saved the city from one flood disaster, should not be expected to do the favour again.[269] He pointed out that the primary function of the Glenmore Dam and Reservoir was to provide the domestic water supply for the city and that it could provide some assistance with flood control, provided the city had sufficient warning that a flood was imminent.

The City of Calgary began to deal with the problem of potential floods on the Elbow River on August 28, 1962, when city engineer C. D. Howard requested that the Department of Water Resources undertake a flood study. Its report, completed in April 1965, provided a profile sheet showing the water levels on the Elbow during various possible floods, along with a set of maps of the Elbow Valley that showed the boundaries between dry land and flooded areas for floods with a 10 percent, 5 percent, and 2 percent frequency. The report was based on the assumption that the Glenmore Reservoir provided no flood control on the Elbow.

The city also initiated the survey first suggested by Robinson in 1951 of the Elbow River Valley to determine the extent of encroachment by residential development, as well as plans to improve the river's carrying capacity. The first project was the resurrection of a plan first proposed in 1912 to remove one of the meanders of the Elbow by cutting a channel through Erlton south of the present-day location of the Repsol Sport Centre. The proposal to construct this channel was revived in 1962 with encouragement from A. G. Martin, the director of the Planning Department.[270] He envisaged the construction of an 80-foot-wide (24-metre-wide) reinforced concrete channel, which was narrower than the original design so would reduce the amount of land required but would cost an additional $350,000. The benefits of a narrower channel included a larger parking area and reduced traffic bridge construction.

In May 1963, the city's plans for the diversion channel were referred to R. E. Bailey, the chief engineer of the provincial government's Department of Water Resources, for comment.[271] Bailey indicated that studies of the Elbow River undertaken by his staff had suggested a similar idea, but they disagreed with the city's choice for the channel's location. Bailey's preference was for a cutoff that began at the bend near 26th Avenue SE and followed the base of the hill to re-enter the river at the bend just above the True-Mix Concrete plant at 25th Avenue SE. This alignment fitted the contour of the land and eliminated any sharp bends, entering and leaving the river with the least possible curvature. The revised alignment also had the advantage of eliminating "a rather narrow, dangerous section of the river" and would improve traffic in the area. The backfilling of the old river channel would provide land for the expansion of the Holy Cross Hospital. The plan's most enthusiastic supporter was the Calgary Stampede and Exhibition Association.

This enthusiasm, however, was not shared by the Elbow Lodge Motor Hotel. In October 1963, F. R. Walton, vice-president of the company that owned the hotel, advised Minister of Agriculture Harry Strom it had invested close to $1 million in 1961, 100 percent of which was Alberta capital. The location of the Elbow Lodge on the banks of the Elbow River had been carefully selected so its "guests are at present able to enjoy this natural beauty and its tranquility, and should that be ever replaced by the uproar of a main highway it requires little imagination to realize what would happen—not only [to] our business but also to the livelihood of our employees."[272] Walton also reprimanded the city for its failure to consult with other landowners about proposed changes in the surrounding terrain until after they had been announced. Should the proposed plans be approved, he concluded, the lodge's business would suffer a very drastic reversal by virtue of the fact that it "would be deprived of the hotel's greatest asset—the Elbow River."[273]

Strom also received a letter from Mrs. Tracey Tupper, who was equally horrified that the "brass at City Hall had been working on a hush-hush project to divert a part of the Elbow River in order to procure the area on which they had decided to build a new racetrack without any community input."[274] Now that the lid was off, she continued, the city without any apology or expression of regret was going to deprive 70 families of their homes. "Mr. Strom," she queried, "do you not see any problem in allowing the city to carry out this 'dirty deal'? If you were one of these residents would it not hit you right in the solar plexus?" Mrs. Tupper also cited the investment she and her husband had made in their Elbow property. Even if they were not included in the area to be used for the channel, they would still "be deprived of the enjoyment of the river and all that it stands for, and in its place will get a race-track." She also suggested the city was contemplating this injustice to Erlton because "the city wouldn't dare to go into the Elbow Park or Elboya districts where the wealth is and divert the river there in order to build a racetrack. We here, having bought our homes and paid for them, have just as much right to the enjoyment of the river as though we were loaded with moola."

Despite these protests, as late as February 1964, the city was pressing on with the project since the Exhibition Association was anxious to proceed. The only causes for delay were the reluctance of the Canadian National Railway to make a deal on the land and the failure of the provincial government to give its approval. The province withheld approval pending further studies, which it recommended should be undertaken by the firm of T. Blench & Associates, consulting hydraulic engineers. In the province's opinion, the idea of a diversion channel had possibilities but further study was required. One problem was the possible erosion of the channel upstream and within the new channel, with the products of erosion deposited downstream, increasing the chances of flooding downstream as a result of the deposition. Design of the cutoff to ensure the flood potential would not be enhanced downstream would require the collection of information on the exact nature of the Elbow River from the reservoir to the downstream end of the cutoff, a hydrological analysis, and discussion with city engineers about the economics of alternative hydraulically acceptable solutions.[275]

In addition to these engineering difficulties, legal issues also arose. As Ivor Strong had explained in 1970, it was felt that the acquisition of the property for the channel would be difficult and costly and that there were legal implications. The legal issue was that as soon as the normal river channel was disturbed or relocated, the city would be held responsible for any damages that might occur as a result of a future flood. To accommodate a future flood, a much larger channel would have to be constructed than the natural channel that presently existed.[276] The idea was briefly resuscitated in May 1970 when G. T. Henderson offered Mayor Sykes land south of the Elbow for Stampede Grounds expansion.[277]

Plans to improve the carrying capacity of the Elbow also included removing the islands owned by the CPR, located at the Mission Bridge, as well as John Tidswell, upstream of the Mission Bridge and across from Elbow Park.[278]

The CPR-owned islands were a legacy of the CPR land grant, which included section 15. The islands had been improved by the Mission Boy Scout troop and officially transferred to the City of Calgary. Trees planted in honour of William Pearce following his death in 1930 were another improvement to the islands, which had been designated as a bird sanctuary during William Reader's term as park superintendent. The Parks Department advised the Engineering Department of the islands' unofficial status as a bird sanctuary but made no effort to provide any protection.

The City of Calgary and the province cooperated on a study that involved the controlled release of water from the Glenmore Dam. Flows of approximately 2,400 cubic feet per second (68 cubic metres per second) were passed early in the week of June 8, 1964. The flow was subsequently increased to 4,000 cubic feet per second (113 cubic metres per second) and 6,000 cubic feet per second (170 cubic metres per second), at which time helicopter inspections were made to evaluate the results. The inspections confirmed concerns going back to 1951 that the channel of the Elbow was shrinking as a result of encroachment by private landowners and the city. The channel was now occupied by gardens and at least one barbecue at the back of private lots, as well as various city construction projects. The Mission Bridge and others also restricted the flow of water. The test releases showed that several buildings were on the verge of being flooded, including an apartment building downstream from the 26th Street Bridge, which was protected to a degree by a piling, though the piling was close to being overtopped. At the Stampede Grounds, footbridge #4 had practically no clearance and would create a serious problem if not raised or pulled out during a flood. There were also numerous examples of waste material being pushed into the Elbow River.

Following the completion of this study, T. Blench & Associates, which had been involved in the controlled release investigation along with the proposed diversion, was hired to investigate "hydraulically acceptable, potentially practical and economic methods of reducing the flood menace of the Elbow River in the City of Calgary."[279] The introduction to the report, which was completed in August 1965, made the familiar points that the Glenmore Dam and Reservoir did not have enough storage to act as a significant flood-reducing structure. Careful manipulation of the reservoir based on hydrographs of the discharge of the Elbow River at Calgary would allow for a reduction of the peak flow downstream of the dam. A flood warning using the Bragg Creek flow data and a meteorological station in the catchment area would allow further reduction of the downstream peak flow. Reduction of the peak discharge below 9,000 cubic feet per second (255 cubic metres per second) was impossible even using flow regulation.

The recommendations for dealing with water flow in excess of 9,000 cubic feet per second (255 cubic metres per second) included general excavation, cutoffs, flow regulation with or without a flood warning system, and upstream storage. General excavation and steepening of the riverbanks would reduce flood levels at once. The report concluded that the most reliable flood protection scheme, although probably the most expensive in direct costs, would be upstream water storage. No work would be required within the city, and the Elbow River channel would be left exactly as it was.

T. Blench & Associates favoured a flood protection scheme using upstream storage since it was the only reliable scheme. Although it conceded that the scheme was costly, the damage that could occur if any of the other plans failed, either because of human error or the occurrence of a flood much larger than designed for, could be largely compared to the costs of upstream storage, especially in the future if there were more development in flood-prone areas. Although T. Blench & Associates did not study the scheme to use upstream storage in detail, it was satisfied that suitable sites were available. The alternatives involved using various means of monitoring water flow into the reservoir, which would permit dam operators to draw down the reservoir to capture the peak flow of the river and reduce the threat of flooding while still providing the necessary water supply. A second alternative was to excavate the river channel below the reservoir and construct a cutoff channel in the Erlton area.

Based on the Blench Report, in April 1965, the city requested that Minister of Agriculture Harry Strom investigate the construction of an upstream dam on the Elbow River above Bragg Creek in the vicinity of Elbow Falls to control flooding. Strom advised the city that the problem had been referred to engineers in the Water Resources Department, and when the various ideas had been "crystallized," they would present the whole picture along with a recommendation for the city's consideration.

To help the engineers in the Water Resources Department, the Montreal Engineering Company was hired in August 1966 to study the flood problem on the Elbow River and Fish Creek. The study was later expanded to include the effects of a flood on the proposed development of the Stampede Grounds in Victoria Park and on a proposed bridge over the Elbow River at 1st Street SE. Montreal Engineering's review incorporated all the previous studies by T. Blench & Associates along with R. T. Hollies' "Report on Possible Dam Sites on the Elbow River," dated March 14, 1961; C. H. and P. H. Mitchel's "Report to the Dominion of Canada," dated August 15, 1911; and Duncan, Durcher & Company's "Report on Proposed Hydro-Electric Development Elbow River," dated June 16, 1914.

The city received Montreal Engineering's initial report on January 20, 1967, along with a transmittal letter noting that its studies indicated that a major flood on the Elbow River constituted a hazard to property in the valley downstream of the Glenmore Dam. In addition, until flood-control measures were undertaken, a warning system such as that proposed by T. Blench & Associates should be considered. Warning would be given when the flow in the upper watershed had reached a predetermined value and would provide the opportunity for residents to move out of the danger area.

The Montreal Engineering Company proposed four schemes to control 100-year floods on the Elbow River. Scheme 1 was to contain the flood within the Glenmore Reservoir by raising the reservoir's full-supply level. This would protect Calgary against 45-year floods and would cost $1.9 million. Scheme 2 was to contain the flood within the Elbow River watershed by constructing upstream storage at the Mitchell Dam site. This would also protect Calgary from a 45-year flood but would cost $4.7 million. Scheme 3 was to contain the flood within both a raised Glenmore Reservoir and the previously proposed Mitchell storage reservoir. This would protect Calgary from a 100-year flood at a total cost of $6.6 million. Scheme 4 was to construct a new spillway from the Glenmore Reservoir to the Bow River so that floodwaters would bypass the city. This would protect Calgary from a 100-year flood at a total cost of more than $12.7 million.

The Montreal Engineering report of January 1967, while using data for a 100-year flood, also raised the spectre of a catastrophic 10,000-year flood. A storm capable of producing this sort of devastation occurred in Montana in June 1964. That event was the result of a large snowpack combined with a late spring and a record level of rainfall. The rain began on the morning of June 7 and continued for 36 hours. Precipitation during that period was as much as 14 inches (356 millimetres). Peak on-stream discharges in the flood area ranged from 2 to 11.5 times the probable 50-year flood levels. The failure of Swift Dam on Birch Creek and Lower Two Medicine Dam on Two Medicine Creek caused the complete destruction of numerous buildings and bridges. The total flood damage in Montana was estimated at $55 million. Thirty lives were lost, 850 people were injured, and about 8,700 people were evacuated during the high-water period. Damage in Canada was in excess of $1 million.[280]

In October 1967, Montreal Engineering, in an addendum to its January 1967 report, provided further recommendations to deal with a catastrophic flood. These recommendations, designated as Schemes 5 and 6, involved the addition of gates on the upstream face of the dam and modifications to the Glenmore Causeway to permit doubling the flow area through the structure.

One strategy not recommend by Montreal Engineering was the diversion of the Elbow River into another watershed. This alternative was suggested by G. Tough at the request of Dr. Louis Hamil. Hamil had been retained by the Parks Department to review future park development. The possibilities identified by Tough included transferring Elbow River water to the Bow River via Fish and Jumpingpound Creeks, Glenbow Lake, and an abandoned irrigation ditch. Montreal Engineering rejected the suggestion as being entirely impractical because of the volume of water involved and the plan's failure to actually solve the problem since it simply transferred the water from one watershed to another.

Following the submission of its Elbow River and Fish Creek floodplain study, Montreal Engineering was hired in May 1967 by the Alberta government to do a similar study of the Bow River. The City of Calgary's review of these reports began in May 1968. City waterworks engineer William Roy rejected the idea that the 1964 Montana flood be used as a standard for planning purposes. He was advised by the weather office that such a storm had never occurred as far north as Calgary, although there was a possibility that it could. The weather office also regarded the extreme snowfall in the Lethbridge area a couple of years previously as a freak storm.

Coping with a flow of 90,000 cubic feet per second (2,550 cubic metres per second) would require raising the dike 13.5 feet (4.1 metres) or doubling the channel through the causeway. The installation of gates on the dam at a cost of $2.2 million would also be required. These changes would allow floodwaters to be passed downstream, causing massive damage. In Roy's opinion, such an event also raised the possibility of the failure of the Glenmore Dam. Gore & Storrie, who had designed the dam and supervised its construction, predicted in a verbal communication that in such extreme conditions, the dam would fail, though Montreal Engineering disagreed. Such an eventuality, in Roy's opinion, would be a natural disaster equivalent to an earthquake or hurricane with which the city could not effectively cope.

The most reasonable course of action was to plan for a 45-year flood, which would result in peak flows of 23,000 cubic feet per second (650 cubic metres per second), something that had already occurred. The cost of preparing for such a flow was not too expensive in comparison to the probable property damage caused by such an event. This contingency had already been provided for in the first scheme suggested by Montreal Engineering in its report. Scheme 1 combined with Scheme 3 was also recommended to deal with a 100-year flood with a flow of 32,000 cubic feet per second (906 cubic metres per second).

Roy recommended the immediate raising of the dike but suggested that other issues be investigated before any more work was undertaken. The issues to be investigated included the legal liability of both the city and the provincial government, the cost of mitigation schemes compared to the probable damage costs to property in the floodplain, flood insurance, the application of development restrictions, and the signing of release forms by owners absolving the the city and the province from any claims for flood damage.

City engineer Charles Howarth's report to J. P. Wilson, the secretary of the Board of Commissioners, passed on Roy's recommendation that the east dike be raised immediately. He also recommended the city continue to improve the warning system and pursue funding options with the provincial government and other agencies to build a dam on the upper Elbow. Summaries of the reports by Montreal Engineering, along with Howarth's recommendations, were identified as secret and provided to the city council at its July 17,

1968, meeting. Without advising residents of the reasons, work began to raise the height of the dike, which led to objections from the community.

With the flood-warning system updated and the raising of the dike completed, the city pursued the long-term mitigation measures recommended by both T. Blench & Associates and Montreal Engineering. The idea of a dam on the upper Elbow River, despite being recommended by the November 26, 1969, meeting of the Standing Committee on Operations and Development, was eventually abandoned since there was no public perception of its necessity. Changes to land use on the floodplain were incorporated into the city's general plan, and park development on the floodplain to prevent flooding problems in Fish Creek was pursued.

Based on engineering studies carried out in the 1960s, the Calgary Emergency Government District prepared a massive flood plan in May 1971. The foreword of the plan noted that the scheme had been developed because the city had no effective plan for such emergencies and had been the victim of floods on eight occasions since 1879. Although there had been no major floods in Calgary since 1932, the possibility still remained and had been confirmed by the city's Engineering Department following extensive research and reports by consultants in 1968 and 1969. The plan was based on the probability of a simultaneous flood on both the Bow and Elbow Rivers because their watersheds were immediately contiguous. The likely cause, based on these reports, was not snowmelt, but sustained heavy rain in the foothills and plains areas. The plan included maps of both the Elbow and the Bow showing the anticipated extent of flooding. The Elbow River maps showed the extent of flooding for flows of 15,000 cubic feet per second (425 cubic metres per second) and 25,000 cubic feet per second (708 cubic metres per second). The plan detailed evacuation protocols for Elbow Park, Glencoe, Victoria Park, Riverdale, Elboya, Stanley Park, Rideau Park, and Roxboro and was subsequently revised and an emergency office created to coordinate its implementation.

NOT QUITE MONTANA

The anxieties of the City of Calgary engineers, Alberta Water Resources engineers, and private engineering consultants during the 1960s came to fruition in 2005 and even more spectacularly in 2013.[281] For the first time since

1932, the city at the confluence of the Bow and Elbow Rivers was devastated by a natural disaster. In June 2005, Calgary experienced the largest amount of rainfall during that month in its history and declared its first state of emergency, which required the mandatory evacuation of 1,500 people from the low-lying areas of Elbow Park, Erlton, Mission, Rideau Park, Riverdale, Roxboro, Stanley Park, and Victoria Park. A record 248 millimetres of rain, three times the June monthly average, fell on the city in three large rainstorms that occurred from June 6 to 8, June 18 to 19, and June 26 to 28. The water level in the rivers was not augmented by snowmelt. In 2005, the snowpack in Calgary's watersheds was significantly lower than the historical norms for the month of May. Records also indicate a gradual and controlled runoff during May, leaving little snow in the mountains by June. The rain, combined with the very limited amount of snowmelt, led to flows on the Bow River in Calgary, the Elbow River at Sarcee Bridge, and Fish Creek near Priddis that were 4, 13, and 60 times higher than the average for the month of June.

The rainfall overflowed rivers and washed out pedestrian bridges and pathways, resulting in flooded roads and neighbourhoods and damage to an estimated 40,000 Calgary homes from a combination of river flooding, basement seepage, and sewage backup. The City of Calgary estimated flooding costs at $17.2 million, which included $13.8 million for infrastructure damage.

The Glenmore Dam, as in previous flood events, was operated to mitigate peak flows below the dam without compromising Calgary's future water supply. The level in the reservoir had been drawn down to 3.1 metres below the crest of the dam by 1:00 p.m. on June 17 in preparation for the coming inflow of water that was already at Bragg Creek. The objective was to hold the water level at 3.1 metres below the crest of the dam as long as possible without exceeding a downstream flow of 170 cubic metres per second to avoid downstream flooding. Once the inflow to the reservoir exceeded 170 cubic metres per second, the reservoir level rose, overtopping the dam. Once the flow started to spill over the dam's crest, the valves that had been installed during the dam's construction were closed to maintain the total downstream flow at 170 cubic metres per second. With the valves fully closed, the flows over the dam could no longer be controlled or mitigated. The Glenmore Dam was overtopped at 3:20 p.m. on June 8 and again at 5:20 p.m. on June 18.

The flood of 2005 was eclipsed by the flood of June 2013. It is the second largest since 1883 in terms of water flow. Flow in the Bow River peaked at 2,400 cubic metres per second, which is eight times the norm. The Elbow River peaked at 1,240 cubic metres per second, which is twelve times its normal rate. The outflow below the Glenmore Dam was seven times the norm at 700 cubic metres per second. At least one newspaper article made the link between this event and the Montana flood of 1964. The dam failures that were the cause of the high number of deaths in Montana did not happen in Calgary. The Glenmore Dam, which was overtopped in 2005 and again in 2013, did not fail as was feared by some people in the 1960s.

Insurable damages for the 2013 flood were estimated at $1.7 billion, making it one of the costliest disasters in Canadian history. Communities in the vicinity of the Bow and Elbow Rivers were placed under a mandatory evacuation order on June 20 and 21. Affecting 75,000 people, it is the largest evacuation order in the city's history. Although none of the city's major highway bridges were damaged, 20 of them were closed. All schools in Calgary were closed as was the downtown. All routes into the downtown core were flooded, and transit service was suspended. Power was shut off to all evacuated areas, including the downtown, and would not be completely restored until June 28. Damage to the transit system included the C-Train tracks in the Erlton area, flooded tunnels, and undermined roads. The city's largest indoor arena, the Scotiabank Saddledome, was among the facilities damaged, and floodwaters reportedly filled up the first 10 rows of the lower seating area.

The post-2013 flood mitigation plans revived all the suggestions made through to the 1960s. These measures included diverting the Elbow River to the Bow above the Glenmore Dam to the Bow River at Ogden. This idea was first suggested in 1929 by Calgary Power and again in 1967 by Montreal Engineering. A tunnel was suggested after 2013 since the option of an overland route had been eliminated by the development of the land between Glenmore and Ogden. An evaluation of the idea by engineering firm Hatch Mott MacDonald indicated that the proposed tunnel could prevent almost $1 billion in property damage and lost business during a 100-year flood.

The construction of dam(s) on the upper Elbow River for the purpose of flood control dates back to 1961. Investigations into dam construction on the upper Elbow for purposes other than flood control date back to the early 1890s. The federal government's irrigation survey during that decade undertook a detailed investigation of the Elbow River and proposed locations for several dams for irrigation purposes.

The idea of diverting water from the Elbow to Fish Creek, which had also been suggested in the 1960s, was again investigated and rejected. The innovative feature of the post-2013 mitigation plan is the inclusion of environmentally sensitive methods of achieving results. This includes the use of vegetation to stabilize riverbanks as a substitute for arming the banks using concrete.

The floods of 2005 and 2013 re-established the Elbow River as both a benefactor and a threat to Calgary. The return of the angry Elbow has made for anxious springs once again.

NOTES

INTRODUCTION

1 John A. Allan, *Geology*, Research Council of Alberta Report 34 (Edmonton: King's Printer, 1943), 111.

2 P. Meyboom, *Groundwater Resources of the City of Calgary and Vicinity*, Research Council of Alberta Bulletin 8 (Edmonton: King's Printer, 1961), 20–25.

3 Michael Wilson, *Once Upon a River: Archaeology and Geology of the Bow River Valley at Calgary, Alberta, Canada* (Ottawa: National Museums of Canada, 1983), 136–59.

4 Surveyor General Edward Deville to Law Clerk, Department of the Interior, 2 October 1913, Library and Archives Canada, RG 15, Vol. 1110 File 30111870.

CHAPTER ONE

5 B. O. K. Reeves, "'Kootsisaw': Calgary before the Canadians" in *Frontier Calgary: Town, City and Region, 1875–1914*, edited by Anthony W. Rasporich and Henry C. Klassen (Calgary: McClelland and Stewart West, 1975), 21–22.

6 Bruce Haig, ed., *A Look at Peter Fidler's Journal: Journal of a Journey Over Land from Buckingham House to the Rocky Mountains, in 1792 & 3* (Lethbridge: Historical Research Centre, 1991), 10.

7 Joseph Burr Tyrrell, ed., *David Thompson's Narrative of his Explorations in Western America, 1784–1812* (Toronto: Champlain Society, 1916), xiv.

8 *Place Names of Alberta*, Geographic Board of Canada, 47.

9 Hugh Dempsey, *Firewater: The Impact of the Whisky Trade on the Blackfoot Nation* (Calgary: Fifth House, 2002), 12.

10 Sam Livingston to Alderman Wright, December 4, 1874, Livingston Fonds, Glenbow Library and Archives.

11 Sheilagh Jameson, "Samuel Henry Harkwood Livingston," *Dictionary of Canadian Biography*, Volume 12: 1891–1900 (Toronto: University of Toronto Press, 2000); Sam Livingston affidavit, PAA Accession 70.313 Film 2000 File 43503.

12 Order-in-council 362(a), April 12, 1875.

13 Hugh Dempsey, "Brisebois: Calgary's Forgotten Founder," in *Frontier Calgary: Town, City and Region, 1875–1914*, edited by Anthony W. Rasporich and Henry C. Klassen (Calgary: McClelland and Stewart West, 1975), 24.

14 *Map of Part of the North West Territory including the Province of Manitoba exhibiting the several Tracts of Country ceded by the Indian Treaties 1,2,3 and 4 to accompany the report of the Honourable the Minister of the Interior*, 20 January, 1875, Glenbow Library and Archives, G3471 E1 1875 C212.

15 The first map to indicate the existence of the Elbow River was entitled *Map of Part of the North West Territory including the Province of Manitoba Exhibiting the several tracts of Country ceded by the Indian Treaties 1, 2, 3, 4, 5, and 6 to Accompany Report of the Honourable D. Mills Minister of the Interior* and published on January 1877. Dominion Topographical Surveyor A. P. Patrick, who surveyed the Stoney Nation reserve in 1877, described his trip to Morley via the Elbow River, along which he observed the farm of Sam Livingston. January 12, 1880, report to Lindsay Russell, Surveyor General of Canada, Appendix No. 8, Annual Report Department of the Interior for 1879, Sessional Papers No. 4, 1880.

16 *Map of the District of Assiniboine and Alberta Showing Dominion Land Surveys to 31 December 1882*, Glenbow Library and Archives, G 3470 1883 C212.

17 Confusion continued through to 1920 when James Nevin Wallace, in an article entitled "Early Explorations along the Bow and Saskatchewan Rivers," indicated that James Hector of the Palliser expedition "followed up the Bow to where Calgary stands and from there travelled some distance up the present Elbow River, which at that time and indeed almost until the arrival of the CPR was known as Swift Creek." This suggestion was incorporated by Irene Spry into her 1961 introduction to the Palliser Papers and has been incorporated into the current literature on the place names of Alberta.

18 Henry Klassen, "I. G. Baker & Co. in Calgary, 1875–1884," *Montana the Magazine of the Western History*, Summer 1985: 12.

19 Peter Darby, "The Integration of southern Alberta with Canada, 1700–1885: An Historical geography" (master's thesis, University of Calgary, 1977), 15–20.

20 Provincial Archives of Alberta, Accession 70.313 Reel 2001 File 84043.

21 William Scollen to parents, ca. 1877–1878, Glenbow Library and Archives, Scollen Fonds M-8873–54.

22 Ibid.

23 Ibid.

24 Ibid.

25 Louis Roselle's homestead application, Library and Archives Canada, RG 15 Volume 632 File 237386.

26 Provincial Archives of Alberta, Accession 70.313 Reel 2001, File 58078.

27 Provincial Archives of Alberta, Accession 70.313 Reel 2000, File 43503.

28 Library and Archives Canada, Record Group 15 Volume 1181 File 2229.

29 Ibid.

30 Library and Archives Canada, RG 15 Volume 284 File 51615.

31 Provincial Archives of Alberta, Accession 70.313 Film 2000 File 43503. Agreement dated September 9, 1882, between Superintendent McIllree and Major E. A. Baynes, permitting the latter to erect a house in the Calgary Bottom near a point on the Bow River known as Shaganappi Point and situated on grounds included in the Police Reserve. Baynes agreed that his settlement on the land gave him no rights to the land and that he would vacant the property and remove the buildings if requested to do so by a government official.

32 North-West Mounted Police Annual Report 1882, 11.

33 Ibid.

34 Ibid.

35 Ibid.

36 Library and Archives Canada, RG 15 Volume 320 File 74920.

37 Library and Archives Canada, RG 15 Volume 283 File 51314.

38 Library and Archives Canada, RG 15 Volume 632 File 237386.

39 Provincial Archives of Alberta, Accession 70.313 Film 2000 File 43503.

40 A. M. Burgess Report, April 14, 1884, Provincial Archives of Alberta, Accession 70.313 Reel 2000 File 43503.

41 Provincial Archives of Alberta, Accession 70.313 Reel 2000 File 43503.

42 Glenbow Library and Archives, Murdoch Fonds.

43 Letter dated August 5, 1883, Glenbow Library and Archives, Isaac Freeze Fonds.

44 *Calgary Herald*, November 9, 1883.

45 *Calgary Herald*, September 14, 1883.

46 *Calgary Herald*, September 7, 1883.

47 *Calgary Herald*, September 28, 1883.

48 Ibid.

49 *Calgary Herald*, October 5, 1883.

50 *Calgary Herald*, October 26, 1883.

51 Ibid.
52 *Calgary Herald,* August 31, 1883.
53 *Calgary Herald,* September 7, 1883.
54 *Calgary Herald,* September 21,1883.
55 *Calgary Herald,* October 12, 1883.
56 *Calgary Herald,* November 2, 1883.
57 Ibid.
58 *Calgary Herald,* November 2, 1883. In Greek mythology, Charon was the ferryman of Hades who carried souls of the newly deceased across the River Styx, which divided the world of the living from that of the dead.
59 *Calgary Herald,* November 9, 1883.
60 Ibid.
61 James Walker to Oswald and Hardisty, November 2, 1883, Library and Archives Canada, RG 15 Volume 310 File 67610.
62 John Hall to Edgar Dewdney, November 22, 1883, Library and Archives Canada, RG15 Volume 310 File 67610.
63 *Calgary Herald,* November 9, 1883.
64 *Calgary Herald,* December 19, 1883.
65 Provincial Archives of Alberta, Accession 83.376 File 490a.
66 Provincial Archives of Alberta, Accession 70.313 Film 2000 file 43503.
67 Ibid.
68 Order-in-council, January 28, 1884.
69 Extract from report by Deputy Minister on claims to lands on and adjacent to the Calgary Townsite, Library and Archives Canada, RG 15 Volume 320 File 74920.
70 Provincial Archives of Alberta, Accession 70.313 Film 2001 File 84043.
71 Ibid.
72 David H. Breen, *The Canadian Prairie West and the Ranching Frontier 1874–1923* (Toronto: University of Toronto Press, 1983), 48–50.
73 Glenbow Library and Archives, Murdoch Papers.
74 *Calgary Herald,* January 30, 1884.
75 *Calgary Herald,* February 20, 1884.
76 Alberta Transportation, Bridge Branch, File 547.
77 *Calgary Herald,* May 8, 1884.
78 Ibid.
79 *Calgary Herald,* July 16, 1884.
80 *Calgary Herald,* July 23, 1884.
81 Ibid.

Chapter Two

82 *Calgary Herald,* February 12, 1885.
83 Alberta Transportation, Bridge Branch, File 547.
84 Father Alberta Lacombe to Lieutenant-Governor Edgar Dewdney, February 20, 1885, Alberta Transportation, Bridge Branch, File 547.
85 Ibid.
86 Ibid.
87 *Calgary Herald,* February 26, 1885.
88 Ibid.
89 Ibid.

90 Father Albert Lacombe to Lieutenant-Governor Edgar Dewdney, May 25, 1886, Alberta Transportation, Bridge Branch, File 547.

91 Father Albert Lacombe to Lieutenant-Governor Edgar Dewdney, August 11, 1886, Alberta Transportation, Bridge Branch, File 547.

92 *Calgary Tribune,* June 17,1887.

93 The regulations referred to may have been bylaw passed in 1887. The territorial government did not pass legislation controlling the use of bridges until 1894.

94 *Calgary Tribune,* June 17, 1887.

95 Ibid.

96 *Weekly Herald,* February 29, 1888.

97 Superintendent of G Division to the Commissioner of the North-West Mounted Police, Library and Archives Canada, RG 18 Volume 1122 File 405–1888.

98 *Calgary Tribune,* July 8, 1887.

99 *Calgary Tribune,* July 12, 1894.

100 *Calgary Herald,* June 17, 1902.

101 *Calgary Herald,* July 28, 1905.

102 *Calgary Herald,* August 4, 1905.

103 Wesley Orr to E. S, Orr, August 8, 1890, Letter book One, Orr Fonds, Glenbow Library and Archives.

104 William Pearce to A. M. Burgess, October 31, 1892, Pearce Papers, File 510, University of Alberta Archives.

105 *Calgary Herald,* December 13, 1892.

106 Ibid.

107 William Pearce Papers, File 9/2/7/3/5, University of Alberta Archives.

108 North Alberta Land Titles District, Plan IRR D.

109 William Pearce Papers, File 9/2/7/3/5, University of Alberta Archives.

110 William Pearce Papers, Files 9/2/7/3/5 and 9/2/7/1/2, University of Alberta Archives.

111 Donald Pisani, *To Reclaim a Divided West: Water, Law and Public Policy 1848–1902* (Albuquerque, NM: University of New Mexico Press, 1992), 102.

112 *Calgary Herald,* July 27, 1894.

113 Ibid.

114 Ibid.

115 William Pearce Papers, File 9–22–7-3–9, University of Alberta Archives.

116 Ibid.

117 Ibid.

118 William Pearce to Peter Turner Bone, February 25, 1895, Pearce Papers, File 9–2-7–3-9, University of Alberta Archives.

119 *Weekly Herald,* July 30, 1896.

120 Ibid.

121 *Calgary Herald,* June 18, 1897.

122 Ibid.

123 Ibid.

124 *Calgary Tribune,* July 8, 1902.

CHAPTER THREE

125 *Calgary Herald,* February 15, 1907.

126 *Calgary Herald,* May 29, 1906.

127 Report to the Mayor and Council from the Joint Fire and Water Committee, June 9, 1906, CCCRA Council Minutes for June 11, 1906.

128 *Albertan*, June 1, 1906.

129 *Calgary Herald*, June 6, 1906.

130 *Calgary Herald*, July 7, 1906.

131 *Calgary Herald*, July 6, 1906.

132 *Albertan* July 22, 1908.

133 *Calgary Herald* July 23, 1908.

134 City Engineer Child to Mayor and Aldermen, May 23, 1910, CCCRA City Clerk's Papers, File 352.

135 Clifford Jones to Frank Oliver, May 6, 1910, CCCRA City Clerk's Papers, File 329.

136 Ibid.

137 City Clerk W. D. Spence to Secretary of the Department of the Interior, December 20, 1910, CCCRA City Clerk's Correspondence, File 328.

138 City Engineer Child's Report, February 22, 1911, CCCRA City Clerk's Papers, File 328.

139 Proposed High-Pressure Gravity System Water Supply for Calgary, CCCRA Council Minutes, June 17, 1912.

140 *Calgary Herald*, August 24, 1912.

141 Report of Commissioners to the Mayor and Council, September 3, 1912, CCCRA Council Minutes, September 3, 1912.

142 Ibid.

143 Commissioners' Report to Council, March 20, 1913, CCCRA Minutes, March 20, 1913.

144 Ibid.

145 Isaac Freeze Fonds, Glenbow Library and Archives.

146 I. G. Ruttle and Dr. Kirby to the Recreation & Playgrounds Committee, CCCRA City Clerk's Correspondence, File 560.

147 *Calgary Herald*, July 30, 1914.

148 Ibid.

CHAPTER FOUR

149 *Calgary Herald*, June 28, 1915.

150 *Herald*, June 29, 1915.

151 Ibid.

152 Ibid.

153 *Calgary Herald*, June 10, 1916.

154 Report dated September 28, 1916, from City Chemist Fred Field to the Chairman, New Water Supply Committee, CCCRA City Clerk's Papers, File 700.

155 Ibid.

156 Ibid.

157 *Calgary Herald*, June 29, 1921.

158 Jack Peach, *Peach Preservers* (Calgary: Sandstone Publishing, 1978), 44.

159 Ibid.

160 The transfer of this island to the City of Calgary was originally requested in 1887 at the same time that Calgary petitioned for the transfer of the islands at the confluence of the Bow and Elbow Rivers to its authority. The transfer was not carried out at that time. The island has had various names in addition to Williams, including "Reservoir," "Archers," and "Bird." It was largely destroyed in the 1960s to provide gravel for riverbank protection.

161 *Calgary Herald*, July 27, 1929.

CHAPTER FIVE

162 In looking at the corporate boundaries of Calgary, the authors observed, as had Thomas Mawson in 1914, that the incorporated area was out of proportion to its population of 90,000, giving a very low density of 3.55 people per acre. This compared to 2.47 for Edmonton and 3.68 for Saskatoon, which were also coping with legacies from their equivalent of the Greater Calgary movement.

163 Nicholas J. Schnitter, *A History of Dams: The useful pyramids* (Rotterdam, Netherlands: A. A. Balkema, 1994).

164 The other major dams built in Alberta prior to 1929 included one at Bassano that diverted water from the Bow River for use in the eastern section of the Canadian Pacific Railway's irrigation project. It is the only example of a buttress dam built in Alberta.

165 Minutes of a special meeting of the Calgary Medical Society, Calgary Medical Association, M 8280 File 3, Glenbow Library and Archives.

166 *Calgary Herald*, November 14, 1929,

167 *West-Ender*, November 15, 1929, CCCRA City Clerk's Papers, File 1529.

168 Ibid.

169 *Calgary Herald*, November 16, 1929.

170 *Calgary Herald*, November 18, 1929.

171 Ibid.

172 *Calgary Herald*, November 19, 1929.

173 CCCRA Agreement No. 2792.

174 William Storrie to City Engineer Chapman, February 12, 1930, CCCRA City Clerk's Department Fonds, File 1384.

175 *Calgary Herald*, November 19, 1929.

176 CCCRA Agreement No. 2980.

177 *Calgary Herald*, November 14, 1929.

178 *Calgary Herald*, July 26, 1930.

179 William Gore, "Calgary's New Waterworks System," *Journal of the American Waterworks Association* 26, no. 8 (1934): 991.

180 J. G. Bennett to the Mayor of Calgary, November 24, 1930, CCCRA Council Minutes, November 24, 1930.

181 N. G. McDonald to Bennett & White, April 17, 1931, CCCRA City of Calgary Archives, Engineering Fonds, Accession CR92–007 Box 3.

182 Ibid.

183 CCCRA Agreement No. 3027.

184 CCCRA Agreement No. 3143.

185 CCCRA Agreements No. 3096, 3100, and 3132.

186 Fred A. Filteau, "Report on valuations to the judicial inquiry regarding the Glenmore Dam," CCCRA RG 26, City Clerk's Papers File 1528, p. 29.

187 Ibid.

188 "Report of the Honourable Mr. Justice Ewing of the Supreme Court of Alberta upon an inquiry held pursuant to a resolution of the Council of the City of Calgary passed under Section 155 of the Charter of the City of Calgary," CCCRA City Clerk's Papers File 1524, p. 12

189 E. B. Nowers to Mayor of Calgary, November 25, 1931, CCCRA City Clerk's Papers File 1522.

190 The Department of Indian Affairs file on Sarcee land surrenders documenting the land surrenders of the Tsuu T'ina Nation deals with the period of 1901 to 1929. For further information on the purchase of the land for the Glenmore Reservoir, see Law Department Report Re: Glenmore Reservoir Lands 1982 June in Information File at City of Calgary Corporate Records Archives.

191 E. B. Nowers to the Mayor, November 25, 1931, CCCRA City Clerk's Papers File 1522.

192 1933 Chapter 62, An act to amend the Acts and Ordinance constituting the charter of the City of Calgary assented to April 11, 1933, Chapter 11, that the council of the City of Calgary is hereby authorized to capitalize and to issue debentures for $350,000 to cover over expenditures on the Glenmore Waterworks.

193 *Calgary Herald*, May 26, 1925.

194 Alderman Savage to Mayor Davison, September 12, 1932, CCCRA Council Minutes, September 12, 1932.

195 *Calgary Herald*, June 24, 1931.

196 Ibid.

197 *The Mention*, April 14, 1932, CCCRA City Clerk's Papers File 1529.

198 *Calgary Herald*, May 6, 1932.

199 Petition to the City Council, CCCRA City Clerk's Papers File 1512.

200 *Calgary Herald*, October 12, 1932.

201 *Calgary Herald*, November 8, 1932.

202 *Calgary Herald*, November 10, 1932.

203 *Calgary Herald*, November 16, 1932.

204 Fred A. Filteau, "Report on valuations to the judicial inquiry regarding the Glenmore Dam," CCCRA RG 26, City Clerk's File 1528, p. 1.

205 CCCRA Bylaw 2746.

206 N. C. Francis to the Mayor of Calgary, December 10, 1931, CCCRA Council Minutes, December 19, 1931.

207 H. C. Francis to J. M. Miller, January 4, 1932, CCCRA Council Minutes, January 4, 1932.

208 The problem caused by the exchange rate is covered in Edward M. Bredin, QC, "Calgary's Foreign Exchange Crisis of 1933," *Alberta History*, Summer 2008.

209 January 4, 1933, entry in engineering daily journal.

210 City Comptroller to Alderman J. W. Russell, January 12, 1914, CCCRA City of Calgary Papers, Box 33, File 317; City of Calgary Comptroller to Alderman R. H. Weir, May 25, 1937, City of Calgary Archives, City of Calgary Papers, Box 33, File 321.

211 CCCRA Council Minutes, May 3, 1933.

212 October 13, 1933, Report of Finance Committee, CCCRA Council Minutes for October 16, 1933.

213 CCCRA Agreement No. 3418.

CHAPTER SIX

214 CCCRA Council Minutes, May 14, 1934.

215 CCCRA Council Minutes, October 16, 1939.

216 CCCRA Council Minutes, June 10, 1940.

217 M 7942 Special Constabulary Mounted Division, Glenbow Library and Archives.

218 Report of the Air Raid Precautions Committee, March 2, 1942, CCCRA Council Minutes, March 2, 1942.

219 CCCRA Parks Department, 1932 Annual Report, 25.

220 CCCRA Parks Department, 1935 Annual Report, 16.

221 Ibid.

222 CCCRA Council Minutes, May 14, 1934.

223 CCCRA Agreement No. 3676.

224 CCCRA Parks Department, 1933 Annual Report, 12.

225 CCCRA Parks Department, 1932 Annual Report, 3.

CHAPTER SEVEN

226 CCCRA Agreement No. 5964.

227 CCCRA Agreements No. 5788 and 5813.

228 CCCRA Agreement No. 8675.

229 R. T. Hollies Report, March 14, 1961, CCCRA Planning Fonds, Series I File 6268.2.2.

230 There are no actual personal accounts of people picnicking in the Elbow Valley, but a number of photographs from the Glenbow Library and Archives photographic collection document this activity.

231 Letter 7, J. C. Leslie to City Council, October 11, 1945, CCCRA Council Meeting, December 10, 1945.

232 Ibid.

233 CCCRA Council Minutes, July 2, 1946.

234 Draft Agreement in City of Calgary CCCRA Council Minutes, October 11, 1955.

235 Ibid.

236 *Calgary Herald,* January 24, 1956.

237 Ibid.

238 Ibid.

239 *Albertan,* January 25, 1956.

240 *Calgary Herald,* January 25, 1956.

241 *Calgary Herald,* February 2, 1956.

242 Ibid.

243 Ibid.

244 *Calgary Herald,* February 6, 1956.

245 CCCRA Council Minutes, March 19, 1951.

246 CCCRA Plan M0003205.

247 Letter 24, W. E. Robinson to J. M. Miller, City Clerk's Files October 10, 1946, CCCRA Council Minutes, October 15, 1946.

248 William E. Robinson to J. M. Miller, October 10, 1946, CCCRA Council Minutes, October 15, 1946.

249 Letter 12, W. H. Hill to J. M. Miller, City Clerk, October 23, 1946, CCCRA Council Meeting of October 28, 1946; Letter 8, W. H. Hill to J. M. Miller, November 1, 1946, Council Meeting of November 12, 1946.

250 W. J. Ross to J. W. Miller, August 14, 1952, CCCRA Council Minutes, August 18, 1952.

251 Clarence Pautzke to Gordon Cummings, October 23, 1950, CCCRA Council Minutes, August 18, 1952.

252 *Calgary Herald,* August 21, 1952.

253 *Calgary Herald,* September 2, 1952

254 Ibid.

255 City Solicitor Bredin to Alderman Upton, December 12, 1952, CCCRA Law Fonds, File G 6 32.

256 CCCRA, March 26, 1954, Commissioner's Report Council Minutes, March 29, 1954.

257 David Milne to Special Committee regarding Glenmore Dam, September 16, 1952, CCCRA City Clerk's Papers, File 3051.

258 CCCRA Minutes, May 9, 1955.

259 CCCRA Commissioners Fonds, Series IV Box 62 File G3, Glenmore Park 1957–1958.

260 *Calgary Herald,* December 19, 1956.

261 These terms were incorporated into Bylaw 4990, passed on August 19, 1957.

262 Bylaw 4999.

263 The details of the new plan were provided by the city commissioners in two reports dated March 29 and April 12. Details of the new plan were also outlined in a map published in the *Calgary Herald* on April 17.

264 CCCRA Agreements No. 11492, 13056, 29512, and 33439.

265 Eric Harvie to D. E. Bachelor, May 26, 1961, CCCRA Board of Commissioners Fonds, Series V Box 136 File 4795, Glenbow Foundation 1961.

266 *Calgary Herald*, June 21, 1960.

267 Dale Stamm, "The Impact of Community Strategies Upon Planning Policy in Calgary" (master's thesis, University of Calgary, 1979).

268 CCCRA Planning Fonds, Series I File 6268.2.2.

269 CCCRA Planning Fonds, Series I File 6268.2.2, Elbow River.

270 A. G. Martin to Mayor Hays, December 11, 1962, CCCRA Planning Department Fonds, Series I File 6268.2.2.

271 CCCRA Commissioners Fonds, Series V Box 229 File 6200, Elbow River Diversion 1965.

272 F. R. Walton to H. E. Strom, October 31, 1963, CCCRA Board of Commissioners Fonds, Series V Box 229 File 6200.5, Elbow River Diversion 1970.

273 Ibid.

274 Mrs. Tracy Tupper to H. E. Strom, November 6, 1963, CCCRA Board of Commissioners Fonds, Series V Box 229 File 6200.5, Elbow River Diversion 1970.

275 Dr. T. Blench to City Engineer Howarth, June 29, 1964, CCCRA Commissioners Fonds, Box 229 File 6200.5, Elbow River Diversion 1970.

276 Commissioner Strong to G. T. Henderson, June 5, 1970, CCCRA Board of Commissioners Series V Box 229 File 6200.5, Elbow River Diversion 1970.

277 Ibid.

278 CCCRA Board of Commissioners Fonds, Series V Box 229 File 6200.5, Elbow River Diversion 1966.

279 Flood Protection—Elbow River Calgary, T. Blench & Associates Ltd., August 30, 1965, City of Calgary Land Information and Mapping Library Report, PR 65003.

280 F. C. Boner and Frank Stermitz, Floods of June 1964 in Northwestern Montana Geological Survey Water-supply Paper 1849-B, United States Department of the Interior.

281 2005 Flood Report, City of Calgary's Report on the 2005 June Flooding in the Elbow and Bow River Watersheds.

Bibliographical Essay

The geological history of the Elbow River is covered in the *Report on the region in the vicinity of the Bow and Belly rivers, North-West Territory, embracing the country from the base of the Rocky Mountains eastward to longitude 110°45*, and *from the 49th parallel northward to latitude 51°20*, published in an 1884 report written by George Mercer Dawson. The evolving relationship between the Elbow and the Bow Rivers is dealt with in a 1943 Research Council of Alberta publication by John Allan entitled *Groundwater Resources of the City of Calgary and Vicinity*, by P. Meyboom Research, and *Once Upon a River: Archaeology and Geology of the Bow River Valley at Calgary, Alberta*, by Michael Wilson.

The literature on the human history of the Elbow River begins with an article by Gerry Oetelaar and David Meyer entitled "Movement and Native American Landscapes: A Comparative Approach" which was published in the *Plains Anthropologist*, volume 51, Number 199, along with a second article by Gerald Oetelaar entitled "River Crossings and Cottonwood Groves: Alluvial Geoarchaeology and Native American Landscapes," which was first presented as a paper at the 36th Annual Chacmool Conference in 2003. The article "Early Explorations Along the Bow and Saskatchewan Rivers" by James Wallace, which was published in the Summer 1961 issue of *Alberta History*, gives an inaccurate description of the exploration of the Elbow Valley. Max Foran has written several valuable works on the beginnings of Calgary and the land development process. These include "Early Calgary 1875–1895: The Controversies Surrounding the Townsite Location and the Direction of Town Expansion," which was part of *Cities in the West: Papers of the Western Canada Urban History Conference, University of Winnipeg, October 1974*, and published in the Mercury Series by the National Museum of Man; "Land Speculation and Urban Development: Calgary 1884–1912, which was published in *Frontier Calgary*; and "Fred Lowes: Booster Extraordinaire," which appeared in the Spring 1989 issue of *Alberta History*. The early history of the Mission District is outlined in an excellent work by Marie Byrne entitled *From the Buffalo to the Cross: A History of the Roman Catholic Diocese of Calgary*. The life of Sam Livingston is the subject of an entry by Sheilagh Jameson in the *Dictionary of Canadian Biography*. His role in the settlers' revolt of 1885 is covered in David Breen's book, *The Canadian Prairie West and the Ranching Frontier: 1874–1924*. The history of the Calgary Golf and Country Club is the subject of Tyler Trafford's *The Calgary Golf and Country Club, 1897–1997: More Than 18 Holes*. Three excellent community histories dealing with Erlton, Mission, and Elbow Park have been written by David Mittelstadt. An examination of how a portion of the land around the Glenmore Reservoir was developed is detailed by Dale Stamm in his master's degree thesis entitled "The Impact of Community Strategies upon Planning Policy in Calgary." The role of whisky traders and the arrival of the North-West Mounted Police is outlined in "Brisebois: Calgary's Forgotten Founder," which appeared in *Frontier Calgary* and in *Firewater: The Impact of the Whisky Trade on the Blackfoot Nation*. Hugh Dempsey also wrote an account of the events leading up to the creation of the Tsuu T'ina Reserve entitled "How the Sarcees Came to Calgary," which appeared in *Calgary: A Living Heritage*. The history of the Glenmore Waterworks system is the subject of Harry Sanders' book *Watermarks: One Hundred Years of Calgary Waterworks*. The history of the I. G. Baker Company in Calgary was covered in Henry Klassen's article in the Summer 1985 issue of *Montana: The Magazine of Western History*.

By contrast to the relative lack of secondary sources that deal specifically with the Elbow River, the primary sources are very rich. The City of Calgary holdings on this subject include the records of the city council, the city clerk, and the city commissioners, as well as those of the Engineering, Parks, and Law Departments. Of particular significance are the engineering records related to the construction of the Glenmore Dam. These include the journal maintained by the engineering office during the construction period, progress reports, photographs, and correspondence between the contractors, consultants, and city officials. The Glenbow Library and Archives has an extensive collection of photographs on the Glenmore Dam's construction, as well as on other activities along the Elbow River such as skating and swimming. The collection also includes letters home by William Scollen and Isaac Freeze, North-West Mounted Police reports, and daily issues of the *Calgary Herald* beginning in August 1883, plus an extensive map collection. The Murdoch Fonds include Scollen's diary, which documents his arrival and first years in Calgary. There is also a collection of his articles from the *Calgary*

Herald that reveals his interest in the natural history of the Calgary area. The Provincial Archives of Alberta has two significant collections relative to the Elbow Valley, one of which, Accession 70.313, has important documents relative to land claims issues. The second collection consists of survey records, which include the notebook of D. L. S. LaRue. Library and Archives Canada has important Department of the Interior files relating to land claims and the Calgary cemetery.

INDEX

Page numbers in bold refer to illustrations and maps.

About the Author

A Calgary-based historian and writer, John Gilpin has a BA and an MA in history from the University of Alberta and a PhD in economic history from the University of Leicester, England. His interests include the settlement of western Canada, with a particular emphasis on transportation, water resources, and urban development. His publications include *Edmonton, Gateway to the North: An Illustrated History; Quenching the Prairie Thirst: A History of the Magrath, Raymond, Taber and St. Mary River Irrigation Districts; Roads to Resources: A History of Transportation in Alberta; Doing What's Best for Kids: 1912–2012: A History of the Fort McMurray Public School District; Prairie Promises: History of the Bow River Irrigation District;* and "The Land Development Process in Edmonton Alberta, 1881–1917." in *Power and Place: Canadian Urban Development in the North American Context.*